DATE DUE

APR 2 2 2003

Bush v. Gore

BUSH v. GORE

The Question of Legitimacy

EDITED BY BRUCE ACKERMAN

YALE UNIVERSITY PRESS
NEW HAVEN & LONDON

Copyright © 2002 by Yale University. All rights reserved. This book may not be reproduced, in whole or in part, including illustrations, in any form (beyond that copying permitted by Sections 107 and 108 of the U.S. Copyright Law and except by reviewers for the public press), without written permission from the publishers.

Designed by Nancy Ovedovitz and set in Scala type by Keystone Typesetting, Inc., Orwigsburg, Pennsylvania. Printed in the United States of America by Sheridan Books, Ann Arbor, Michigan.

Library of Congress Cataloging-in-Publication Data
Bush v. Gore : the question of legitimacy / edited by Bruce Ackerman.
    p.   cm.
Includes bibliographical references and index.
ISBN 0-300-09379-9 (cloth : alk. paper)
ISBN 0-300-09380-2 (paper : alk. paper)
1. Bush, George W. (George Walker), 1946—Trials, litigation, etc. 2. Gore, Albert, 1948—Trials, litigation, etc. 3. Presidents—United States—Election—2000. 4. Contested elections—Florida. I. Title: Bush versus Gore. II. Ackerman, Bruce A.
KF5074.2.B874 2002
342.73′075—dc21
2002000918

A catalogue record for this book is available from the British Library.

The paper in this book meets the guidelines for permanence and durability of the Committee on Production Guidelines for Book Longevity of the Council on Library Resources.

10 9 8 7 6 5 4 3 2 1

Contents

PART TWO POLITICAL QUESTIONS

BRUCE ACKERMAN

Introduction: The Question of Legitimacy

Talk of constitutional crisis conjures up some great disturbance in the larger society—revolution or war, economic depression or massive movement for social change. The mighty social forces unleashed by these events disrupt existing constitutional arrangements and threaten to overwhelm political and legal elites. The question, simply put, is whether existing leaders can channel these forces into constructive forms, or whether the Constitution will be fractured beyond recognition.

But there is another kind of crisis—generated not by social pressure but by the machinery of government itself. Some part of the machine misfires, then another, then another. The general public is bewildered, the elites are uncertain about the next step.

Time marches on—decisions must be made, they are made, and then?

Anxious reappraisal, followed slowly by a consensus on how the system performed. If the collective judgment is positive, the participants

Many thanks are due to Dean Tony Kronman, of Yale Law School, who provided financial support for the talkfest as part of the university's celebration of its tercentenary.

celebrate the glories of their constitutional inheritance and look forward confidently to future challenges.

But if it is negative, a gnawing sense of illegitimacy eats away at the fabric of mutual confidence.

Consider Watergate. No great social force generated this crisis. Nothing compelled Richard Nixon to bug the headquarters of the Democratic National Committee. But he did, and the question was how the rest of the system would respond. Each step was controversial —from the congressional hearings to the discharge of Special Prosecutor Archibald Cox to the Supreme Court's decision to the president's resignation to his pardon by President Ford. Yet after the smoke cleared, and after much debate, a clear consensus emerged: the system worked, not perfectly, but well enough.

Will we be saying the same thing about *Bush* v. *Gore*? Or will the decision cast a darkening cloud over the Bush presidency and the Supreme Court of the United States?

The answer begins, but does not end, with the legal merits of the majority's decision. Part One of this book, "The Rule of Law?," opens with a spirited pair of essays by Charles Fried and Jed Rubenfeld. A professor at Harvard Law School, Fried confronts the decision on the basis of a distinguished career that includes service as solicitor general under Ronald Reagan and as associate justice of the Massachusetts Supreme Court. He argues that the Court's decision was entirely reasonable—it is the harsh academic reception that is extreme. Professor Rubenfeld of Yale Law School then enters the field with a powerful essay that exemplifies the emerging critique.

Both writers aim for a large audience and set the tone for the book. The contributors refuse to hide behind mind-numbing legal minutia, presenting the key questions in straightforward terms. You don't have to go to law school to get to the heart of their dispute. It is enough to be a thoughtful American.

This initial exchange is followed by two writers whose special experience deepens the debate. Professor Laurence Tribe's role as Al

Gore's counsel before the Supreme Court is part of a unique career as the leading scholar-advocate of his generation. Judge Guido Calabresi, formerly dean of Yale Law School, is the most distinguished academic appointed by President Clinton to the United States Court of Appeals.

Tribe describes how television transformed the Court's perceptions of the stakes. Intervening without an adequate legal record, the justices allowed TV images to create a false sense of crisis and to distort their understanding of the constitutional requirements of equal protection. Tribe places the Court's decision in a real-world context, revealing the bankruptcy of its media-driven formulations. No less troubling is the Court's imperative need for order and its disdain for the political branches. He argues that the Court was wrong to assume the decisive role the Constitution assigns to Congress in electoral disputes and concludes with the fear that the decision may become "our judicial Vietnam"—undermining confidence in the judiciary even when major interventions are actually required by constitutional principle.

Judge Guido Calabresi begins with a sketch of three possible opinions that might have resolved *Bush v. Gore* in a principled way—one favoring Bush, one Gore, and one indeterminate at the time the Supreme Court decided the case. The trouble is that the Court failed to take any of these models seriously, awarding the presidency without committing itself to any coherent constitutional principle. Calabresi is no absolutist, and concedes that unprincipled decision making may sometimes be acceptable, even wise. But the problem confronting the Court did not remotely authorize such a breach with established judicial norms. It is only by committing themselves even more firmly to legal principle that federal judges may ultimately undo the harm caused by the aberrational character of the Supreme Court's decision.

We are reaching a crucial question: Is *Bush v. Gore* just another controversial decision, or does it represent a decisive breach with the rule of law? Owen Fiss of Yale Law School vigorously rejects the more disturbing answer. On his view, the case is no different from many others decided by the Rehnquist Court. He rejects the claim that its unprincipled character places the decision "on a different moral plane." Fiss believes that the Court's decision is principled. While he considers those principles to be mistaken and wrongly applied to the facts, he maintains that this is true of many decisions reached by many courts. The fallibility of judicial reason should not shake our collective faith in the rule of law, and in the judicial effort to hold power accountable to principle.

Robert Post and Margaret Jane Radin take a darker view. For Post, a professor at the University of California at Berkeley, the decision "conspired to inflict a searing and disorienting vision of a world without law, a nation subject to courts who command without accountability." Even as passions cooled over the following months, the case continues to pose the ultimate question confronting all teachers of law. If they present *Bush* v. *Gore* in classroom discussion as an ordinary, if flawed, decision, this may merely confirm their students' most cynical suspicions about the legal process. Is it not wiser to announce that the Supreme Court's decision was a fundamental breach with the rule of law, and challenge the next generation to place our national commitments on a firmer foundation?

Stanford's Margaret Jane Radin understands the fundamental question in similar terms but provides a more straightforward answer. Americans will never reconstruct the rule of law unless we candidly recognize how profoundly it was shaken by the Supreme Court's decision. As professionals most concerned with the future of constitutional development, law professors have an obligation to speak these uncomfortable truths to the larger public.

For all its themes and variations, Part One focuses on a tightly interconnected set of questions: Does *Bush* v. *Gore* have a solid—or even plausible—foundation in legal principle? If not, how to reestablish the nation's confidence in the rule of law?

Part Two, "Political Questions," confronts this legalistic focus with a series of political issues—beginning with the authority of the Court to oust politicians from the center stage of the electoral process. Professor Steven Calabresi sensitively explores the ways in which political efforts to break the "tie vote" in Florida were systematically discredited in the media, while judicial efforts were consistently glorified. Calabresi juxtaposes this pro-judicial bias of the media with the classical legal principles governing the "political question doctrine." He concludes that the Court had a constitutional obligation to defer to the political branches, and that it was up to Congress, not the Court, to resolve the ultimate conflict. Calabresi is one of the founders of the Federalist Society and an advisor to George W. Bush's campaign; his challenge to the Court is to be taken with special seriousness. Whatever else one may say about it, his defense of politics doesn't seem to be politically motivated!

According to Jeffrey Rosen, Calabresi is very much the exception. The most striking fact about the decision is how politically polarizing it is. If the Court is to save the rule of law, it must rethink its approach to political questions. Rosen traces the way the classical doctrine of principled restraint, elaborated by Calabresi, has been transformed into an invitation to judicial heroism. He challenges this new doctrine by confronting one of its primary defenders, Judge Richard Posner. Posner's efforts to defend *Bush* v. *Gore* on "pragmatic" grounds only demonstrate how speculative and dangerous the new interventionism has become.

Both Calabresi and Rosen seek to save the rule of law by reviving the political question doctrine. Mark Tushnet, in contrast, evaluates the decision in explicitly political terms. There is nothing particularly surprising about "five Republican Justices award[ing] the presidency to the Republican candidate." The only real question is whether the Court played its part in a politically savvy way. Tushnet doubts this. The justices lost a great deal of support by issuing an opinion that offended rule of law myths too blatantly. They also seem to be gambling too heavily on the success of the Bush presidency to restore their future reputations. Moving beyond this narrow political calculus,

Tushnet considers the extent to which the opinion expresses a conservative distrust of democracy and an embrace of technological solutions to political problems.

The first three chapters in this part focus on the Court and the super-politicization its decision has generated. But the solution to the problem, if there is one, can be found only in more politics, most obviously the politics involved in appointing the next generation of Supreme Court justices. Cass Sunstein frames the issue against the larger context of the Rehnquist Court's efforts to revolutionize constitutional doctrine. Given the Rehnquist Court's general tendency to denigrate the legitimacy of democratic solutions, the Senate has a responsibility to assure the appointment of justices who will demonstrate greater appreciation of the virtues of political decision making. But this would have been true even if *Bush* v. *Gore* had not been decided. He denies that this case should fundamentally change the Senate's approach to the process of "advice and consent."

Bruce Ackerman disagrees. The Court's intervention in the presidential election places an unprecedented constitutional obligation on the Senate. The Supreme Court nominations of presidents are normally entitled to substantial deference because the president has a direct connection to the national electorate. But *Bush* v. *Gore* has disturbed this electoral relationship, transforming the Senate into the only popularly elected institution that can control a runaway Court. During the current period of constitutional disequilibrium, the Senate should exercise its authority to prevent any new appointments to the Court. It should require President Bush to demonstrate that he can win the election of 2004 fair and square before allowing his Supreme Court nominees to determine the future direction of constitutional development.

Jack Balkin sets this debate in a larger comparative context. If America had operated under a parliamentary system, the problematic outcome of 2000 would quickly generate a call for new elections, permitting the selection of a leader with a clearer democratic mandate. But the American system operates on a fixed electoral calendar. This means that legitimacy questions will recur repeatedly over the next four years. Sometimes, as in the case of judicial appointments, the issues will return to the very surface of public argument, but they will never be entirely absent from other debates as well. Scratch the surface of most normal conflicts and you will find anxieties about constitutional legitimacy. The terrorist attacks of September 11, 2001, have given George W. Bush a remarkable opportunity to resolve doubts about his leadership. But as the examples of Lyndon Johnson and George H. W. Bush suggest, a warlike foreign policy is no cure-all for domestic political predicaments. The legitimacy question will remain a part of the debate framing the elections of 2002 and 2004. The enduring verdict on *Bush* v. *Gore* will very much depend on who wins these elections.

The contributors to this book regard these chapters as a small part of this larger process of democratic resolution. The first wave of books on the election crisis were written in a rush during the first few weeks after the decision. We decided to take more time to think the issues through. Most of us came to New Haven, Connecticut, for a weekend of intensive discussion in late April 2001. Sustained dialogue probably sharpened the disagreements expressed by the assembled company, but it enabled everybody to hear the best arguments from the other side(s) before returning home to begin writing.

This "talkfest"—as the participants came to call it—not only permitted the essayists to transcend a variety of knee-jerk reactions. It has also allowed them to write a much more unified book. Before putting pen to paper, each writer knew where his or her contribution fit into the larger conversation—yielding a complex whole that is larger than the sum of its parts.

None of us suppose that this book represents anything like the last word. But we do hope it helps move the debate beyond instant analysis and encourages Americans to recognize that the troubling questions raised by *Bush* v. *Gore* will be with all of us for a long time to come.

PART ONE

The Rule of Law?

CHARLES FRIED

An Unreasonable Reaction to a Reasonable Decision

"You hick! . . . I take a nobody, see? . . . Get his name in the papers and pay for his campaign expenses. . . . Get my boys to bring the voters out. And then count the votes over and over again till they added up right and he was elected."—Edward G. Robinson (as gangster Johnny Rocco) explaining Florida politics to John Rodney (as Deputy Clyde Sawyer) in *Key Largo* (1948).

At the close of the polls on November 7, 2000, the presidential election was for all intents and purposes a tie. Everything depended on the outcome in Florida, where the first tabulation showed Governor Bush ahead by a few hundred of the six million votes cast there. The next day, as required by Florida law, the ballots were counted again and Bush was again the winner. Protests were lodged and a third count began. The Florida Supreme Court extended the lawful deadline in a decision that was later unanimously vacated by the Supreme Court of the United States (in Bush I). By the time that vacated deadline had arrived, Bush was still ahead and the secretary of state certified him

Several friends and colleagues have offered suggestions on drafts of this chapter. The secret of their identities is safe with me. David Ware of the Harvard Law School Class of 2002 provided research assistance.

the winner. Gore went back to court. A lower court threw out his suit, but the Florida Supreme Court ordered yet another recount. The Supreme Court of the United States in Bush II first stayed the Florida decision and then reversed it, effectively ending the count. Gore conceded. And the left had a cow.[1]

A leading constitutional scholar has called the decision "vulgarly partisan." Six hundred seventy-three law professors signed a statement condemning the Supreme Court for its affront to the rule of law. The cover of the *New Republic* showed a picture of the Supreme Court over which was pasted the banner "Disgraced." A distinguished participant in the discussions opined that the Court's intervention was an act so lawless that it could be justified only on pragmatic grounds, and then only had the case been *Bush* v. *Hitler.* Another constitutional scholar posted an online note calling the justices in the majority "absolute, utter, contemptible fools." And I don't know how many law teachers have rent their garments and declared that they cannot again look their students in the eyes and teach constitutional law as a serious subject. I will buy lunch for any of these legal scholars who voted for Bush. I will buy dinner for any who favored the Rehnquist Court's decisions on subjects like racial preferences, federalism, and criminal law. And I will send on a 'round the world cruise any of the critics who were hoping that a President Bush would replace present justices who voted for these things with younger justices who were similarly inclined.[2]

My attitude is somewhat different. I applaud—I have even argued for—decisions like *Croson* and *Adarand* (limiting racial set asides),

1. The labor pains had begun earlier. Professors Ackerman, Dworkin, Dershowitz, and I know not how many others had complained right after the election about the Palm Beach County butterfly ballot, and some attached their names to advertisements for a proposal for a revote so complex and so constitutionally preposterous that they quickly disavowed any connection with it.

2. These offers are void where prohibited by law. They are also void where permitted by law.

Shaw (disciplining racially gerrymandered voting districts), *Lopez* and *Morrison* (finding that the Constitution's commerce power is not a grant to Congress to regulate anything which that day strikes its fancy), and *Boerne* (refusing to allow Congress to overrule the Court's interpretation of the Constitution). And in this very case I filed a brief on behalf of the Florida legislature making just the arguments that so upset the left-liberal academic establishment. But nonetheless it seems to me now—and did then—that there were two sides to these arguments, that Professor Tribe and his colleagues presented a well-argued brief for the other side. And what is the hotly contested constitutional case where this has not been so?[3] I believe the case was correctly decided, but it presents so many intricacies that it is quite possible, as the discussion continues, that doubts may enter and convictions reverse. That, too, is normal. This collection is not the place to attempt a thoroughgoing technical defense of the Court's decision. That has been done excellently and in detail in a book by Richard Posner, and in essays by Nelson Lund in a forthcoming symposium in the *Cardozo Law Review*,[4] and by Richard Epstein, Michael McConnell, and John Yoo in a collection to be published by University of Chicago Press.[5] Rather, I shall only try to convince you of the reasonableness of *Bush* v. *Gore*, of its rightful place among the large number of important Supreme Court decisions on which reasonable minds might differ.

It has been a common theme of the denunciations that the Court's

3. I recall Herbert Wechsler's great essay, "Towards Neutral Principles of Constitutional Law," questioning the reasoning in *Shelley* v. *Kramer* and *Brown* v. *Board* and the large number of essays responding to its challenge to find a principled basis for those decisions. The best, perhaps, was Charles Black's. Whatever else was said, few if any questioned the motives of the Court or of the participants in the debate. They stuck to the merits.

4. I posted on a chat group for law professors my recommendation of Lund's essay as the best detailed defense of *Bush* v. *Gore* I had seen. It is a sign of the degraded state of debate on this subject that Lund's article and my posting were immediately condemned as "propaganda."

5. Cass R. Sunstein and Richard A. Epstein, eds., The Vote (2001).

decision was a brutal intervention in the political process transparently designed to assure the selection of a president whose nominees to the Supreme Court would continue the agenda of the present majority. If this were not "vulgarly partisan" enough, the accusation adds the suggestion that some of the justices did not want to see their rumored plans for retirement within the next four years thwarted by the prospect of uncongenial replacements. Only such indefensible motives could explain a decision the critics stated to be inadequately reasoned, devoid of principle, and inconsistent with the doctrinal commitments to federalism and sparing use of the equal protection clause the majority had elsewhere espoused when it suited its reactionary agenda.

Arguments from motive invite a reciprocal search for strategic motives moving those who make them. And if one were inclined to such a search, in this case the motive would not be hard to find: generate public, media, and political hostility in order to stiffen resistance to an uncongenial president's uncongenial judicial appointments (Bruce Ackerman's proposal that no justices be confirmed until 2005 is an example of such an attempt at mobilization).[6]

There is the deeper danger in this descent into accusations of bad faith: it erodes the high respect in which courts are held in this country and so degrades a precious national asset. Justice Stevens's stern warning against this danger of course contributed to it. Gratifying as it is to hunt for ulterior motives, we should be engaged in the more ordinary task of debating the correctness of the case's reasoning, as we do with other Supreme Court decisions.

Some critics seem to think that a case with such big practical consequences should proclaim a principle of equivalent grandeur: prominence in the history books should be matched with equal billing in the

---

6. If a majority of senators could be persuaded to announce such a novel posture, the president would have a ready justification for using his power to make recess appointments.

case books. *Bush* v. *Gore* certainly offers no spectacular breakthroughs in constitutional doctrine, nor did it deal with other problems that have come to light in the Florida vote but were not part of this case. That is because the case was the creature of the lower court decisions it reviewed. The key to seeing the normalcy of this case is just that. There is a good reason why the Court did not consider whether our system of choosing presidents accords with the principles of democracy, or whether the Constitution requires that all who arrive at the polls and attempt a choice should have their votes taken into account, or any other such large proposition. The Court considered the questions presented in a petition for certiorari to review a decision by the Florida Supreme Court.[7] That is what the Court is supposed to do, and that is what it did.

If I insist on viewing *Bush* v. *Gore* as regular Supreme Court litigation, then, the critics ask, was not the decision to grant certiorari itself irregular? Justice Breyer opens his dissent: "The Court was wrong to take this case." And Justice Souter: "The Court should not have reviewed . . . this case." Other critics have taken up this refrain. The Court has complete control over what cases it takes. The decision not to take a case needs no explanation and is without precedential value. The court has published rules to guide litigants in applying for certiorari. The usual occasion for a grant is some clear and stark conflict in the decisions of the lower federal courts or between those courts and the highest court of a state, crying out for a decision that restores uniformity to the law. The Court's rules also say that review may be granted if the decision below conflicts with one of its own decisions— again a necessity to maintain the structural integrity of the system. And there is the much rarer ground that there is a question of exceptional national importance that requires resolution at the highest level of the judiciary just because it is the highest.

---

7. Technically, the stay application was treated as a petition for certiorari (an accepted procedure in cases on a short fuse).

But these are rules only for the guidance of litigants—rules of thumb. The Court may do what it wants, and regularly ignores them. I am sure that the critics of *Bush* v. *Gore* applaud the Court's decision in the *Virginia Military Institute* (*VMI*) case, but there was no conflict in the circuits in that case and a quite unusual set of circumstances. On the other hand these same critics may have heaved a sigh of relief when the Court denied review in the *Milwaukee* case allowing the use of state paid vouchers in church-related schools—a decision on a frequently recurring issue of great importance that has put the law into considerable uncertainty. And few complain if the Court occasionally grants review and overturns a decision that seems egregiously wrong or unjust—in a death penalty case, for instance—even though there is no disuniformity in the law or a matter of general importance. Finally, if the Court senses that a decision below distorts or even fails to show proper deference to one of its own prior decisions, no matter how lacking in general significance, it may pounce to enforce respect. Or it may not.

The proper role of pragmatism and principle has long been a staple of Supreme Court commentary. The Court's authority depends on its adherence to principle, and principle is displayed in the coherence and transparency of the reasons it offers for its decisions. In *Bush* v. *Gore,* the critics say, the Court got it exactly wrong. It failed to act in a statesmanlike way in the one area where statesmanship is authorized: "The Court was wrong to take this case." And then, having taken the case, it acted in a political, unprincipled way in its actual decision, the point where principle alone should rule. This harsh judgment is unjustified. As I have shown, the Court's decision to take the case was in accord with past practice. Its resolution of the case was as well reasoned as many cases resolving sharply controverted issues. For sheer transparency of reasoning *Bush* v. *Gore* stacks up quite well against, say, *Romer* v. *Evans* (the Colorado gay ordinance case).

Recall the actual case, the actual petition, that the Court was called to act upon. Only five days earlier (in Bush I) the Court had unanimously vacated an earlier judgment of the Florida Supreme Court and asked the Florida court to clarify the basis for it. The Florida court in Bush II had disregarded the Supreme Court's mandate, and without even adverting to it, had given important effect to its own previous, now vacated, decision. What counsel of prudence dictated that the Court should turn the other cheek to such a clear act of insubordination? Surely not that the selection of the next president of the United States might in part depend on it. If care for the Court's standing bears on its exercise of discretion to take a case, then letting this pass would count as cowardly avoidance of difficulty, of controversy, and of the risk of just the obloquy that the disappointed losers have been heaping on the Court ever since. Cowardice is not prudence.

The critics say that this only locates the Court's folly at the earlier time when it granted certiorari in Bush I. Justice Souter: "The Court should not have reviewed either [Bush I] or [Bush II]." There is some more plausibility to that, although it is undercut by the fact that Bush I was decided by a unanimous Court. But the petition in Bush I had a lot to be said for it too: it presented difficult and important questions of interpretation of provisions of the Constitution (principally Article II, Section 1) and federal law (Title 3 of the U.S. Code). And even the argument I made on behalf of the Florida legislature—that these questions were not justiciable but should be left in the first instance to the state legislature and ultimately to the Congress—might have elicited an important and illuminating response from the Court. (In any event, the Court ignored and therefore may be said to have rejected that argument—surely a significant result in itself.) And to urge a lack of a conflict with other decisions on a question so unlikely to arise, but so important when it does, is irrelevant to the point of captiousness.

But there is more. The Florida court, in a dispute that touched the whole nation, acted in a strangely irregular way. That court had issued a stay no one had asked for and then extended a statutory deadline for certification of election tabulations, relying only on its claim of inherent equitable powers. This was troubling for two reasons. First, it is a serious constitutional question (to which there are certainly two sides) whether state courts are under a special obligation to hew closely to their legislatures' directions in respect to matters bearing on the selection of presidential electors. This question becomes acute when a court not only interprets the relevant state statute in an arguably aberrant way but also takes on an active managerial role nowhere set out in legislation and assigned by law to the secretary of state. The framers rather explicitly rejected putting the control of election procedures for the presidency in the hands of courts, so their specification (in Article II, Section 1, Paragraph 2) that the electors in each state shall be appointed "in such manner as the legislature thereof may direct" may be taken to have been a more pointed conferral of power on legislatures than would have been an assignment of the task to the states generally. (The same is true of the assignment in Article V of special responsibilities to state legislatures in the amendment process.) In its unanimous opinion the Court took this argument seriously:

> As a general rule, this Court defers to a state court's interpretation of a state statute. But in the case of a law enacted by a state legislature applicable not only to elections to state offices, but also to the selection of Presidential electors, the legislature is not acting solely under the authority given it by the people of the State, but by virtue of a direct grant of authority made under Art. II, § 1, cl. 2, of the United States Constitution.

Second, there had already been two tabulations of the vote, and the intervention of the Florida Supreme Court in Bush I to prolong the process and make time for still a third count gave rise to a reasonable concern that this was partisan manipulation. (As the Bush people put it: Keep on counting until Gore wins.) Although such a suspicion of partisanship was strenuously kept out of the briefs, oral argument and ultimate decision, it was understandable for the Bush lawyers to raise it in the petition seeking review, to get the Court's attention. Clearing the air of such suspicions—one way or the other—when so much was at stake would be an additional and entirely proper reason for the Court to take Bush I.

It is only against the background of the Court's unanimous opinion, vacation, and remand order in Bush I, and of the Florida court's decision in Bush II, that the Supreme Court's decision in the Bush II case can be judged. Bush II is not some abstract pronouncement of political science (or political preference) but a response to a petition to review a particular decision of a subordinate court. Against that background the decision of the Florida court may be characterized as somewhere between debatable and indefensible. Three of the seven Florida justices (including the chief justice, who had joined the court in its earlier opinion) this time dissented in very strong terms, anticipating the grounds for reversal given by the Supreme Court in Bush II. That circumstance alone should draw the teeth of the charge that the Supreme Court's decision was indefensible, unprincipled, beyond the pale, and so on.

At the oral argument of Bush II several of the justices were palpably annoyed. They were annoyed not only that the Florida court had not responded to the remand order—after all, they might yet get around to that—but also that it had treated the remand as a nullity by ordering that votes counted during the extended recount be added to Gore's total. The Florida court's order extending the recount period had been vacated, so that whatever had occurred pursuant to it should not have been given legal effect. The Florida court simply ignored this point. There are many cases—trivial and important—in which the Court drops its usually distant and deferential posture toward an inferior court because it senses its mandate has not been respected. (Justice O'Connor has been particularly insistent that lower courts respect the Court's mandate, in one case harshly clipping the wings of a circuit court that had repeatedly defied the Court's mandate in order to thwart an execution and in another case rebuking a state court that had failed to follow the Court's mandate in order to speed an execution. Thus she has been inconsistent only if viewed through the vulgar journalistic lens of political consistency.) The stay of the Florida court's decision granted on December 9 can best be explained as a response to the disrespect implicit in that decision.[8] That four justices noted their dissent from that stay—when in another case they might have shared the majority's sense—does not necessarily reflect badly on the Court and well on them. Maybe the four dissenters had joined in the prior unanimous opinion, which had been "dissed" by the Florida court, only because they wanted to avoid a divided Court in such a highly charged case. I know nothing of that, and whatever I hear I relegate to the category of gossip. What we have is Bush I and the Florida court's subsequent behavior. I also relegate to the realm of gossip the altogether plausible conjecture that Justices O'Connor and Kennedy agreed with the chief justice's concurrence but did not join it because they wanted to state a ground—the denial of equal protection —on which seven justices agreed. But most of all I dismiss as gossip the conjecture that Justices Souter and Breyer didn't really mean it when they, too, found the Florida court's decree violated the Constitution, that they had only expressed that view in the hope of peeling off Justices Kennedy and O'Connor to their stated preferred resolution of yet another remand to the Florida court, and that somehow they had been outmaneuvered into stating their agreement with the majority's substantive decision.

So at last we come to the holding of the case that the voting scheme

8. The outrage against the stay by 673 law professors is, to say the least, overwrought. If the decision on the merits was justified, the stay becomes irrelevant. Yes, it did shut down the counting three and a half days earlier, but by hypothesis that counting was being done in an unconstitutional way. Moreover, if the Court had already decided on the basis of the stay papers that the Florida court's order was clearly wrong and in defiance of its own remand order, then a stay would be justified.

instituted by the Florida court violated equal protection. On that score, don't listen to me. Here is what Justice Souter says:

> It is true that the Equal Protection Clause does not forbid the use of a variety of voting mechanisms within a jurisdiction, even though different mechanisms will have different levels of effectiveness in recording voters' intentions; local variety can be justified by concerns about cost, the potential value of innovation, and so on. But evidence in the record here suggests that a different order of disparity obtains under rules for determining a voter's intent than have been applied (and could continue to be applied) to identical types of ballots used in identical brands of machines and exhibiting identical physical characteristics (such as "hanging" or "dimpled" chads). See, e.g., Tr., at 238–242 (Dec. 2–3, 2000) (testimony of Palm Beach County Canvassing Board Chairman Judge Charles Burton describing varying standards applied to imperfectly punched ballots in Palm Beach County during precertification manual recount); id. at 497–500 (similarly describing varying standards applied in Miami-Dade County); Tr. of Hearing 8–10 (Dec. 8, 2000) (soliciting from county canvassing boards proposed protocols for determining voters' intent but declining to provide a precise, uniform standard). I can conceive of no legitimate state interest served by these differing treatments of the expressions of voters' fundamental rights. The differences appear wholly arbitrary.[9]

And here is Justice Breyer:

> The majority's third concern does implicate principles of fundamental fairness. The majority concludes that the Equal Protection Clause requires that a manual recount be governed not only by the

9. It is beyond me how, having written this, Justice Souter can also write that he is "in substantial agreement" with Justices Stevens's and Ginsburg's root-and-branch rejection of the Court's decision.

uniform general standard of the "clear intent of the voter," but also by uniform subsidiary standards (for example, a uniform determination whether indented, but not perforated, "undervotes" should count). The opinion points out that the Florida Supreme Court ordered the inclusion of Broward County's undercounted "legal votes" even though those votes included ballots that were not perforated but simply "dimpled," while newly recounted ballots from other counties will likely include only votes determined to be "legal" on the basis of a stricter standard. In light of our previous remand, the Florida Supreme Court may have been reluctant to adopt a more specific standard than that provided for by the legislature for fear of exceeding its authority under Article II. However, since the use of different standards could favor one or the other of the candidates, since time was, and is, too short to permit the lower courts to iron out significant differences through ordinary judicial review, and since the relevant distinction was embodied in the order of the State's highest court, I agree that, in these very special circumstances, basic principles of fairness may well have counseled the adoption of a uniform standard to address the problem. In light of the majority's disposition, I need not decide whether, or the extent to which, as a remedial matter, the Constitution would place limits upon the content of the uniform standard.

That makes seven justices in agreement that the Florida court's decree either instituted or ratified a constitutional violation. Yet the Court's many ferocious critics complain that this conclusion is "indefensible," "unprincipled," and a menace to the rule of law. It is said that the judgment of unconstitutionality implies far more than the Court would be willing to accept in other contexts. The judgment implies that our system of highly various, decentralized, locally controlled vote tabulation systems are all unconstitutional, so that hardly an election in the country is valid under the Court's strictures. Then it is said that the Court itself understood this and explicitly disavowed any principle its decision might imply. It explicitly embraced lack of principle, ad hocery, vulgar partisanship: "Our consideration is limited to the present circumstances, for the problem of equal protection in election processes generally presents many complexities."

These harsh accusations are quite unjust. There is an obvious difference between the regime the Court struck down and the rational universe of diverse and divergent election procedures. True it is that the methods of tabulation in our country vary from state to state and even from precinct to precinct. But these differences are ordained before any particular election is held, and, existing ex ante, they do not systematically disfavor any candidate or group of voters.[10] The Florida court by contrast set in motion a system of disparities *after* the election had been held, when it was known just what depended on every subjective judgment, every change of standard from one moment to the next in counting the ballots. It is this difference between ex ante random disparities and the too easily manipulable variable standards set up after the fact that prompted the Court's limiting language so gleefully and maliciously quoted against it. After all, both Justices Souter and Breyer in the passages quoted above mark the same distinction. (Justice Breyer: "The use of different standards could favor one or the other of the candidates.") And every student of the Supreme Court knows that it is canonical for the Court, when it decides for the first time an issue on an unusual set of facts, to issue such a caveat. It is almost boilerplate. Those who charge the Court not just with error but with bad faith on this score are open to condemnation in kind.

Finally, there is the remedy. This is the most vulnerable part of the

---

10. It might be said that poorer precincts may use less accurate machinery, but that inaccuracy ex ante may also be random relative to any candidate. Or that they systematically lead to a larger number of invalid ballots, so that a class of voters is systematically undervalued. If that is true it would certainly constitute an equal protection violation, but that kind of claim was not made in this case—though perhaps it might have been.

Court's opinion, but it is at least as defensible as scores of Supreme Court remedial "snappers" in all sorts of cases. On the whole I think the Court has the better of it, but I am open to persuasion on this point.[11] The objection is that, even assuming the correctness of its equal protection analysis, the Court should have vacated the Florida court's scheme and remanded the case to it to attempt to devise one that accorded with equal protection. Instead the Court famously wrote:

> Seven Justices of the Court agree that there are constitutional prob-
> lems with the recount ordered by the Florida Supreme Court that
> demand a remedy . . . Because the Florida Supreme Court has said
> that the Florida Legislature intended to obtain the safe-harbor bene-
> fits of 3 U.S.C. § 5, Justice Breyer's proposed remedy—remanding to
> the Florida Supreme Court for its ordering of a constitutionally
> proper contest until December 18—contemplates action in violation
> of the Florida election code, and hence could not be part of an
> "appropriate" order authorized by Fla. Stat. § 102.168(8) (2000).

True it is that the December 12 "safe harbor provision" is just that, an option available to the states, not a requirement of federal law. But the Court also did not just make it up that the Florida court had stated several times its interpretation of Florida law as requiring compliance with that deadline. It is also true that these references were made by the Florida court when it did not anticipate that it would be used against it in this way. That strengthens not weakens it as an authorita-tive exposition of Florida law, and the Court was justified in holding it to that interpretation.

---

11. It is in part because of my doubts on this score that I preferred the concur-ring opinion's analysis in terms of the Florida court's subversion of the Florida legislative scheme and thus its violation of Article II, Section 1. I commend the analysis along these lines—written by my colleague Einer Elhauge—in our brief on behalf of the Florida legislature in Bush II. On that basis an outright reversal would have been more appropriate.

In any event, the Court did not reverse outright; it did "remand for further proceedings not inconsistent with this opinion." The next move, therefore, was up to the Florida court. It's just that the requirement that it comply with the wishes of the Florida legislature—in this the per curiam took a leaf from the concurring justices' book—made that move (as they say in chess) a forced move. Perhaps even the Florida court would have come to that conclusion, with at least one more judge of that court abandoning the sinking ship. Instead, as also happens in chess, rather than moving into checkmate, Gore resigned.

If reasonable people might differ about the importance of the December 12 date in Florida law, there is much less doubt about December 18 as a milestone date: Section 7 of Title III of the United States Code states that "the electors . . . of each State shall meet and give their votes" on a fixed date, which in 2000 was December 18. And though it might have been possible to devise a uniform scheme of vote counting to be completed by that date, it would have been quite impossible to do so in a way that complied with established Florida law. The new vote count would have had to proceed under the Florida laws governing election contests. These require judicial review—including court challenges, trials with witnesses, and appellate process—for each contested vote. In much simpler circumstances these contests have taken as long as sixteen months to resolve. The Court adverted to this:

> It is obvious that the recount cannot be conducted in compliance with the requirements of equal protection and due process without substantial additional work. It would require not only the adoption (after opportunity for argument) of adequate statewide standards for determining what is a legal vote, and practicable procedures to implement them, but also orderly judicial review of any disputed matters that might arise. In addition, the Secretary of State has advised that the recount of only a portion of the ballots requires that the vote tabulation equipment be used to screen out undervotes, a function for which the machines were not designed. If a recount of

overvotes were also required, perhaps even a second screening would be necessary. Use of the equipment for this purpose, and any new software developed for it, would have to be evaluated for accuracy by the Secretary of State, as required by Fla. Stat. § 101.015 (2000).

This leaves Justice Stevens's argument that the only real deadline is January 6, when the votes are opened and counted in Congress under the Twelfth Amendment. He adduces for this proposition the precedent of Hawaii in the election of 1960 being allowed to change its electoral vote on January 4. This is mere persiflage. Nothing turned on Hawaii's electoral vote in that election. The wording of Section 7 is mandatory, and, unlike Section 5, it is not directed only at dealing with the difficulties that may arise when a state appoints conflicting slates of electors. But the Court did not rely on Section 7 and the impossibility of completing a recount by alternative procedures in six days without rewriting Florida law. And neither the Florida court nor the Supreme Court of the United States may simply make up such procedures and still comply with Article II, Section 1, Paragraph 2. So if this is the point it all comes down to, it is far too fine a point on which to rest so vast an edifice of denunciation.

The critics also argue that this was a nakedly pro-Bush ruling because the members of the majority abandoned their usual hostility to the protections of the equal protection clause, their insistence that only intentional violations may be corrected under that clause (as per *Washington* v. *Davis* and *United States* v. *Morrison*) and their deference to state law. Once again this is partisan persiflage. First, there is no intent-test problem at all. The complaint was that different voters were treated differently, and that *that* disparate treatment was the very counting scheme the Florida court ordered.[12] Then it is just false that

---

12. Also the court's order provided that only some ballots be looked at for yet a third time: only the so-called undervotes, not the overvotes and not the votes that

the Court majority regularly devalues equal protection claims. It is the majority who insist on the rigorous application of equal protection in cases of racial preferences. The closest precedent is *Shaw* v. *Reno*. But the critics and dissenters don't like those cases either. Now you might say that this doesn't really count: a justice is *really* favorable to equal protection only when it favors certain groups. Give me a break! And as to deference to state law, it is the Bush majority justices who have refused—just as they did in this case—to allow states to hide behind aberrant interpretations of state law to defeat constitutional property right protections. And in those cases it is the dissenters who have raised the banner of deference to state law. The majority may or may not have been right in those cases, but the charge that the majority in Bush II acted opportunistically and abandoned principles it elsewhere follows regularly is palpably wrong.[13]

Finally, the Court's detractors ask archly whether the majority's decision would have been the same if a state court had been caught trying to steal the election for George Bush. Who knows? Based on what I have been arguing, I have reason to hope that the majority would have decided the same way even if its decision would have made Al Gore president. May I also hope that in that mirror image case, Justices Stevens and Ginsburg would have written the same dissents they did in this one.

---

had been previously tabulated as legal votes but which on manual inspection might be judged invalid.

13. True, in the property rights cases the minority voted to save programs favorable to the environment and legal services to the poor, and in this case it protested a decision that defeated Al Gore. But that is hardly the kind of consistency the critics are talking about.

Not as Bad as *Plessy*. Worse.

I swore never to write an essay like this one. Who is served by another demonstration that *Bush* v. *Gore* was, as a legal matter, utterly indefensible? Those who agree do not need it. Those who disagree will not believe it.

But the colloquy among the contributors to this book has persuaded me that something important about *Bush* v. *Gore* has still been missed —by its (many) critics and (few) supporters alike—something that can be uncovered only by going over, yet again, the illegality of the Supreme Court's opinion.

What has been missed is the feature of *Bush* v. *Gore* that distinguishes it from other Supreme Court decisions with which one might powerfully disagree. Depending on one's views, such decisions might include on the one hand *Plessy* v. *Ferguson* (in which the Court, a century ago, upheld racial segregation) or on the other *Roe* v. *Wade*. Disagree as we might with such decisions as *Plessy* or *Roe*, the breathtaking indefensibility of *Bush* v. *Gore* is of an entirely different order. To be sure, the wrongness of *Bush* v. *Gore* may be much less consequential, given the very real possibility that Bush would have become president in any event. But at bottom *Bush* v. *Gore* is worse even than the notorious *Plessy*, and it makes *Roe* look like an exemplar of principled decision making. I will try to say why.

This chapter addresses *Bush* v. *Gore* only from a legal point of view. Some supporters of the Court's decision defend it not legally, but pragmatically and politically. They say that the presidential election controversy threatened political "chaos" and that the nation needed "closure." In other words, we are told to throw the law out the window and think about the "good of the country." I will have nothing to say about such claims here. Perhaps *Bush* v. *Gore* is defensible as a political (rather than legal) decision, perhaps not. But throwing the law out the window when it comes to the decisions of the United States Supreme Court does not seem to me a likely recipe for the country's good.

There were three major legal components of the Court's decision in *Bush* v. *Gore*: (1) the famous stay, which temporarily enjoined the statewide hand-counting of votes in Florida pending the Supreme Court's decision; (2) the Court's finding that this hand-count violated the equal protection clause, primarily because of the lack of specific rules for determining which ballots were to be deemed legal votes; and (3) the Court's ultimate decision to halt the manual recount for good (rather than remanding to the Florida Supreme Court to cure the equal protection violation).

I am not going to discuss the stay at all, although many lawyers consider it astonishingly egregious. And I am only going to say a few words—later—about the equal protection violation. My focus, rather, will be on the decisive, final piece of *Bush* v. *Gore*.

The *Bush* v. *Gore* majority said it had to halt the counting of votes because there was insufficient time to establish satisfactory vote-counting rules and still complete the recount by December 12, 2000. This was incontrovertibly true, especially because the Court had stayed the count on December 9 and then issued its opinion approximately two hours before midnight on December 12. There was, however, one question to be answered: Why did the recount have to be completed by December 12?

Florida's election laws do not mention a December 12 deadline. They do not even hint at it. Nor is any such deadline imposed by federal law. As everyone understood, the pertinent federal statute made December 12 not a deadline but a "safe harbor" date.

Under the federal statute, states are given an incentive to resolve any disputes about who won their electoral college votes by December 12. If they do so, their resolution of such disputes becomes immune from certain challenges when, in January, the vice president and the members of Congress convene to count up all the states' votes. But federal law does not *require* states to do anything by December 12. Most of the states in this election submitted their electoral votes after December 12. In fact, in Hawaii in 1960, a court-ordered recount— declaring that John F. Kennedy had won the state's election, not Richard M. Nixon, who was initially declared the victor—was not completed *until December 28.*[1]

So the December 12 deadline was not required by federal law. Did the *Bush* v. *Gore* majority say otherwise? No. The majority ruled that extending the count beyond December 12 would transgress *state* law (it would be "a violation of the Florida election code"). But if the question was a matter of state law, how could the United States Supreme Court decide it?

It couldn't, and every single justice knew it. How, then, did the majority come up with a December 12 deadline? The opinion says

1. Hawaii initially certified Nixon as the winner by 98 votes. A state court ordered a recount, despite protests by Nixon supporters that the recount could not be completed by the federal safe-harbor date. On December 28, Kennedy was officially declared the winner by 115 votes. In January, when all the states' votes were tallied in Washington under the supervision of Vice President Nixon, Hawaii's electoral votes were duly counted in favor of Kennedy

only one thing on this crucial point, and what it says defies the credibility of a child (I know, because I have an eight-year-old daughter who took a preternatural interest in the case). The majority said that they had to honor the December 12 deadline out of deference to—was it the United States Constitution? The Florida legislature? No, it was out of deference to the Florida Supreme Court.

That's right: the Florida Supreme Court, that august authority to which the United States Supreme Court refused to defer on virtually any other point of law in the entire controversy. The Florida Supreme Court had been wrong (we were told) about the state-law deadline for certifying the election results. The Florida Supreme Court had been wrong about the rules governing the manual recount. According to at least three of the five members of the *Bush* v. *Gore* majority, the Florida court had also been wrong about the state-law standard of review applicable to election contests; wrong about the state-law definition of a "legal vote"; wrong about the appropriateness under state law of a statewide manual recount; and wrong about the degree of deference due under state law to Secretary of State Katherine Harris. But on the dispositive, count-ending, election-determining issue of the December 12 deadline, the majority's hands were regrettably tied by their respectful regard for the Florida justices' unquestionable power to declare that date to be the deadline under Florida law.

Unfortunately, there was one more little problem. The Florida justices had *not* declared December 12 to be the deadline. On the contrary, they had merely ordered the manual recount to proceed "forthwith." They had not set any deadline by which the recount was to conclude.

To be sure, the Florida justices were probably hoping, perhaps even trying, to get the count finished by December 12. But they had never imposed any strict December 12 deadline. Nor had they said anything about what would happen, under state law, if the count could not be completed by December 12.

Did this little difficulty trouble the majority? Not a bit. They got over it in a single sentence. The Florida Supreme Court, the majority observed, had held that Florida law was designed so that Florida could "participate fully in the federal electoral process." If that's not a clear embrace of a strict December 12 deadline, what is? I repeat: Florida was to "participate fully in the federal election process." On the basis of those words from the state supreme court—and that's the exact and only quotation offered—the *Bush* v. *Gore* majority declared that the Florida justices had authoritatively read Florida law to call for a final vote count by the federal safe-harbor date of December 12.

Readers quite probably will not believe me. They will think that there must be something more in the majority's opinion on this point. Surely it could not have been that bad. Well, look it up. Read it— carefully—and judge for yourselves:

> The Supreme Court of Florida has said that the legislature intended the State's electors to "participate fully in the electoral process," as provided in 3 U.S.C. § 5. That statute, in turn, requires that any controversy or contest that is designed to lead to a conclusive selection of electors be completed by December 12. That date is upon us. . . . Because the Florida Supreme Court has said that the Florida legislature intended to obtain the safe-harbor benefits of 3 U.S.C. § 5, Justice Breyer's proposed remedy—remanding to the Florida Supreme Court for its ordering of a constitutionally proper contest until December 18—contemplates action in violation of the Florida election code.

Even those who have defended *Bush* v. *Gore* have called this passage "not . . . very persuasive."[2] Something stronger needs to be said. This passage—on which the entire decision turns—is not merely unpersuasive. It is deceptive and indefensible.

In the second sentence quoted, the majority uses language that

---

2. Michael W. McConnell, "Two-and-a-Half Cheers for *Bush* v. *Gore*," in The Vote (Cass R. Sunstein and Richard A. Epstein, eds. 2001).

would lead all but the most expert readers to believe that federal law "*requires* that any controversy or contest . . . be completed by December 12." In fact, federal law does no such thing. As noted above, under federal law, December 12 is only a safe-harbor date—which the Court itself acknowledges in the last sentence quoted.

As a result, the majority is obliged to say that *Florida* has chosen to make the December 12 safe-harbor date into a strict deadline as a matter of state law. To achieve this result, the majority uses language suggesting that Florida statutory law creates a December 12 deadline. Thus in the last quoted sentence, the Court says that a recount beyond that date would be "in violation of the Florida election code." But the Florida election code says nothing about a December 12 deadline.

As a result, the majority is obliged to say that the *Florida Supreme Court* read the December 12 deadline into the Florida election code. But the Florida justices did no such thing. Therefore, the five members of the *Bush* v. *Gore* majority take the phrase "participate fully in the electoral process" and *pretend*—there is no other word for it—that this phrase somehow amounted to a judicial finding that the state legislature intended to make December 12 a state law deadline for the counting of votes.

The full truth is even worse. Remember that only a week earlier, the United States Supreme Court had reprimanded the Florida justices for their earlier decision setting a November 27 deadline for the "certification" of the election results. What had the Florida justices done wrong in their earlier decision, which the Supreme Court vacated? They had, precisely, dared to assert a power to *read into Florida election law a deadline not expressly specified in Florida's election code.* Which undoubtedly explains why, one week later, the majority in *Bush* v. *Gore* had to defer to the Florida Supreme Court's asserted power to *read into Florida election law a deadline not expressly specified in Florida's election code.*

In other words, to decide *Bush* v. *Gore* the way it did, the majority had to do something it pretended it *wasn't doing* and *couldn't* do (decide a matter of state law) by pretending that the Florida justices had done something they *hadn't done* and, supposedly, *couldn't* do (set a deadline of December 12 for the completion of the election contest, even though this deadline was nowhere expressed or even implied by Florida's election code).

There was no December 12 deadline. The majority made it up. On this pretense, the presidential election was determined.

Now turn to the Court's finding that the hand-counting of votes ordered by the Florida Supreme Court violated the equal protection clause. I will say only a little about this holding.

To be clear: this finding was *not* legally indefensible. The absence of clear vote-counting rules in the manual recount created obvious risks of arbitrariness, unequal treatment, and partisan subjectivity. As the *Bush* v. *Gore* majority observed, "dimpled chads" in at least one county were apparently being deemed legal votes, while identical ballots in other counties were not.

It is certainly defensible to hold that an electoral process is arbitrary when different counties apply different rules to identically situated votes or voters, with the result that some people lose their votes simply because they happen to live in one county rather than another. We can all think of numerous examples of such unequal treatment that would seem blatantly unconstitutional.

For example, surely the Court would never have let different counties use different rules for deciding which citizens were legal voters, so that in one county a large number of voters—disproportionately minority voters—could be wrongly turned away from the polls. Nor, surely, would the Court have let one Florida county use a ballot totally different from and more confusing than the ballots elsewhere, resulting in thousands of people in that county losing their votes. And most clearly of all, under the principle of *Bush* v. *Gore,* the Court would never have permitted a county-by-county system of discretionary decisions about whether to count *absentee* ballots, so that officials in one county could deem certain absentee ballots to be legal votes although technically in violation of Florida law, while officials in another county deemed identical ballots invalid.

All these things happened in Florida, in this election. Nor were they discovered only after the fact; on the contrary, all were the subject of lawsuits before or at the time *Bush* v. *Gore* was decided. But not one of these other disparities and inequalities—all of which favored Bush, and every one of which involved a disputed number of votes potentially large enough to alter the election result—was dealt with by the Supreme Court or any other court in terms of the equal protection reasoning announced in *Bush* v. *Gore*.

Once again, the point is not that the finding of an equal protection violation in *Bush* v. *Gore* was legally indefensible. It *was* defensible (although mistaken, in my view). But it was also *suspicious*.

By saying so, I do not mean to impugn the majority's motives. I am not concerned here with the majority's motives. The question is objective. The question is whether the Supreme Court's resolution of the 2000 presidential contest can or cannot (for whatever reason) be taken seriously in the legal terms in which it is presented. From this point of view, a certain suspicion about the equal protection finding, which was literally unprecedented, is inevitable. The suspicion is twofold.

First, reasonable people may feel that the *Bush* v. *Gore* majority, regardless of whether they were acting in subjective good faith, used the language of equal protection to rationalize a wholly unprincipled decision. On this point, many have highlighted the majority's statement that its consideration of the equal protection issue was "limited to the present circumstances." Critics say this statement tells lower court judges not to apply the reasoning of *Bush* v. *Gore* to other cases, which would plainly be an illegitimate instruction. I think too much has been made of this point. We do not know whether or how the Court will apply its reasoning in the future. What we do know, however, is that this reasoning was *not* applied to other disputed Florida aspects in *this* election. And that is very troubling, because it leaves thoughtful citizens suspicious about whether the election contest was decided in accordance with law.

Second, reasonable people may also feel that the equal protection principle did not accord with the settled convictions of the very members of the Court who decided *Bush* v. *Gore*. On this point, critics have cited the many decisions by the current Court espousing a "federalist" agenda. The claim here is that the majority's decision in *Bush* v. *Gore* contradicts the majority's own expressed commitments to state autonomy. I am again dubious about this claim, because the Court's federalism can be understood as a commitment to the autonomy of state *legislatures* (not courts), and it is easy enough to describe *Bush* v. *Gore* as protecting the Florida legislature (from a wayward Florida Supreme Court).

But insufficient attention has been paid to a different kind of case, much more closely on point, in which members of the *Bush* v. *Gore* majority do not seem to have taken the same position that they took here. Twenty years ago, when John Anderson mounted a third-party presidential campaign, Ohio refused to let Anderson's name on the state's election ballot. Ohio's reason was that Anderson had failed to obtain the number of signatures required by state law for third-party candidates. Anderson brought suit. He pointed out that Ohio required more signatures for third-party candidates than for major-party candidates. This disparity, Anderson argued, violated the equal protection clause and the First Amendment.

The case was not decided by the Supreme Court until 1983, long after the election. No immediate election-changing consequences were on the line, meaning that the decision was essentially prospective, not retrospective. As a result, the justices presumably decided the case based on their actual legal views. Anderson won (on First Amendment grounds).[3]

---

3. The case was *Anderson* v. *Celebrezze*, 460 U.S. 780 (1983).

But there was a strong, four-justice dissent in the case. The dissent essentially argued that exacting constitutional scrutiny of Ohio's electoral processes was improper because *state* law governs elections, even presidential elections. According to the dissent, the only role for federal courts in such matters is to ensure that the state has acted "rationally." Who wrote this rational-basis dissent? William Rehnquist. Who joined it? Sandra Day O'Connor.

Given the extreme closeness of the election in Florida and the significant evidence of machine failure, the Florida Supreme Court's statewide manual recount was almost certainly legitimate under a mere-rationality test. Did Rehnquist, in his *Bush* v. *Gore* concurrence, say anything about the *Anderson* case? Yes. In fact, his concurrence begins with a quotation from that case. The concurrence emphasizes, quoting *Anderson,* that state regulations of presidential elections "implicate a uniquely important federal interest" demanding careful constitutional scrutiny. Rehnquist neglects to mention that he is quoting a decision from which he himself vigorously dissented.

But what about the merits of the Rehnquist concurrence, putting aside the question of whether it reflected its author's genuine legal views? Some supporters of *Bush* v. *Gore* argue that all the problems in the majority opinion can be avoided, and the Court's decision placed on much firmer grounds, by adopting the reasoning offered in the concurrence.

Post hoc rationalization is standard operating procedure in legal thought. Sometimes the reasoning in a concurrence is belatedly recognized as superior to that in the majority opinion. But in *Bush* v. *Gore,* there was a good reason why the concurring opinion did not command a majority. In the majority opinion, at least the substantive constitutional holding—the finding of an equal protection violation— was within the ambit of legal defensibility. By contrast, in the concurrence, the constitutional holding itself is indefensible.

The concurrence argues that the Florida Supreme Court's order of a manual recount strayed so far from the clear dictates of Florida statutory law that it violated the Constitution's command that a state's electors be selected "in such Manner as the Legislature thereof may direct." To support this argument, the concurring justices could not merely claim that they had found a superior reading of Florida's election laws, under which the recount was wrong. (Recall that federal courts, including the Supreme Court, are not authorized to second-guess a state supreme court on matters of state law.) Instead, the concurrence had to claim—and did claim—that "the Florida Supreme Court's interpretation of the Florida election laws impermissibly distorted them" beyond the reasonable bounds of "fair reading."

This is an extremely difficult case to make. Florida's election contest statute expressly vests in the state judiciary the broadest possible legal discretion: "to ensure that each allegation in the complaint is investigated, examined, or checked, to prevent or correct any alleged wrong, and to provide any relief appropriate under such circumstances" (Fla. Stat. § 102.168(8)). Obviously this language did not compel the ordering of a statewide manual recount in *Bush* v. *Gore.* But just as obviously, a reasonable judge could decide that such a recount was "appropriate" "to ensure" that each allegation of error was "investigated" and that "any alleged wrong" was "corrected." The Florida justices' order, in other words, was well within the extremely broad ambit of the statutory language.

Against this conclusion, the concurrence's main argument, repeated by such academic supporters as Richard Epstein,[4] was that the Florida justices had gone fundamentally wrong on a state law procedural point. The Florida justices had treated the election contest as a "de novo" proceeding, when, we are told, the proper standard of review in a Florida election contest is merely to decide whether the

---

4. Richard Epstein, " 'In Such Manner as the Legislature Thereof May Direct': The Outcome in *Bush* v. *Gore* Defended," in The Vote (Cass R. Sunstein and Richard A. Epstein, eds. 2001).

decisions made in the earlier "protest" and "certification" proceedings amounted to an "abuse of discretion."

Under Florida law, county canvassing boards initially tally the votes within their respective counties. If parties "protest" these tallies, the canvassing boards "may" conduct manual recounts before submitting final returns to the secretary of state, who officially calculates the totals and "certifies" the winner. Only then can an election "contest" take place. According to the *Bush* v. *Gore* concurrence, the contest should merely review the earlier protest/certification proceedings for abuse of discretion. By treating the contest as de novo, says the concurrence, the Florida Supreme Court "emptie[d] certification of virtually all legal consequence," a result said to be in manifest violation of the statutory scheme.

This reasoning simply overlooks a critical fact about the Florida election code. Once this fact is recognized, it becomes perfectly reasonable to treat the election contest as a de novo proceeding, without "empt[ying] certification" of "legal consequence" at all.

Florida's protest and contest rules govern the election not only of federal officers, but also, and much more numerously, of state officers. State officeholders can differ from their federal counterparts in an important respect. Federal senators and representatives do not take office until January, two months after a November election. By contrast, at least some of Florida's elected officers take office immediately after election.

With respect to such state officials, if there were no expeditious determination of the election results *prior* to an election contest, there could be situations in which no one could authoritatively take office. There might be no legislators in vacated seats. There might be no mayor or city council in a given municipality. When the term of an outgoing officeholder expires on or just after election day, and when the newly elected officer is to take office forthwith, it is obviously essential to have *someone* expeditiously and authoritatively, even if only provisionally, declared a winner.

As soon as one sees the need for an expeditious provisional determination of the election winner, it becomes perfectly reasonable to make the election contest an essentially de novo proceeding. The protest-and-certification process is, by design, expedited and utilitarian. It serves the goal of producing an authoritative result in short order, to ensure that *someone* can take office. That is why state law provides for a seven-day certification deadline in most cases. Indeed, Florida even gives its secretary of state discretion to reject a recount submitted on the eighth day following the election, apparently without regard to whether the recount is accurate and would change the certification result.

The contest process, by contrast, is concerned with ensuring to the extent possible that the true, lawful result of the election is discovered and respected. That is why the contest statute empowers judges to "investigate" "each allegation" of mistake or wrongdoing that might have occurred in the necessarily expedited protest/certification proceedings, to "correct any alleged error" made in those proceedings, and to order any "appropriate" relief. This way of looking at Florida's two procedures is fully consistent with treating the contest as de novo, because the purpose of the contest is to allow judges to investigate and correct errors potentially made in the haste of certification.

From this point of view, decisions made by the county canvassing boards or the secretary of state should be reviewed under the lenient abuse-of-discretion standard with respect to an election *protest*, but not with respect to an election *contest*. Moreover, while time-consuming hand-counting might well be *disfavored* during the *certification* process, it would be perfectly plausible to *favor* hand-counting in the *contest* phase, at least if there was evidence of machine error.

From this perfectly reasonable viewpoint, the concurrence's chief claim—that a de novo contest proceeding "empties certification of virtually all legal consequence"—is simply mistaken or confused. The certification would ensure that *someone* is seated in office expeditiously, and it would determine *who* is to do so. These are very important "legal consequences." The certified winner would wield all the powers of his office at least during the pendency of the contest. And under Florida law, contests can take as much time as the judiciary deems "appropriate"—over a year in some prior cases.

The most one can reasonably say is that Florida's two processes are both ill-tailored to the exceptional position of presidential elector. The electors do not require an expeditious certification, because they do not take office immediately. But a very lengthy contest would be equally inappropriate, because the electors exercise the power of their office only once—in January, two months after the election—and never again.

These considerations, however, do not cut against the Florida Supreme Court's decisions. They cut in favor. The haste of the certification deadline had caused at least one county (according to its own statements) to halt a manual recount of votes that was turning up errors in the machine count. Other counties, however, had not been asked in the protest proceedings to hand-count their votes at all. Hence a statewide recount could easily be deemed "appropriate" to "investigate" "each allegation" of error and to ensure, as best the judiciary could within the time available, that the true result of the election would be discovered and respected.[5]

This interpretation of Florida's protest and contest proceedings is, of course, not mandatory. The concurrence's alternative view, in which the contest exists merely to ensure that there have been no abuses of discretion in the protest/certification proceedings, is another possible interpretation (although, I think, inferior to the one

5. This analysis also suggests that Secretary of State Harris might indeed have abused her discretion when she insisted upon the one-week certification deadline, because the one good legal reason for insisting upon so expeditious a certification process did not apply (the electors do not take office immediately). But whatever one says about the Florida justices' *certification* decision, their subsequent *contest* decision was plainly within the ambit of the Florida code, under the interpretation offered above.

described above). But the concurrence's claim that the Florida Supreme Court's decision was legally "absurd," or that its "interpretation of the Florida election laws impermissibly distorted them" beyond the bounds of reason, is insupportable.

Within a short time after the Supreme Court decided *Bush* v. *Gore,* the case dropped off the front pages and the nightly news. Whether there was simmering public discontent with the decision, or instead widespread indifference, is another matter. I suspect indifference.

One reason is that the public does not expect Supreme Court decisions to be free from deep political or ideological divisions. After all, if the Supreme Court made up the December 12 deadline in *Bush* v. *Gore,* didn't the Court equally "make up" the right of privacy announced in *Roe* v. *Wade?* A number of commentators have endorsed the idea that *Bush* v. *Gore,* if legally indefensible, is no more indefensible than a case like *Roe.* If, the argument seems to run, one wants to support "judicial activism" in *Roe,* one had better be prepared to take the bitter with the sweet.

In these final paragraphs I address the comparison between *Bush* v. *Gore* and other cases, like *Roe* or *Plessy* v. *Ferguson,* with which one might powerfully disagree. As noted above, I believe that *Bush* v. *Gore* is not comparable to these cases. In one important respect, *Bush* v. *Gore* is in fact much worse.

Critics of *Roe* say that the Court in that case read into the Constitution a right that the justices favored but that cannot be squared with the Constitution's text, history, or any other legitimate source of constitutional interpretation. Supporters of *Roe* say the opposite. They hold that the case rests on principles fully justifiable, textually and historically, as a matter of legitimate constitutional interpretation.

People can have differing views about this. But at the end of the day, their disagreement is a disagreement of a certain kind. It is a disagreement about constitutional principle.

The question is whether a certain freedom should or should not be recognized as a constitutional right. Supporters of *Roe* ardently defend the fundamental, constitutional status of this freedom. Opponents reject the idea that abortion is a constitutionally fundamental right; some think of abortion as affirmatively evil.

The same can be said of *Plessy*. Most of us abhor *Plessy* and believe that the equal protection principle announced in *Brown* v. *Board of Education* (which overturned *Plessy*) is the right one. But there can be no doubt that *Plessy* was a decision articulating a firmly held constitutional principle, whether right or profoundly wrong. To disagree with *Plessy* is to disagree about a matter of constitutional principle.

This is as it should be. Constitutional law elaborates over time the meaning of the nation's fundamental legal commitments. It is, therefore, fundamentally concerned with deep disagreements Americans have over the basic principles that govern their polity. From the very inception of constitutional law, there have been intense disagreements over the principles for which the Constitution stands. (A very early and famous example was the dispute between Jefferson and Hamilton about the constitutionality of a national bank.) The Supreme Court cannot avoid taking a stand on some of these disagreements. Resolving them is its very function.

Bush v. *Gore,* however, is not about constitutional principle. When the *Bush* v. *Gore* majority made up a December 12 state law deadline, they were not announcing a fundamental principle or freedom or anything else in which anybody passionately believed. Correct me if I'm wrong, but I haven't heard any Bush supporters marching in the street proclaiming the right of state supreme courts to make December 12 the deadline for resolving election contests.

This is why *Bush* v. *Gore* differs profoundly from cases like *Roe* or *Plessy*. At least the justices in *Roe* and *Plessy* were insisting on constitutional principles in which they and their supporters genuinely, probably passionately, believed. *Bush* v. *Gore* had nothing to do with such principles. It had to do with one thing: who won the election.

That's why post hoc rationalization is inappropriate here, even though it is standard operating procedure in many constitutional contexts. In a case like *Roe* (or *Plessy* or *Brown*, for that matter), the real issue isn't whether a particular plaintiff wins or loses. The real issue is whether the Constitution does or does not stand for some very important principle. For this reason, it makes good sense for supporters of the decision to continue to think through the best possible justifications for the Court's decisions long after those decisions are on the books. Because what really matters—what the case is really about—isn't whether the Court properly dealt with the individuals referred to as Roe or Plessy or Brown, but rather whether a certain principle should be part of the nation's enduring constitutional law.

Bush v. *Gore* is a different kind of case. No one cared in any large, prospective sense about whether Florida had or hadn't set a December 12 deadline for its election contest. All that turned on that question was—the presidency of the United States.

Thus when the majority made up this deadline on completely indefensible grounds, one does not go looking for post hoc rationalizations to explain why Florida really had made December 12 its deadline, even if the Court didn't itself give very good reasons. No question arises of whether post hoc rationalizations can be found for this proposition, because there is no question of this proposition becoming part of the nation's enduring constitutional law.

On the contrary, all one can say is that the majority rendered an enormously illegitimate decision—and be done with it.

What is to be done?

First, the illegitimacy of *Bush* v. *Gore* does not translate into an illegitimate presidency. It is not Bush's fault that the Supreme Court acted illegally. The Bush team acted properly in bringing its case before the Court, and once the majority had rendered its decision, it was necessary for all to abide by it. Especially given that Bush might well have become president regardless of the Court's decision, the majority's indefensible behavior provides no basis for acting as if the nation now has no legitimate president.

The fault is the Court's—or more particularly five members thereof —and the hammer, if there is to be one, should fall on the Court's bench. I therefore firmly support the proposals to block all appointments to the Supreme Court during this presidency. It is not that the *Bush* v. *Gore* majority should be "punished" for their behavior. But our justices must have the strongest possible incentive not to intervene in presidential controversies except on unmistakable legal grounds.

As Paul Carrington has observed, in the hearts of most justices is a desire to see their views made into law and to see the law they have made carried forward after they are gone, not in dissenting opinions, but in the opinions of the Court. This desire—entirely aside from any crude considerations of partisanship—can exert a deep and improper influence when the justices undertake to decide a presidential election. It might make them intervene on thin or indefensible grounds, prompting them to announce unprecedented constitutional law and even to make up state law deadlines in order to reach the desired result. All this could happen without the slightest subjective bad faith. The only sensible policy is to ensure that justices who yield to these temptations do not profit from their license.

Second, on the jurisprudential front, scholars may need to consider the possibility that other decisions rendered by the *Bush* v. *Gore* majority can no longer be taken seriously as matters of constitutional principle either. These same five members of the Court have issued path-breaking and sometimes quite surprising constitutional decisions in recent years. They have held, for example, that the Eleventh Amendment, which bars certain suits brought against a state by "Citizens of *another* State," also bars suits brought against a state by citizens of that *same* state (last I checked, "another" and "the same" were opposites). They have held that the Boy Scouts have a right under the First Amendment, which protects the "freedom of speech," to exclude homosexuals (if the Boy Scouts are "speaking" when they exclude homosexuals, is an all-white homeowners' association also "speaking" when it excludes blacks?).

The usual scholarly practice is to evaluate, debate, and carefully analyze Supreme Court decisions in the doctrinal terms in which they present themselves. The usual practice, in other words, is to take these cases seriously as matters of constitutional interpretation and argue about them accordingly. In light of *Bush* v. *Gore*, we may want to think carefully about whether, when it comes to decisions rendered by these five members of the Court, this practice has stopped making sense.

LAURENCE H. TRIBE 3

eroG .v hsuB: Through the Looking Glass

Once upon a time, an aroused and active citizenry gathering political support for a favored cause or candidate didn't seem terribly alarming to the Supreme Court. In 1986, when I represented a group of Berkeley activists agitating for rent control against landowners who felt threatened by that grass-roots effort, the Court, in *Fisher* v. *City of Berkeley*, ruled 8–1 for my clients, rejecting the argument that such citizen-based action was preempted by the Sherman Act. But barely a decade later, the landscape had changed. In *Timmons* v. *Twin Cities Area New Party*, I represented a minority political party challenging a state ban on "fusion" candidacies (in which two parties, usually a minor party and one of the two major parties, nominate the same candidate) that the major parties saw as threatening to their dominance; the Court's 6–3 decision upholding the state's power to assure political stability by preserving the shared hegemony of those two parties decisively awakened me to the drumbeat sounded by a cohesive Court majority:[1] Chief

I am grateful to Bruce Ackerman, Mike Dorf, George Fletcher, Heather Gerkin, Dan Geyser, Tom Goldstein, Tara Grove, Pat Gudridge, Sam Issacharoff, Jonathan Massey, Joel Perwin, Rick Pildes, Ben Souede, and Scott Turow for helpful suggestions. All errors are, as the saying goes, my own.

1. This trend has been noted elsewhere. See, e.g., Richard Pildes, Democracy and Disorder, 68 U. Chic. L. Rev. 695 (2001).

Justice Rehnquist and Justice O'Connor, both of them members of the *Fisher* majority, joined by Justices Scalia, Kennedy, and Thomas, supported quite often by Justice Breyer (as in *Timmons*) and at times by Justice Souter as well (dissenting in *Timmons*, but on narrowly procedural grounds), have coalesced around an alliance whose signature concerns are the avoidance of political ferment and fragmentation, the preservation of order and hierarchy, and the imposition, whenever possible, of relatively simple and abstract rules in preference to complex or contextual standards. I had decided to make these increasingly evident preoccupations—and their subtext, a perplexing distrust *of* democracy—a central theme of my new law school course, "The Court and the Constitution at the Turn of the Millennium," when serendipity struck in the form of what was to become Exhibit A: *Bush* v. *Gore*.

What I find most interesting about *Bush* v. *Gore* isn't just how wrong its legal reasoning seems but what shaped the Court's perceptions and why it plunged with such zeal into that presidential thicket in the face of such evident obstacles. Right after we all learned of the infamous "butterfly ballot" in Palm Beach County, I wrote a *New York Times* editorial urging patience while Florida's legal processes determined who was disenfranchised and what to do about it. I thought we'd "have an opportunity, as Dec. 18 approached, to think about just what to do if the irresistible force of litigation meets the unmovable obstacle of time."

Little did I suspect that the institution which would prove unable to resist the "force of litigation" would be the U.S. Supreme Court, or that I'd find myself plunked in the middle of the whole affair, writing the briefs as Vice President Gore's Supreme Court counsel and presenting his case in the first of the two Supreme Court oral arguments, on December 1 I can't pretend I didn't get a kick out of being at the center of attention, but there was a gnawing question: "Should this *be* the center? Are people like me supposed to be playing the lead roles in this show? Should people like *them*—the nine justices questioning me—be calling the shots here?" Dozens of senators and representatives were sitting in the public gallery listening to the dialogue. "Shouldn't they be more than *spectators* to this drama?"

Although I have little basis for comparison—*Bush* v. *Gore* is the only case I've ever studied in real time, teaching it and beginning to write about it at the very moment I was litigating it—my total immersion may have given me a clearer view of the way Bush v. Gore the political contest became *Bush* v. *Gore* the lawsuit, which in turn captivated the nation as a televised spectacle that forever changed the image, and ultimately the reality, of all it touched.

To get our bearings, it may be helpful to begin with the situation that led to and surrounded the litigation, when what the public saw, and what every participant in this legal saga experienced, began with the first premature TV announcement of Gore winning Florida's crucial electoral votes on Tuesday evening, November 7. That faded into the "never mind" mea culpas from the media announcing in the predawn hours of November 8 that the winner was in fact Bush. That in turn blurred into the embarrassed explanations shortly thereafter that the election in Florida, and thus the nation, was too close to call.

The sight of elderly voters, many of them Holocaust survivors and their relatives, crying that the butterfly ballot had misled them to vote for Pat Buchanan when they had meant to vote for Al Gore, coupled with televised pictures of a specimen butterfly ballot, made clear to millions of Americans how easy it would have been to lose one's franchise in Florida. The rapidly growing sense that nothing could be done about that particular outrage even though it doubtless cost Gore thousands of votes—more than enough to make up the Bush margin of victory—underscored the urgency and, for many, the justice of letting Gore hunt for uncounted legal votes wherever he could find them in Florida. But the Bush spinmeisters outspun those of Gore, as the televised reality lingered lastingly and mockingly over the painstaking effort to recount ballots manually in counties where protests had been lodged by Gore and his supporters, deriding that on again— off again effort as a thinly veiled attempt to change the election's rules in the middle of the game in a lawless process that involved trying to guess what a mark or an indentation on a ballot might say about a voter's intent, with "dimples" and "hanging chads" becoming household words that evoked images of election fraud to many, while conjuring images emblematic of democracy and reminiscent of the 1960s struggles over voting rights to others.

The TV cameras zoomed in as self-important talking heads gravely intoned predictions of "constitutional crisis" at the thought that Congress, heaven forbid, might be drawn into the endgame unless we could be delivered from that supposed evil, and from what many evidently perceived as the dangers of democracy, by the deus ex machina of the Supreme Court, to which journalists referred in hushed tones suggestive of a latter-day Wizard of Oz. The saga closed, finally, with a made-for-TV ending that featured the scramble of scattered reporters, clutching that Court's "final answer" as they dashed down its marble steps, illuminated by banks of floodlights in the crisp December night, and handed the pages of the opinion to newscasters and network anchors who struggled to decipher, live and on camera, the Court's deliberately obscure bottom line less than two hours before midnight, December 12, when the Court ruled the recounting had to end, bringing the presidential election of 2000 to a suitably dramatic, if dramatically undemocratic, close.

This succession of television images does more than represent the case of *Bush* v. *Gore;* it profoundly shaped the Supreme Court's understanding of the stakes involved and its ultimate holding that the Florida Supreme Court's December 8 order—which mandated a statewide recount of ballots that had registered no vote for president but gave no specific guidelines for their evaluation, merely instructing election officials to discern the clear intent of the voter—violated the Fourteenth Amendment's equal protection clause. Take, for instance, the televised close-ups that became the enduring legacy of the entire dispute—the close-ups of election officials holding partly perforated ballots up to the light, squinting to see what dents or holes or hanging chads they might detect and quarreling over how to tally those ballots as possible votes in the presidential race. That this meant ballots *identical in appearance* could end up being *counted differently* in different counties or in the same county at different times, perhaps for partisan reasons, required no formal proof to anyone who had seen all that on screen: in time-pressured, breathlessly conducted litigation, with unheard-of deadlines crowding what would normally be six weeks of briefing into a weekend and what would normally be months of judicial reflection into a matter of hours or at most days, those pictures were worth not thousands, but tens of thousands, of words.

Six Dimensions of the Seen and Unseen

Hidden Variables   But there were a number of crucial things the TV screen *couldn't* show. One important dimension of the case not captured by the television cameras was the impossibility of ever articulating uniform rules for accurately translating—into votes for Bush, Gore, someone else, or no one—the infinite variety of marks that voters might have left in pencil or ink or with a stylus on the ballots cast in the forty-one of Florida's sixty-seven counties that used optical scanners (equipped in only twenty-four of those forty-one counties with mechanisms to give voters a second chance if the ballot they attempted to cast was rejected by the machines as invalid) or, for that matter, on the punch-card ballots used in twenty-four counties (none of which was equipped with any second-chance capability). If uniform and accurate statewide rules could be articulated, surely the single judge assigned by the December 8 order to review the county-by-county recounts would be as well positioned as the state's highest court to articulate them. Yet only Justice Stevens, dissenting, thought the concerns raised by different counties using similar voting systems but "differing substandards for determining voter intent" could be relieved by that "single impartial magistrate," whose potentially harmonizing image was evidently eclipsed for the Court by the ever-present spectacle of election officials holding ballots in the air to divine each voter's intent—officials whose subsequent consultations with a state magistrate were destined to be conducted out of camera range. The illusion of a technical "fix" in the uniform set of rules the state's high court was faulted for not having promulgated was of a different order. Evidently the justices who acted as though machinelike algorithms could workably replace human judgment in deciphering the machine-rejected ballots were tuned in to breakthroughs in artificial intelligence and computerized pattern-recognition unknown to the rest of us.

The Overshadowed Duality of Errors   A second dimension—one not exactly hidden from the TV viewing audience and yet somehow lost on the Court—was the significance of the fact that election officials can err in at least two diametrically opposed directions: they can *wrongly fail to count* a vote that someone intended to cast as such; or they can *wrongly attribute* a vote to someone who either intended to cast no vote at all or, worse still, intended to cast a vote but for an opposing candidate. Machines can do that too, of course—as they did to the Palm Beach citizens who intended to vote for Gore and unwittingly became "Buchanan supporters." And, in just the same way, an error during a manual recount can turn a "none of the above" voter into a phantom supporter of one of the leading candidates ("false inclusion"), or can turn a supporter of either of those candidates into an imaginary supporter of the other ("false reversal"), or can turn someone who intended to vote for one of those two into a "didn't cast any vote for president" statistic ("false exclusion"). This makes it impossible to treat *differing degrees of leniency or severity* in the recount standard being used in different places with the same kinds of vote tabulation equipment as though they corresponded to *differing degrees of accuracy* in discovering previously uncounted votes.[2] Thus, when the Court im-

2. See Ronald Dworkin, "A Badly Flawed Election," New York Review of Books, Jan. 11, 2001, at 53–55; " 'A Badly Flawed Election': An Exchange," *id.* at 9–10, Feb. 22, 2001.

plied that the use of a more stringent recount standard in Palm Beach County had violated the "one person, one vote" principle by diluting the votes of people in the more Republican-leaning county of Palm Beach relative to the votes of people in the more Democratic-leaning county of Broward, where a "more forgiving standard" was able to uncover "almost three times as many new votes [as in Palm Beach], a result markedly disproportionate to the difference in population between the counties," the Court was acting as though any recount technique with a lower per capita yield of "new votes" in a given county would somehow mean a higher disenfranchisement rate for the voters of that county, whereas in truth no such equation is possible.

The Court in effect allowed the duality of errors to be overshadowed by the mirage of geographic comparisons. Once we eliminate that shadow, it becomes clear that any uniform set of statewide standards cannot begin to account for all the differences in the design and thickness of ballots; in the form and maintenance of tabulation equipment; and in the age, political leanings, and other demographic characteristics of distinct areas that would yield tendencies toward either false exclusion or false inclusion (including its most extreme variant, false reversal) and thus *cannot* in the end minimize the aggregate number of errors or come closest to approximating what the Court deemed the applicable ideal of "one person, one vote."

Missing History Those many differences are encompassed by another dimension absent from the TV screen. This third dimension consists of the unique *histories* lying *behind* the similar-looking ballots that the election canvassers were inspecting visually on camera, and makes plain why uniform statewide counting rules would necessarily introduce their own distinct inequalities. In one precinct, for instance, more of the punch-card voting machines might be outdated or in poor repair, or the chads might have been less recently cleared out, or more of the voters might be elderly or frail, or voting instructions, which were supposed by law to have been printed in Spanish as well as English, may have been written in English only—as was the case in

Osceola County, with a 29 percent Hispanic population. For an election canvasser in such a precinct, to count a mark or a perforation as a vote under a standard more forgiving than the one applied by a canvasser in another precinct—where an identical-looking ballot's history is likely to have been different—could be a way to honor, not violate, the principle of "one person, one vote." Remembering that it's "one *person*, one vote," not "one *ballot*, one vote," is rendered more difficult by the fact that it's the *ballot* one sees being held in the air and scrutinized with squinted eyes; the person who cast that ballot, and the story connecting that person to the machine he or she encountered at a particular time and place—the machine that registered no vote for president in that encounter—must be constructed in the mind's eye.

Florida's highest court, from its vantage point closer to the action, presumably recognized how futile, and almost certainly counterproductive, would have been any effort to mechanize, standardize, and ultimately dehumanize the process of assessing from a ballot's appearance what the voter who cast that ballot probably intended. Imagine, for instance, rigorously enforcing a rule saying a punch-card ballot counts only where the chad has been detached on at least two corners. Suppose that in one county the ballots were printed on such thick cardboard that *no* chads were detached on more than a single corner, and most were merely indented. Or suppose that in another county hundreds of ballots were found with no detachments but with the name "Bush" or "Gore" clearly circled, obviously violating the instructions but making the voter's intent unmistakably clear. If you reply that the uniform standards would, of course, make exceptions for such cases, then you've given up on the quest for objective criteria articulable in advance, because the only way to *detect* cases that merit exceptional treatment is to demote the uniform rules to the status of mere guidelines, all to be applied with a dollop of subjective judgment and a pile of plain old common sense.

Even if the county boards' *initial* choice of recount standards wouldn't always have been calibrated to those underlying variations, the supervising state judge would have been there to compel them to take such important variations into account. That task might have been performed imperfectly, but one thing is certain: straining all these multifaceted background facts through a uniformly metered sieve will yield an unequal stream of results, *not* a stream that flows evenly in accord with the formula: one person, one vote. The equal protection holding of Bush preserves at best the surface appearance of equality. And the Court's evident assumption that this surface appearance is what it takes "to sustain the confidence that all citizens must have in the outcome of elections" reflects a genuinely pathetic view of the American electorate.

The Due Process Plight of the Beleaguered Ballot   How could so deeply flawed and problematic an equal protection claim have prevailed? Answering that question exposes a fourth dimension of the problem. Part of the intuitive appeal and rhetorical force of the equal protection claim, which as we've observed was far easier to connect with what one could *see* on television than were the logical counterarguments, was the ease with which the elusive concept of "one person, one vote" could be deployed to straddle the macro and the micro levels of inquiry, leaping back and forth between two values. The first was the architectural, or *systemic,* value of assuring that apportionment schemes and other election-related institutional designs and arrangements do not systematically dilute the weight or influence of any discernible group of voters (say, urban voters as opposed to their country cousins). The second was the quite distinct *individualistic* value of procedural fairness to each voter apart from any assessment of the comparative weight of the votes of various groups or communities.

In the end, the Court's opinion perched unsteadily on the cusp between the sweep of the electorate as a whole, and the imagined individual voter; much of the opinion's work is done by borrowing doctrinal imagery from each realm in order to shore up the inadequacy of the argument in the other. Thus, according to the Court, because the issue isn't "whether to believe a witness but how to interpret the marks or holes or scratches on an inanimate object," the supposed result is that the "search for intent can be confined by specific rules designed to ensure uniform treatment." The Court observes that the absence of such rules "has led to unequal evaluation of ballots in various respects," listing examples in which "standards for accepting or rejecting contested ballots might vary not only from county to county but indeed within a single county from one recount team to another." The picture the Court's verbal sketch is calculated to project is one in which individual *persons* are deprived, one at a time, of something to which they are entitled but without the process that is due when such deprivations occur, while *ballots,* depicted almost as though they *were* persons in their own right, are grouped and counted according to criteria that deliberately and avoidably risk diluting their weight should they happen to be cast in counties adopting one measure of voter intent rather than another. The fact that, unlike the "one person, one vote" decisions in the Court's canon, this case did not involve *grouping* voters, by geography or otherwise, for disparate representation or for the application of disparate standards—that *Bush* v. *Gore* is no *Baker* v. *Carr*—is neatly papered over by an insistence that the right to equal protection of the laws, like the right to procedural due process, belongs to individual voters, not to groups.

But, as the Rehnquist Court has never tired of insisting, unless the positive law of the state confers an entitlement to have a given interest vindicated once certain objective facts are established, *no process is due* beyond whatever process the positive law of the state makes available. Thus the Court in *Bush* v. *Gore* faulted Florida for failing to provide something the Rehnquist Court has repeatedly held that due process requires no state to provide: the conversion of (1) the individual voter's interest in having her vote counted if her ballot manifests a clear indication of her intent as evaluated in the discretion of whichever officials state law entrusts with recounting ballots, into (2) a full-fledged "liberty" or "property" interest in having a neutral adjudicator evaluate her ballot by applying objective criteria that the state has never supplied. That such objective, impersonally applicable criteria could reduce the room for partisan manipulation more than might the availability of judicial review is undeniable. But that's invariably true whenever a state chooses to confer an interest subject to an official's discretion—something of which instances abounded during the initial vote count—rather than an entitlement girded with objective criteria. Besides, partisan considerations could just as easily enter into the state supreme court's selection of supposedly objective criteria for various types of ballots—a selection that six justices thought would overcome all constitutional objections.

The Untold Story of the Underlying Count   Nor was the Court willing to grapple with the multiple defects in the vote count that its decision left in place—which brings us to the fifth dimension: the comparative analysis so conspicuously missing from the Court's opinion. All seven justices who saw equal protection problems in the recount process were guilty of assuming that they could validly put to one side, and relegate to another day and another lawsuit, the multitude of errors and inequities, all occurring off camera and none visible on the TV screen, that made a mockery of the underlying vote count leading to the certification of Bush as the winner by 537 votes out of over 6 million cast. Some have argued that because the irreducible margin of error exceeded that minuscule margin of victory, simple prudence dictated finding some excuse for blowing the whistle without further ado. But any such theory has to assume the *underlying* vote count is worthy of belief and entitled to be treated as authoritative despite all the flaws in the process generating that vote count—including ample opportunities on the part of state and local officials to tailor the processing of voters and the handling of ballots to the latest reports of how the election was going and how their adoption of one practice rather than another could shape the outcome—and despite the equally obvious likelihood that adjusting the underlying count with the results of the recount, *whether with its supposed flaws or with the state being given time to correct them*, would at least yield a *more* reliable determination of who won.

To offer a few telling examples: Florida law unambiguously mandated at least one initial recount in all sixty-seven counties because the vote totals in the initial count came within half of 1 percent of one another. Yet eighteen of Florida's counties *did no such recount.* And there's no doubt that other differences among the counties, many of which were understood to be positively correlated with socioeconomic status and thus with likely ethnic background and political affiliation, rendered the initial count not only less reliable than Florida law required but also less than politically and racially neutral in the distribution of error rates. Thus, for example, far more ballots were rejected in the twenty-four punch-card counties (3.9 percent) than in the twenty-four optical-scan counties with second-chance capability (0.6 percent); in the fifteen optical-scan counties without second-chance capability, the rejection rate was highest of all (5.7 percent). Minority voters were roughly *ten times* as likely not to have their votes correctly counted in this election as were non-minority voters, and that's to say nothing of the larger and more difficult to document phenomenon of obstacles that prevented minority voters from even obtaining a ballot that anyone *could* count. In some of the forty-one optical-scan counties, ballots had been counted as valid in the initial counting process even when voters simply checked or circled a candidate's name; other counties had excluded all ballots that were not machine-readable. Moreover, eleven counties used the infamous "butterfly" ballot (Palm Beach) or some other confusing form of "wraparound" ballot that *no* amount of recounting could translate into a vote mirroring the voters' actual intent. Yet only Justice Ginsburg's dissent put the logically crucial *comparative* question: What was there in the Court's opinion or in the dissenting opinions of Justice Souter or Justice Breyer that demonstrated "that the recount adopted by the Florida court, flawed as it may be, would yield a result any less fair or precise than the certification that preceded the recount" or any less fair or precise, I would add, than a recount under some uniform set of specific rules for particular ballot configurations? The inescapable answer is: nothing.

Nor is it enough, in response, to extol the possible virtues of decentralized decision-making with respect to the choice of how much to spend on better voting equipment as opposed to such things as better computers for the public schools, as Justice Souter seemed to suppose. *First,* even if the interest in equality of opportunity with respect to public schooling may properly be sacrificed on the altar of local autonomy (as it was in 1973, in *San Antonio Board of Education* v. *Rodriguez*), the reason is only that the Court has yet to treat *equality of educational opportunity* on a par with *equality of the franchise,* which is, of course, the right that the Court says the Florida recount sacrificed. *Second,* any interest in localism that the Court or those agreeing with its equal protection holding deem cognizable with respect to differences in underlying voting mechanisms, ballot designs, or automatic recount practices should be no less cognizable with respect to differences in how ballots were to be recounted under the December 8 order. There is no mystical difference between the count and the recount for equal protection purposes. If there were, a nice question would be: How should the automatic recount mandated by Florida law but actually undertaken in just forty-nine of Florida's counties be classified in this election? Third, whatever weight any justice may have given to the distinctively *legislative* character of the judgment to decentralize decision-making with respect to the underlying vote, it's clear that the terms of the Florida Supreme Court's recount order derive, as every justice with the exception of the Rehnquist Three presume, from the legislation enacted to discharge the state's duty under Article II, Section 1, Clause 2, to choose presidential electors as the state's legislature directs.

Changing the Rules Midway through the Game   Focusing on the latter presumption exposes yet another difficulty with the theory that equal protection mandates the adoption of more specific criteria than the "intent of the voter." For, as the Court could not deny, the December 8 recount order, in directing all the canvassing boards to apply that general standard and *not* any statewide set of uniform substandards or rules, carried out the electoral ground rules that the people of Florida, through their legislature, had put in place before election day. And Article II, Section 1, Clause 2 makes the rules laid down by each state legislature the binding guide to how the state's presidential electors are picked. The "fix" proposed by the Court and by Justices Souter and Breyer would thus appear to require adopting *new* rules in mid-election—one of the cardinal sins that Bush accused the Florida Supreme Court of having committed. So there's considerable tension between the equal protection theory that attracted seven justices and the universally accepted importance of judging an election's results in accord with standards and methods adopted in advance.

A "One-Time-Only" Equal Protection Offer   But the inequities and inaccuracies of the underlying vote count and the certification embodying it cannot, as we've already seen, be so simply swept under a rug emblazoned with the motto "Another problem for another day." Because a presidential election cannot be rerun after its flaws have been extinguished (3 U.S.C. §1 requires that all presidential electors be chosen on November 7), to strike down the recount is to uphold the count itself; the two are joined at the hip and cannot be severed. Talk of the "fundamental right of each voter" cannot be permitted to obscure that what is at stake is *the aggregation of votes into a single result.* Yet, as we've seen, the Court tried to obscure just that, by subtly transposing the wide-angle picture truly before it—a picture in which candidate Bush seeks to secure electoral victory by halting the statewide recount of legal votes—into a close-up shot of a beleaguered voter who intended to register a presidential preference but marked her ballot in a way that wasn't machine-readable and is now at the mercy of officials left free to apply an "intent of the voter" standard as they see fit.

At the end of the day, the Court gave only one reason for failing to approach the problem from a comparative perspective—for failing to ask whether the state court's recount order would yield an outcome less fair or precise than the certification preceding that outcome, or than uniform statewide standards, might yield—and for thus focusing solely on the arrangement of the deck chairs rather than on the plight of the *Titanic* itself. According to the Court, that reason was: "the problem of equal protection in election processes generally presents many complexities" supposedly absent when one focuses on "the minimum procedures necessary to protect the *fundamental right of each voter* in the special instance of a statewide recount under the authority of a single state judicial officer."

Ballots as Castaways Yet after all that talk about "fundamental rights" and "minimum procedures," in devising a remedy for the alleged equal protection and due process violations the Court decided that the *Titanic*'s deck chairs might as well go down with the ship, too. This becomes painfully clear when we examine a sixth dimension not captured by the television cameras: the invisible spectacle of thousands upon thousands of ballots being jettisoned into oblivion by the Court's order that the recount be stopped before all legal votes could be counted.

The Court's only justification for ending the recount rather than allowing the Florida Supreme Court to try fashioning a remedy for the supposed defects in its December 8 order was the state's interest in finality. The Court claimed that it had to defer to the Florida Supreme Court's finding that the state legislature, to ensure that Florida could "participat[e] fully in the federal election process," wished to avail itself of the safe harbor offered by 3 U.S.C. §5, a federal statutory provision indicating that Congress would accept without challenge the presidential electors from any state that by December 12 had fully and finally resolved, in accord with the rules and procedures in place on election day, any election-related "controversy or contest." And the Court treated that supposed state judicial finding about what the Florida legislature wanted as tantamount to a mandate to end the recount on December 12. Chief Justice Rehnquist's concurring opinion, joined by Justices Scalia and Thomas, didn't agree. The chief justice argued that, in conferring power specifically on the *state legislature,* the Constitution's mechanism (Article II, Section 1, Clause 2) for directing each state's choice of presidential electors limited the degree to which the Court could properly defer to the state judiciary's reading of the state's election code. But the concurring opinion's "independent" analysis of Florida's election statutes somehow led it to the same bottom line: given the benefits of resolving all election contests in time to fit within the Safe Harbor Act, the Florida legislature, in empowering state courts to grant "appropriate" relief, "*must have meant relief that would have become final by*" December 12.

That simply won't wash. You can read the Florida statutes backward and forward without finding the slightest clue that the state legislature ever decided all recounts in a presidential election must stop by December 12 or, for that matter, at any time before the electors meet to give their votes on December 18. And the Florida court's own alleged treatment of December 12 as a drop-dead deadline, assuming there was some reason to defer to it, was at best ambiguous.

It required no high-powered psychologist or political scientist to figure out that the state legislature wanted the state's electors to get counted in the national tally, but coming in within the December 12 safe harbor wouldn't in any event guarantee that Congress, in counting the electoral votes on January 6 in accord with its own constitutional responsibility, would honor the promise made by the 1887 Congress that passed the 3 U.S.C. §5, and, as Justice Ginsburg's dissent pointed out without rebuttal from the Court, the 1887 Electoral Count Act, under which the January 6 count was to be conducted, contained later deadlines and alternative ways of getting an electoral slate bullet-proofed for the congressional count. The one thing anyone could say for sure was that, if anything deprived Florida of a shot at the benefits of the Safe Harbor of 3 U.S.C. §5, it wasn't the *Florida court's* December 8 recount order but the *Supreme Court's* December 9 *stay* of that recount order. For it was that stay that guaranteed Florida could not produce by December 12 any final resolution, using the rules and procedures in place on November 7, of the electoral contest that the stay had interrupted.

Worse still, even if we could pretend with the Court that bringing the recount to a permanent halt on December 9 would have left Florida's electors, as previously certified on November 26, sailing right into that safe harbor—something we know isn't so—reading the laws of Florida (or, for that matter, of the United States) to mandate this purchase of electoral security at the price of essentially ditching into the sea thousands of ballots that clearly expressed a voter's intent but didn't happen to get counted before they were tossed overboard would, by the Court's own criteria, have been flatly unconstitutional. Only Justice Stevens, dissenting, made that point, but it was a telling one. The Court had, after all, acknowledged that under Florida law "all ballots that reveal the intent of the voter constitute valid votes," so under the Court's own reasoning no legislative or judicial determination to put the state's interest in finality above the rights of those voters to have *all* their ballots counted could stand. As the Supreme Court itself had told the Florida high court: "The press of time does not diminish the constitutional concern." And it would be question-begging to say that the rights of *all* the voters, including those whose ballots would never be counted, would be safeguarded by shielding from challenge the electors certified on November 26—because, of course, the whole question was whether counting the remaining ballots would have shown that the wrong electors had been certified!

The supreme irony in all this must surely be that the Supreme Court's decision to stop the counting of legal votes at a point when the pending election contest could no longer be resolved by December 12 not only deprived the state of the one benefit that alone was said to justify that extraordinary act, but also arbitrarily distinguished between seemingly identical ballots all of which reflected legal votes but only some of which had the good fortune to get counted before the Court called "time." And the Supreme Court did both things in the name of a federal constitutional pronouncement that was without precedent and certainly wasn't based on any rules or principles in place on the date of the election. Supreme irony, for those were the very sins that the Court and the concurring opinion accused the Florida Supreme Court of committing. To borrow an image the Court once used in another context, the justices failed to "step through an analytical looking glass" to reflect on the inequities that, *under their own reasoning,* were rife in their own opinions and actions.[3]

Compressed onto a Single Screen

It bears repeating that the televised image, which showed only the surface reality, was essentially all that both the viewing audience and the Supreme Court's justices, deciding on the thinnest of records and the most truncated of schedules, had palpably before them. The briefing on the equal protection issue barely scratched the surface of this analysis, and the oral argument of December 11, the first time the Court agreed to consider the equal protection issue (having denied certiorari on that question the first time the case reached it for argument on December 1), mentioned in passing that some counties had more accurate voting machines than others, but it otherwise left untouched this vast yet invisible terrain. And it is this terrain that, once plowed, exposes the multiple, independently fatal flaws in the Court's superficial assumption—perfectly reflecting what the televised picture

3. *NCAA* v. *Tarkanian,* 488 U.S. 179, 192–93 (1988).

misleadingly suggested—that treating the same way all those ballots that look the same is the essence of what equal protection requires.

I suppose this could be why seven justices and numerous commentators in this book and elsewhere have assumed it was at least *plausible* to hold, as a matter of equal protection, that similar-looking ballots emerging from similarly designed machines need to be counted the same way. Any plausibility in such a holding is a mirage. The truth is that mathematical regularity and mechanical standardization, whatever their technocratic appeal, may achieve surface equality only at the expense of preserving or even exacerbating a deeper inequality; that in this realm, as in many others, "2, 4, 6, 8's not the way to litigate";[4] and that "sometimes the grossest discrimination can lie in treating things that are different as though they were exactly alike."[5] But those insights tend to fall on deaf ears when the eyes are dazzled by shallow images of an easily achieved surface sameness.

The Mystery of the Court's "Unsought Responsibility"

Are we expected to overlook or forgive all these gaping flaws in the Court's argument just because of the insufficiency of the record and the time pressures under which the Court's "unsought responsibility," as its opinion puts it, forced it to work? *"Unsought responsibility"*? Get real! The Court talks as though, simply because the "contending parties invoke[d] the [judicial] process," it had *no choice* but "to resolve the federal and constitutional issues [it] ha[d] been *forced* to confront." Really? The cases are too numerous to cite in which the Court, extolling the virtues of abstention or avoidance, has let a cup laced with far less poison than this pass from its lips. For the nation to be lectured about "the vital limits on judicial authority," and to be told that "[n]one are more conscious of [those] limits . . . than are the

4. See Laurence H. Tribe, Trial by Mathematics: Precision and Ritual in the Legal Process, 84 Harv. L. Rev. 1329 (1971).

5. *Jenness* v. *Fortson*, 403 U.S. 431, 442 (1971).

members of this Court," in a case where the Court has reached out to grant discretionary review—and has then said not a word to explain why *it*, rather than Congress, is the proper decision maker—is insult enough. Expecting the nation to endure that lecture from a Court that feels obliged to insist that "none stand more in admiration" than it does "of the Constitution's design to leave the selection of the President to the people, through their legislatures, and to the political sphere," goes over the top.

What, precisely, *is* the Court's justification—even assuming, counterfactually, that its ruling on the merits had been defensible—for first interrupting, and then bringing to a close, the national conversation that was Bush v. Gore—for making it into a court case and then ending the game before the matter could reach Congress? Florida Chief Justice Wells, dissenting from the 4–3 recount order of December 8, quoted a mathematician's view that the "margin of error in this election is far greater than the margin of victory, no matter who wins." With every recount, the state would emerge with just another conclusion, not necessarily a closer approximation of the truth. For Wells, given the futility of identifying an unambiguous winner, the game wasn't worth the candle; worse, "prolonging [the] judicial process in this counting contest propels this country . . . into an unprecedented and unnecessary constitutional crisis" that "will do substantial damage to our country, our state, and to this Court as an institution."

Rescuing Their Chosen Candidate—From What? The Supreme Court was less forthright than Wells had been but evidently had much the same thing in mind. Exactly what "crisis" it feared on the road ahead, however, remains mysterious. I part from the cynics who imagine that "crisis" to have been the presidency of Al Gore. Had the Court cared only about averting that outcome, it must have known at the time that it could almost certainly have avoided it while simply letting the December 8 recount continue. If that recount emerged with a victory, however narrow, for Bush, that would have ended the matter. Had it instead emerged with what Florida's highest court was prepared to certify as a victory for Gore, there was every indication that the Florida legislature stood ready to certify a slate of Bush electors notwithstanding any such judicial decision, something the Court's December 12 opinion strongly suggested the state legislature could properly do at any time. The Court should have been more circumspect about the state legislature's authority to take such *ex post facto* action once the voting had taken place and electors had been chosen—given that the relevant congressional legislation empowers a state legislature to direct the choice of a new set of electors only when the state "has held an election for the purpose of choosing electors, and has *failed to make a choice* on the day prescribed by law," not when it has *made* a choice but the choice has yet to be ascertained.[6] But only the Court would have been in a position to stop the state legislature from construing its constitutional mandate more broadly, and the Court could simply have declined to do so. And, even setting the state legislature aside, who would have been in a position to stop Florida's secretary of state, an avidly partisan Republican who had co-chaired the Bush campaign, from herself submitting to Congress the slate of Bush electors that she had been ready to certify since shortly after Thanksgiving? Florida's Supreme Court? Hardly. If that court had sought to interfere with the submission of a slate of Bush electors *either* by the secretary of state *or* by the state legislature, the Supreme Court would have had a far clearer legal basis for intervening than it could possibly conjure up on December 9, for it would then be acting to prevent a state's nullification of federal supremacy by direct obstruction of Congress's ability, acting under the authority entrusted to it by the Twelfth Amendment, to determine which set of Florida electoral votes to count. Supreme Court intervention at *that* point would rest squarely on the Supremacy Clause of Article VI, the glue melding the several states into a single Union.

Had the Supreme Court opted for that course—which would in

6. See 3 U.S.C. §2.

essence have recognized that breaking the virtual tie in Florida was a "political question" textually committed to Congress under the Twelfth Amendment—the odds were great that Bush would still emerge victorious. The 1887 Electoral Count Act contained a labyrinthine procedure by which the Congress that would convene on January 6 was to resolve disputes over election results in contested states and was to break any remaining ties. It's true that even that procedure, untested in the 114 years during which it had been in place, was shadowed by constitutional doubt over the power of one Congress to bind its successors in such matters. But, even so, the relative power of the Republicans and Democrats in the Congress that would do the counting made it overwhelmingly likely that, in the end, Bush would have emerged the winner.

I pursue the point simply to stress that the Court's intervention, its determination even before argument that the counting must stop at once, and its insistence thereafter that the counting not resume need not have reflected a wish to assure a Bush presidency (and hence the appointment of like-minded successors). Nor need the Court's actions have been reflections of an equal protection theory that cannot survive scrutiny and that the Court itself must have recognized was at best rather wobbly. Instead, everything the Court did could well have reflected nothing beyond the dismay of its five-justice majority at the very processes that lay ahead regardless of their result, or a wish by that majority to have the Bush succession unmarred by what Justice Scalia described, in an opinion accompanying the decision of a bare majority of the Court to issue a stay, as "a cloud upon . . . the legitimacy of [Bush's] election."

What Cloud? Presumably, it was the cloud the majority thought might be created by the very knowledge of a mounting number of possible votes for Gore, but that concern seems irreconcilable with the First Amendment inasmuch as the Court could set the record straight by finally announcing that the recounted votes had not been tallied in a lawful manner should that be its ultimate conclusion. As a reason for wanting to bring the entire process to a rapid close rather than bowing out altogether, that concern is no less troubling in First Amendment terms, but it does have greater explanatory power. For had the Court stayed out of the whole controversy, leaving the ultimate resolution to Congress, it would not have retained the ability to clear away whatever shadow it thought might be improperly cast by the cloud of illegal votes that ought never to have been, but might well have been, counted by Florida's highest court and then by substantial segments of the House and Senate en route to Congress's eventual designation of Bush as the next president. Through the eyes of its majority, the Court may well have been making *a deliberate decision to short-circuit the elaborate set of political processes that otherwise lay ahead en route to that highly probable if not altogether inevitable destination.*

A Herculean Pretension And what can have seemed so distressing about that set of processes?[7] One can only surmise that, to this set of justices, images of ballots being counted across the state—images that, for many others, conjured memories of the voting rights struggles of decades past—brought to mind instead thoughts of chaos and mob rule. Anything threatening to stability, good order, the established hierarchy, and business as usual—whether on the ground in Florida or in the halls of Congress—qualified as a "crisis" that was within their inherent jurisdiction to halt. These five were, after all, the same justices who had seen theirs as the sole institution capable of ensuring political stability in *Timmons* v. *Twin Cities Area New Party,* the case in which I had argued unsuccessfully for a First Amendment right of political parties to nominate the same candidate—a practice that the Court treated as threatening to the stability producing

7. The image of "Hercules" is invoked with apologies to Ronald Dworkin, whose ideal of the omniscient Hercules as judge is never confused with the reality of judges who are mere mortals. See his essay Hard Cases, 88 Harv. L. Rev. 1057, 1083–1109 (1975).

hegemony of the two major parties. The key to understanding this Court, I'd concluded in my "Turn of the Millennium" course in whose syllabus *Bush* v. *Gore* had become an unplanned but pivotal addition, was to recognize its towering confidence in its own ability to define and prioritize values of constitutional magnitude, and to decide which measures were needed in order to realize those values. Low indeed on that list of values is an energized, politicized electorate struggling to find its way toward concrete outcomes in such forms as the election of a president.

The Court's self-confidence in what it sees as matters constitutional is matched only by its disdain for the meaningful participation of other actors in constitutional debate. Thus, despite the case that many (including commentators as otherwise divergent as the conservative legal scholar Michael McConnell and I) have made for giving Congress substantial latitude in defining constitutional terms for purposes of exercising power under Section 5 to enforce the Fourteenth Amendment—and for recognizing that Congress needn't be confined by the institutional and federalism-based constraints that properly inhibit the Supreme Court from itself defining the scope of Section 1 of the Fourteenth Amendment as broadly as Congress might—the Court has been rigidly doctrinaire in dismissing out of hand any such pluralistic approach to constitutional interpretation and enforcement. Thus, it has struck down key provisions of the Religious Freedom Restoration Act, the Patent Reform Act, the Trademark Remedy Clarification Act, the Age Discrimination in Employment Act, and the Americans With Disabilities Act, all because it concluded that Congress in those statutes had gone beyond what the Court regarded as the correct understanding of Fourteenth Amendment rights or, having hewed to the Court's understanding, had taken more far-reaching steps than the Court deemed necessary.

A similar hubris was in evidence in *Dickerson* v. *United States*, when the Court gave the back of its hand just months before *Bush* v. *Gore* to Congress's attempt to legislate around the 1966 holding of *Miranda* v.

Arizona. What was striking about the Court's decision was not that a majority led by Chief Justice Rehnquist ultimately invoked principles of stare decisis to conclude that *Miranda*'s warnings, as watered down by intervening decisions, had become such familiar parts of the "national culture" that its constitutional validity should not at this late date be reexamined; rather, what was striking was that the Court proceeded by first determining that, *right or wrong,* the *Miranda* Court had *expressed* its ruling as one it *thought* was grounded in the Constitution, and then concluding that Congress had violated the Constitution simply by flouting the *Court's* word.

A final example is the joint 1992 opinion of Justices O'Connor, Kennedy, and Souter, reaffirming the core of *Roe* v. *Wade* in *Planned Parenthood of Pennsylvania* v. *Casey,* an opinion I otherwise admire as one of the Court's most eloquent explications of liberty and equality, but in which the impatience of the authors with dissent from their wisdom was starkly evident in their announcement that retreating, *especially in the face of continued protest,* from a decision as basic as *Roe* would betray those who had cast their lot with the Court and would put in doubt the legitimacy of that august tribunal as the oracle of last resort on fundamental national matters. Although Chief Justice Rehnquist and Justices Scalia and Thomas protested the imperious tone and anti-democratic substance of that opinion, they have joined two of its three authors (Justices O'Connor and Kennedy) in all but one (*Dickerson*) of the principal cases invoked above for the proposition that the justices in the *Bush* v. *Gore* majority have little but disdain for Congress as a serious partner in the constitutional enterprise, and not much patience with "We the People" as the ultimate source of sovereignty in this republic.

The Forgotten "Rule of Law": The Political Question Doctrine   Given that set of attitudes, the Court's sense that its destiny was to intervene —to take the hit to its short-term reputation, if it had to—need not have been driven even by a genuine fear that the nation was about to go over some constitutional precipice. Enough for this Court would have been the spectacle of perhaps another week of state and local officials holding ballots up to the light and squinting to get a better view of dimpled chads or of partial perforations—images that struck many as displaying democracy at work but that must have struck the *Bush v. Gore* majority as the antithesis of the rule of law—and the further spectacle, down the road, of Congress making the choice in tumult and with an orgy of politics. To those for whom, in Justice Scalia's phrase, "the rule of law is the law of rules," the fact that rules laid down in this case—by the Twelfth Amendment, by Congress in 1887, by the Florida legislature as its words had been construed by Florida's highest court—would appear to have invited this boisterous political brawl must have seemed an oversight by the framers, deserving of no greater respect than a gigantic inkblot.

Even if the Constitution's very architecture suggests that it is a nonjusticiable political question whether the rules governing a particular election have been so fundamentally altered (rather than merely refined and particularized) in midstream as to rend the fabric of republican government, and even if the text of the Twelfth Amendment confirms that conclusion when the subject of the election is the presidency, the Court may well have thought it needn't fret too much over how to justify having the last word on the matter: it didn't so much as mention the political question doctrine! It might even have thought: "Who but a sore loser could complain that we've assumed the burden of a decision fraught with political dangers for any lawmaker who'd have to confront her constituents after choosing one presidential candidate over another? Particularly when an election is a virtual tie, the typical lawmaker would risk alienating half his constituents whichever way he voted; how convenient for all concerned that the nation has *us,* insulated in our splendor from such accountability, to bear the brunt of popular anger!"

The political incentives were thus aligned in favor of decisive Supreme Court intervention to bring closure and relief to an election that had already overstayed its welcome as the Christmas season neared—even if that meant distrusting the people and insulting democracy. And for a Court that believes its own press, having absorbed the TV image of a tribunal above the fray that alone can speak with authority about the Constitution, nothing could have seemed more natural.

An Alternative Vision and Some Lessons for the Future   But there is another vision of the Court's proper relation to democracy, a vision in which the order the Court sought by *avoiding* politics is instead the *work* of politics, in which order is *earned* rather than *decreed*. In this other vision, Congress is less to be feared than challenged; it may or may not rise to the occasion, with ordinary politicians winning for themselves some of the respect that the Court won, if only momentarily, through the obvious intelligence of its oral proceedings and the statecraft reflected in its unanimous remand of December 4, in which it implicitly rebuffed the theory that the Florida Supreme Court had fatally interfered with what Bush claimed was the state legislature's exclusive Article II, Section 1, Clause 2 authority, when the Court gave the Florida court a chance to clarify its stance. Who knows but that a kind of bipartisanship appropriate to a virtually tied election and to a challenge of historic proportion mightn't have developed? And, even if it did not, the meaning of extraordinary challenges encompasses the risk of failure.

To draw a reason to doubt the majesty of law and of the Constitution from the Court's smug assurance that it and it alone could rise to this constitutional occasion and evoke the better angels of our nature would be tragically misguided. That the Court's distressing decision to rescue the nation from democracy was no isolated misstep but a manifestation of pathologies evidenced in all too many other ways is hardly a basis to diagnose either judicial review or the rule of law as moribund or even mortally wounded. The Court has had far better days and will have them again. Nor does *Bush* v. *Gore* make it harder to feel good about studying the Court and teaching about its work: the decision offers a veritable cornucopia of puzzles about doctrine and insights about constitutional law and adjudication.

But drawing sweeping institutional lessons in *any* direction from *Bush v. Gore* and from the politics we have lost seems dangerous. I especially lament the tendency of some to draw from the seemingly Herculean pretension that marked *Bush v. Gore* the lesson that judicial modesty and incrementalism are always the path of wisdom—that the Court that decides the least decides the best. The arguments over when the Court does well to act more boldly—when the time and circumstances are right for a *Brown v. Board of Education,* a *Gideon v. Wainwright,* a *New York Times v. Sullivan,* a *Baker v. Carr,* a *Roe v. Wade*—are too complex and multifaceted to be squeezed into any simplistic generalization that would treat *Bush* v. *Gore* as the right wing's answer to *Roe* v. *Wade.*

The danger of always fighting the last war is too real for us to succumb to any version of the syndrome that would make *Bush* v. *Gore* our judicial Vietnam.

GUIDO CALABRESI **4**

In Partial (but not Partisan) Praise of Principle

Is the Supreme Court's opinion in *Bush* v. *Gore* different from the mass of controversial decisions that courts issue, and if it is, can it nonetheless be justified? These are questions I have asked myself many times since the Court spoke. My answers are: yes, it is unusual though not unique in its total lack of what can be called "principle," and no, I don't think it can be justified. In reaching these conclusions I have no interest in casting aspersions on individual justices or on their motives, and will not do so. My object is simply to discuss the rather complex but crucial role of principle in judicial decision making.

I will contrast the Court's opinion with three hypothetical principled decisions that could have issued. Though each would have been highly controversial and readily criticizable, all would also have been standard court opinions. Significantly, on the basis of what was believed at the time, one of these would likely have given the election to Gore, one to Bush, and one would have left it in uncertainty.

The first, which would seemingly have made Gore the winner,[1] is the most traditional, conservative even, in terms of judicial behavior.

---

1. When I say that this opinion would have made Gore the winner, I am basing my statement on what people believed to be the case at the time, because that is the crucial moment relevant to my discussion.

It is certainly the one that most legal observers expected. It is also the most restrained in its view of the role of courts. Accordingly, I put it in the mouth of Justice Felix Frankfurter, though it might as easily have been written by the justice for whom Chief Justice Rehnquist clerked, Robert Jackson.

This opinion would emphasize the profoundly political nature of elections and the need for courts, and especially federal courts, to stay out of such "political thickets" if they are to preserve themselves and their credibility for those tasks—like protection of minority rights— that they are most qualified to perform. The opinion would then point to two entities that, in our constitutional system, would be better able to deal with the electoral problems at hand. The first (identified after an appropriate bow to federalism) is Florida. It is Florida, in all its political complexity (which includes its governor, its secretary of state, and even its elected Supreme Court), that should decide in the first instance how Florida's electors will be picked. Federal courts have no special grounding or role in Florida's politics. And whatever federal control is appropriate rests best in the second entity, the Congress of the United States. Emphasizing now the majoritarian essence of elections, the opinion would argue that Congress can, and perhaps must, protect whatever national interest there is in such national elections. Let the House and Senate do their job, the Court would conclude, and let the federal courts stay out of issues that they are institutionally not suited to deal with and that can only undermine their capacity to do those things that, in our system, no one else can handle well.

The second opinion—which, at the time, would have left the result uncertain—is the most judicially self-confident and aggressive. It emphasizes the Supreme Court as the ultimate keeper of national values and as the final arbiter of fairness and just process. I put it in the mouth of Chief Justice Earl Warren, though Justice William Brennan would also have enjoyed writing it. The only thing that matters in elections, the Court would thunder, is that every vote count. "One person, one vote" is the essence of electoral justice under the Constitution. Time is of no moment. December 12 is irrelevant, as is December 18. So is January 6, the date when Congress meets to count the electoral votes, and even January 20—as the law provides for an acting president if no one is chosen by that date. What matters is that the election be fair, and fairness requires that every valid vote be tallied. And We, the Supreme Court, will decide what constitutes a valid ballot, presumably after looking at what different states—Texas on the one hand, and Indiana on the other—had said about hanging chads and dimples. Chief Justice Warren would characteristically derive this newly defined federal requirement from the equal protection clause of the Constitution. And, having done so, he would close by ordering Florida—its courts and its counters—so to tally the vote.

I put my third opinion, which would have given the election to Bush, in the mouth of Chief Justice John Marshall, no less. It is, in some ways, the most sophisticated and elegant of the three. It would begin by saying that federal courts should stay out of political questions whenever possible. But it would quickly add that where there is federal law, federal courts cannot avoid their duty to enforce that law. In the case before the Court, the great chief justice would proceed, the law is plain. First, it requires that the grand electors, the members of the electoral college, be chosen on a day certain—this year, November 7. And if no choice occurs on that day, a reelection on another day to cure the matter would be illegal and invalid. (And this makes sense, he would add, because that reelection would not replicate the original one—for example, would people vote for Ralph Nader a second time when the national result was clearly in play; would the turnout be totally different, etc., etc.?) This does not mean, Marshall would continue, that we must know, on election day, who was chosen as grand electors. That clearly could take time to determine. But the choice, if it is to be made directly by vote of the people, must nonetheless be made on the appointed date.

What then should be done if for any reason—hurricane, flood, fire, or accidental destruction of the ballot boxes—no election takes place on election day? Again, John Marshall would magisterially proclaim, "The law provides." It says that if no electors are chosen, then the choice should be made by a body that is answerable to, because elected by, the people. This body could have been the state's congressional delegation, but, under the actual law, the state legislature has been given this awesome task. That legislature must select the grand electors, and must do so before the whole nation, but, most especially, before the people of the state who can, if their legislature picks unwisely, throw the legislators out.

The state legislature—in the election before us, the Florida House and Senate—has no power to act if the grand electors were in fact directly selected by the people on November 7. (Hence, all the premature posturing—about choosing electors—that occurred in the Florida legislature before the Supreme Court acted in *Bush* v. *Gore* would be decried in this opinion.) But if no valid choice occurred on November 7, only the Florida legislature can legally decide who should represent Florida in the electoral college. In making that selection, Marshall would explain, the legislators need not attempt to replicate what would have happened on November 7, as that would be impossible to determine. They must, rather, exercise the independent authority given to them by the law, and be answerable to their constituents—and thereby, indirectly, to the nation—for how they exercise that authority.

What, the chief would continue, can be said about this election? He could—and in my fantasy would—hold, that as to this election, we do not know, and never will know, whom the people of Florida picked on November 7 to be grand electors. The margin of votes is smaller than the margin of error in machine counting, and so the machine tally cannot determine who won. And hand-counting, though potentially more accurate, is also not capable of telling us who won, at least in a state in which dimples may be counted in some counties. For that hand-counting can itself create those very dimples, albeit inadvertently.

The fact of the matter, Marshall's opinion would conclude, is that the November 7 Florida election was a tie, and hence resulted in no electors being chosen. Accordingly, and most unusually, the task falls on the Florida legislature to select the Florida members of the electoral college. If that choice happens to decide the presidency, so be it. The law must be served!

Of course, all three opinions that I have outlined[2]—and many possible variations on their themes—might be "result-oriented," that is, written to achieve results their authors strongly favored. And of course, each could be strongly criticized on these or other grounds. (I shall shortly indicate what such criticisms would look like.) But all these things are true of many "major" court opinions and do not much matter. What does matter is that every one of the three decisions above described stands for something, for a principle that will affect—or even perhaps determine—the result in future cases. And these future results may well be anathema to the present opinion's authors. What is more, the criticism that can be directed at each of these opinions is itself likely to be focused on the principle adopted by the Court in that opinion—either on its future undesirability or on why it was wrongly applied in the present case. These attributes crucially differentiate the actual Court opinion in *Bush* v. *Gore* from my three hypothetical holdings, and it is their absence in *Bush* v. *Gore* that makes *Bush* v. *Gore*—though not unique—unusual and hence subject to unusual criticism.

Unlike the hypothetical judgments of Frankfurter, Warren, and Marshall—and those of most courts—the actual opinion in *Bush* v. *Gore* is not based on any principle that means to govern a future case. Indeed, the opinion expressly limits itself to this election and no other.

---

2. I make no claim of originality with respect to these three hypothetical opinions. The first two, in one form or another, have been much bandied about both before and after *Bush* v. *Gore* issued. Aspects of the third can be found in Charles Fried's amicus brief to the Supreme Court in Bush's first appeal from the Florida courts to that Court. And my colleague Paul Kahn, of Yale Law School, has also developed a fully worked out opinion of this sort.

It is, as some have described it, a ticket valid on one day only. And, as such, it imposes a result for that day and for no other.

This is not the case with many other opinions that have been seriously questioned. The reasoning and the policy behind the *Dred Scott* case, like those underlying *Brown* v. *Board of Education,* were attacked at the time and have been since. But no one can doubt that each expounded a principle, or that each stood for something with future consequences. Similarly, *Roe* v. *Wade,* at the time it issued, stood for a principle about constitutional rights to privacy in sexual matters. The decision was perhaps wrong or perhaps right, perhaps novel or perhaps presaged in earlier decisions, but it surely expressed a legal point of view. And the principled character of *Roe* did not abate when the Supreme Court—in cases like *Bowers* v. *Hardwick,* upholding the constitutionality of anti-sodomy laws—subsequently declined to follow the logic of *Roe's* "right to privacy" principle. This meant only that a later Court was left scrambling to find another principle which might support *Roe.* (And this the Supreme Court did, again for better or for worse, in *Planned Parenthood of Southeastern Pennsylvania* v. *Casey.*)

As Arthur Corbin—the greatest and most conservative of the legal realists—once said: an opinion that holds that the rich must always win (or always lose, for that matter) is not unprincipled. It reflects what may be a terrible principle, and one that should be excoriated. But its problem is not that it is lacking in principle.

The same is true of cases like *Korematsu* v. *United States,* upholding the wartime consignment of Japanese Americans to concentration camps. It too has been bitterly—and in my view appropriately—criticized. But it has not been decried because it stood for nothing. Unlike some of the other cases just mentioned, it is not even the principles that *Korematsu* pronounced that have been subjected to devastating attack. The most effective critique has focused on the way one of *Korematsu's* principles—that of heightened judicial scrutiny for racial classifications—was applied to the facts of the case. In such a situation, the Court can be blamed for the result it reached. And such criticism, like criticism that is addressed directly to the principle that the Court adopted, is standard. Cases that err in their choice of principle, or in how facts are applied to a principle, are inevitable and are not—however horrible the particular outcome may seem—either that rare or that systemically virulent.

It is not much different when a particular judge joins or writes an opinion containing principles that contradict his or her prior commitments. My favorite instance is *Bolling* v. *Sharpe*, which was a companion case to *Brown* v. *Board of Education* and which struck down segregation in the District of Columbia. Justice Black joined that opinion, but on his philosophy, on his principles, he should not have done so. Black—as is well known—was a literalist who required some appropriate constitutional language before invalidating a law. He also believed that the due process clause was not an open-ended grant of constitutional authority but simply incorporated the imperatives of the first eight amendments to the Constitution. He had no problem with *Brown* v. *Board of Education* because he believed that the Fourteenth Amendment's requirement of "equal protection" provided sufficient textual basis to invalidate state segregation laws. But the Fourteenth Amendment, by its express terms, applies only to the states and not to the federal government. And the District of Columbia is a federal entity. The Fifth Amendment, which imposes due process limitations on the federal government, has no companion clause dealing with equal protection. As a result, unless equal protection is part of a concept of "ordered liberty" that, though unspoken, somehow inheres in substantive "due process"—a notion that was anathema to Justice Black—no verbal hook was available on which he could hang *Bolling*. And yet he joined that opinion.

No one can doubt that Black violated his principles in *Bolling*. He knew it, and he said so when I questioned him. His reason for doing so will be worth considering when I discuss, anon, whether *Bush* v. *Gore*, though unprincipled, can still be justified. In any event, Black recognized that whether or not his joining *Bolling* was the right thing to do, he was properly subject to criticism merely for doing so. That being said, the opinion in *Bolling* was not unprincipled (even if Black was for joining it). It stood for the notion, accepted then and followed since, that due process requirements that apply to the federal government are, to some extent, open-ended and can include not merely preexisting notions but also some latter-day fundamentals, like those embodied in the equal protection clause. Again, one can argue with whether this is, or is not, a proper view of the due process clause. And one can attack Black for his inconsistency on this matter. But one cannot deny that *Bolling* embodies a principle, and one to which the Court, by deciding the case as it did, committed itself.

Unlike these cases and unlike my three hypothetical opinions, this is not true of the actual decision in *Bush* v. *Gore*. Each of my three decisions can be criticized either for its principle or for how that principle was applied. *Bush* v. *Gore* cannot.

The Frankfurterian opinion can be questioned on the ground—among others—that it is an awful policy to let states get away with any manner of electoral theft in the name of "political question," "federalism," or "judicial restraint." Nor can Congress be relied upon to control even the most egregious cases of thievery, especially if it is divided among the parties. No, the criticism would continue, only federal courts can assure the fairness of the ballot, at least in national elections, and they must therefore do so. (Of course, replies to such criticisms are also available, but that is beside the point I am now making.)

Similarly, my Warren-style opinion can be attacked because it makes the Supreme Court the ultimate "counter" in all federal elections, and by doing so, it numbs the political bodies and allows the people's representatives to shirk responsibilities that ultimately only majoritarian entities can exercise. On what basis, this criticism would add, can an unelected priesthood assert that it can define what is and what is not fair in so profoundly populist and political an event as an election? (Answers to this attack are, naturally, also available, but again they are not here germane.)

Finally, the Marshallian opinion can likewise be criticized, both for its principle and for how it applies that principle. Is it really true, opponents might say, that a new election on another day is prohibited, or is less appropriate than a decision by a body that was picked at another time and with completely different issues in mind? And even if it were true, is it correct to say that this election was a tie, and that we do not know, and never will know, whom the citizens of Florida selected on November 7?

I will not answer these challenges. Nor will I say which of the three opinions seems to me most appropriate. This chapter is not about such questions. My point is rather that the discussion of each of these opinions (like that which followed on *Dred Scott, Brown, Roe, Korematsu,* and *Bolling*), turns on whether the principles that the cases stand for, as applied to their facts, will bring about good, bad, or catastrophic results when similar situations occur in the future. The discussion also turns on whether the principle applied was new or precedented, had a basis in language or tradition, or was instead the result of a novel, and hence willful, imposition of the Court's values. But, and this is the crucial point, even a highly willful and result-oriented judge (as no less an authority than Justice Antonin Scalia has pointed out) is significantly and almost inevitably restrained by the knowledge that a principle pronounced and applied in one case will likely govern, or at least affect, the outcomes of later cases. It is the fear of potentially dreadful future results that keeps the willful judge from giving free rein to his or her wishes in the instant case. Nothing else restrains a judge as much!

What is more, and as important, the existence of a principle means that the Court's decision not only is restrained, but can also be evaluated, discussed, defended, and challenged on the basis of competing principles. This is true of each of the aforementioned opinions. But it is not true of *Bush* v. *Gore*, which in its own terms proposes to stand for nothing. *Bush* v. *Gore* states no principle that it intends to guide subsequent cases. To the contrary, it expressly says that whatever it did is not meant to apply to the future.

Now, of course, clever lawyers will seek, and are already trying, to derive principles from *Bush* v. *Gore* that can be applied in future situations, and I wish them very well. But that does not alter the fact that as written, *Bush* v. *Gore* was designed by its authors neither to constrain them through fear of future effects, nor to permit the opinion to be challenged as representing a point of view, a principle, that is wrong or undesirable because of the law it creates, because—that is—of its possible future consequences.[3]

The great constitutional scholar Alexander Bickel said that opinions that lack principle are per se wrong. They need to be savaged for what they are, since they cannot be challenged for what they hold. I am a teacher of a common-law subject—torts—and I have seen more than my share of unprincipled, self-contradictory, one-event-ticket-only, opinions. More, I expect, than did a scholar like Alexander Bickel, who focused primarily on constitutional cases. And I am not as absolutist as Bickel. As a result, I am not prepared to say that unprincipled opinions are inevitably wrong. I do agree, however, that such opinions must, in the first instance, be attacked, and severely so, for what they

3. Some have tried to defend *Bush* v. *Gore* by pointing out that three of the justices who joined it also wrote a separate opinion, which these defenders deem principled. But that defense fails. The fact that the Court could have (but didn't) reach its result in a way that stood for something cannot justify reaching the same result in a way that stands for nothing. Both in terms of constraints imposed by future events and in terms of capacity to criticize, it is what the Court actually did and not what hypothetically it might have done that counts.

Others have asserted that *Bush* v. *Gore* did purport to assert a principle that might have some limited future application. But they have also pointed out that any such principle was incoherent and contradicted in the opinion itself. To the extent this last is true, however, the opinion must be criticizable precisely as if it made no such attempt but was a "one case only" holding. See note 4 *infra*.

are . . . for their very being. Let me briefly reiterate why, before I turn to justifying the occasional use of unprincipled opinions.

Bickel is correct, that an opinion that stands for nothing is dangerous. If permissible, it would allow its authors to obtain the results they desire, without any adverse consequences. It would let judges act, plain and simply, according to their wishes, their values, and subject to no effective restraint. One could, of course, have a polity in which a group of Unelected Worthies wielded ultimate power. More than one society has given just such authority to variously denominated priesthoods. We have traditionally declined to do so. (And even those polities that have, have tended to justify the power given as deriving from, or being limited by, no less than the Almighty.) We do allow juries, to some extent, to impose results that stand for nothing other than what particular jurors value. But the jurors are, after all, meant to be one's peers, and hence to represent the unspoken (even if occasionally unspeakable) values of the polity. Judges have no similar grounding and, the traditional view goes, cannot be similarly empowered. They must be constrained, and the only effective constraints are (1) the fact that what they hold today has effects on future cases, and (2) the fact that what they hold today can be attacked for the rule established. Judges are constrained, that is, solely by the fact that they must issue principled decisions.[4]

It follows that when—as I contend occurred in *Bush* v. *Gore*—courts hand down an opinion that stands for nothing, they must be excoriated for that very fact! Were this not so, judges would become, even

4. In conversations with me, Bickel did not distinguish between opinions that were self-consciously limited to the single case before the court and those that were simply self-contradictory. To him—and I agree—both are equally unprincipled and must be attacked as such. An incoherent opinion, no less than one that intentionally stands for nothing, has no future legal consequences, and hence is incapable of restraining its authors or of being criticized on account of those consequences.

more than they are, uncontrolled priestly guardians. Without future consequences to limit them, and without the possibility of criticism of the principles they enunciate, judges would be free to give full vent to their own, unrepresentative, policy preferences. To prevent this from becoming the case, it is necessary, it is essential, that any unprincipled opinion be decried long and loud by all and sundry, and that its authors be pilloried for issuing an opinion that stands for nothing. For such opinions cannot be effectively attacked on any other ground. And if they cannot be effectively attacked, judges—who are, after all, human and like power—will resort to them again and again.[5]

Does this mean that all such opinions are necessarily undesirable, that judges should never engage in ad hoc law making? Alex Bickel thought so. Both as a "positive" and as a "normative" matter, I am not so absolutist. First, unprincipled opinions have been delivered by judges since the dawn of law. *Bush* v. *Gore* is not the first nor will it be the last. Not only have individual judges—like Justice Black in *Bolling* v. *Sharp*—contradicted their own principles, but whole courts have issued decisions that were incoherent and stood for nothing. And second, as Black said to me in explaining his position in *Bolling* v. *Sharpe,* it was simply unthinkable that the Court could strike down segregation in the states and leave it standing in its own backyard. The District of Columbia, though a federal enclave, was in fact governed by the House of Representatives Committee on the District of Columbia, which was dominated by rural, white Southerners who were delighted to create a situation that would permit critics to say segregation is outlawed everywhere, except of course where the Court sits! Any principle that led to that result, however worthy the principle would be in

5. Some Legal Realists, critical legal scholars, and even Judge Richard Posner in his most "pragmatic" effusions have either sought to justify such unprincipled judicial behavior or asserted that this is what judges do. This chapter is not the place to take on their views except to say, first, as a factual matter my experience as a judge suggests quite the contrary and, second, were it so, the manner through which judges are currently chosen would be indefensible.

most cases, had to yield in this case. And if Black was unable to reconcile the correct result with the principle that he still felt was proper in almost all cases . . . so be it!

So far as Black was concerned, *Bolling* v. *Sharpe* was a case in which he had to say "Hier stand ich. Ich kann nicht anders. Gott hilfe mier." So, inevitably, must whole courts in some cases. If, instead of *Bush* v. *Gore* the case were *Bush* v. *Hitler,* and if no principled way of barring Hitler's victory were available, are we really prepared to say that a Court that issued an opinion for Bush was wrong? I, for one, am not.

Nor is it only great cases and dire moments that have called forth unprincipled—but perhaps wise—opinions. It is said—though I have never found the case—that Chief Judge Cardozo's great colleague and adversary on the New York Court of Appeals, Judge Andrews, was once faced with an impossible garble in New York law dealing with stocks and bonds. He responded by writing an unintelligible opinion that, while gibberish, resolved all the problems in a sensible fashion. It is also said that, for reasons lost in New York history, no legislative solution to the mess was feasible. It is finally said that, thereafter, Andrews's decision was cited approvingly by many courts—near and far—and was inevitably referred to as "the well reasoned opinion of Judge Andrews."

No, it is not the case that unprincipled opinions are necessarily undesirable, and it is equally not the case that they are invariably wrong. It may even be the case that because they don't establish any principle, they can be the least dangerous decision a court can make when faced with a particularly intolerable situation. (This is especially so if the decision marks a first tentative, common-law step down a road that may in time enable a later court to establish a sound principle, and to do so less willfully because cognizant of, and reliant on, a number of past judicial fiats.)

It follows, I submit, that judges must on occasion be permitted to issue decisions that lack principle. And yet, if unprincipled opinions are to be kept in close check and not transform judges into uncontrolled guardians, if they are—in other words—to be the relatively rare exceptions that serve a system of law and not become the harbingers of a system of magistocracy, their every manifestation must in and of itself give rise to criticism.

My point is simply this. There is no rule that can define—a priori— those situations, large and little, in which an unprincipled opinion is justified. There is, therefore, no way of keeping judges from abusing their power to issue such decisions except by making it clear to them that whenever they emit such a ruling they are acting at their peril. Whenever, that is, they do so, they will be vigorously denounced, and properly so, for violating the only thing that justifies their authority . . . subservience to principle. It is only fierce condemnation of unprincipled decisions that serves to constrain judges and to some degree helps them resist the temptation to wield power. If severe criticism automatically attaches to such opinions, a judge who is inclined to write one will hesitate. For that judge will be aware that critical disdain can easily lead to historical infamy, and can cause even a glorious judicial career to be scorned. And that is as it should be.

Yet, acting at one's peril has its rewards. A judge who decided *Bush* v. *Hitler*—correctly, but in an unprincipled way—and then resigned because that very decision made him or her unfit to rule in ordinary cases—would surely be a heroic figure, and acknowledged as such. And so might a judge who stayed on, recognizing the peril of what he or she had done. History would determine whether it was worth it, whether the jurist was Pilate or Solomon. History has not treated Hugo Black badly for his "lapse" from principle in *Bolling* v. *Sharpe*. Nor should it.

What, then, can one say about the opinion in *Bush* v. *Gore?* I believe it to be unprincipled. Was it nonetheless justified? Will history hail the courage—the willingness to risk obloquy of Justices O'Connor and Kennedy in writing an opinion that was designed to self-destruct? Will it understand and forgive the chief justice and Justices Scalia and Thomas for joining up, even though their view of the case was quite obviously different? It is always risky to foretell history, but, at my peril, I hazard the guess that it will not treat them well.

Bush v. *Hitler,* the case certainly wasn't. Hyperbole about culture wars notwithstanding, this was an election between two relatively ordinary and not especially interesting, let alone frightening, politicians. One can feel very strongly that one of them would be much better for the nation than the other but still admit, as I think one must, that if the choice between these two contenders justified deviation from principled decision making, then there are no real limits on judges' use of unprincipled decisions. Whatever the stakes in this election, the danger to the Court as an institution from its reliance on an unprincipled holding seems to me to be unmistakably greater. No, I very much doubt that the members of the majority in *Bush* v. *Gore* will be viewed in distant retrospect as profiles in courage because, by their stand on that December night, they elected Compassionate Conservatism rather than Gorish Grace.

Still, as I said at the start of this chapter, I have no interest in, and no intention of, impugning judicial motives. I will not play the game—so popular in liberal circles—of asking whether anyone thinks the majority would have issued the same ruling had the case been *Gore* v. *Bush,* or whether anyone doubts that the dissenters, instead, would have written in that case exactly as they did in this. I am quite ready to believe that the majority thought it needed to act as it did to avoid a constitutional crisis. And I know all too well how difficult it is for judges to act wisely when under extreme pressures of time. I am, finally, also ready to accept the notion that the majority was affected by a deeply held belief—whether or not justified—that the Florida Supreme Court had itself acted in a partisan and unprincipled way. All this is by way of saying that in criticizing, as I do, the Court's decision, I do not wish to personalize my criticism or to assert that I, or other critics, would have done better in analogous circumstances. I would like to think so, but who can really say?

In the end, all that is irrelevant. The fact remains that *Bush* v. *Gore* was a dangerously bad decision. It was *bad*, not because its result was necessarily wrong but because it was unprincipled. It was *dangerously* bad because its lack of principle was naked and in a case that had the very highest visibility. And as such, it can all too readily serve to legitimate and make standard unprincipled decisions. It must, therefore, be criticized every bit as severely as it has been. Nor, I believe, can it resist historical obloquy. The grounds that occasionally justify legally incoherent outcome-determinative holdings do not come near to saving it. The stakes at play were penny ante compared to the harm the decision risked doing to the enormously hard task of constraining judges and, as a result, to the stature of the Court.

Characteristically, the most plausible defense of *Bush* v. *Gore's* lack of principle is, at once, its most devastating indictment. Its most sophisticated defenders, Robert Bork for example, argue that *Bush* v. *Gore* was justified because only by acting as it did could the High Court cope with the Florida Supreme Court's own unprincipled partisanship.[6] For purposes of this argument, I will assume that the Florida court's actions can be so described. But even so, I still wholeheartedly deny that the Florida court's behavior can justify the United States Supreme Court's actions.

After *Bush* v. *Gore* was delivered, many students and colleagues asked me what I, as a judge, would do in the face of so unprincipled a holding. My answer was immediate. "I would try to act in yet more principled a fashion." That is, and must be, the only possible judicial response to unprincipled judicial decisions. Any other answer generates a declining spiral leading, at the bottom, to the destruction of judges as proper participants in limited and principled policy making. The fact that the authors of *Bush* v. *Gore*, if their staunchest defenders are right about their motivation, did not recognize this is very sad indeed. But if the rest of the judiciary does recognize it

6. Robert Bork, Sanctimony Serving Politics, 19 The New Criterion 4, 6 (March 2001)

and responds by embracing principle even more tenaciously, then the opinion, though terribly wrong and perhaps a personal tragedy for its authors, will in time be treated as an aberration. And then *Bush* v. *Gore* will become as relatively insignificant as its immediate political consequences.

The Fallibility of Reason

Adjudication is the process through which ideals embodied in author-itative legal texts are elaborated and concretized. It requires the judge to listen to the presentation of facts and the law, to decide who has the best argument, and then to justify his decision. In this endeavor, the judge is not free to rely on any reason. He cannot invoke some rea-sons that might be wholly acceptable to legislators—for example, party loyalty—but instead is limited by a set of rules imposed on him by the professional community to which he belongs. The reason of the judge is thus constrained, or as Lord Coke put it, "artificial," but reason itself remains the source of the judge's authority. The judge stands before the community as the instrument of public reason, and his work is judged accordingly. The correctness of a judicial decision depends on our capacity to justify that decision on the basis of reason embodied in legal principle.

Judges have made mistakes and will do so in the future. Like any-thing human, judges and the public reason they embody are fallible. The process of criticizing judicial decisions and pointing to the errors they contain is a common endeavor for all lawyers and the central work of law professors. In fact, through the Socratic method, law students

I am happy to acknowledge the contributions of Matthew Lindsay and Nich-olas Daum to this chapter and to my work on *Bush* v. *Gore* in general.

are initiated into the profession by being taught to criticize judicial decisions for failure to comport with publicly acceptable reasons.

The Supreme Court's decision in *Bush* v. *Gore* is clearly susceptible to this sort of criticism, yet many critics wish to place it on an entirely different plane. Not only did the Court err, so they claim, but the decision put the authority of law in question and caused a crisis of legitimacy. Writing in the January 8, 2001, issue of *The Nation*, Professor Sanford Levinson of the University of Texas Law School reported that *Bush* v. *Gore* triggered "the deepest intellectual crisis—at least for people who profess to take law seriously—in decades."

In making this claim, Professor Levinson and a number of other critics, some of whom are represented in this book, place *Bush* v. *Gore* in a world apart from other recent controversial, politically charged Supreme Court decisions, such as those curbing affirmative action, striking down a key provision of the Violence Against Women Act, permitting the imposition of the death penalty or, on the other side of the political divide, limiting the power of states to regulate abortions. All these decisions have been criticized as lacking adequate justification, some with good reason, but none have been accused of offending the law or causing a crisis of any sort. The question I therefore put to myself is whether *Bush* v. *Gore* is truly unique and, if so, whether this uniqueness compromises the authority of the law.

The Supreme Court set aside a decision of the Florida Supreme Court that had ordered a manual recount of thousands of ballots in several Florida counties in order to correct for deficiencies of machine counting. On the basis of the machine count giving the Republican presidential candidate, George W. Bush of Texas, an edge, the State Elections Commission had certified a slate of Republican electors. Although the Florida governor, the younger brother of the Republican candidate, had recused himself from any participation in the proceedings of the commission, once the commission acted he signed the certificate required by federal statute and transmitted it to Washington. The manual recount ordered by the Florida Supreme Court might have changed the outcome of the state popular vote in favor of

Vice President Al Gore, the Democratic candidate, and thus required the certification of a slate of electors pledged to him.

The United States Supreme Court first stayed and then finally set aside the order of the Florida court, thereby leaving in force the slate of electors certified by the governor. The Florida Supreme Court had issued its order on Friday, December 8; that order was stayed by the Supreme Court on Saturday, December 9, and set aside at 10:00 PM on Tuesday, December 12. On Wednesday evening, December 13, Vice President Al Gore conceded defeat. Although he narrowly won the popular vote nationwide (by 500,000 out of 100,000,000 votes cast), the Constitution makes electoral votes, allocated on a state-by-state basis, decisive. With the Florida electoral votes, Governor George W. Bush of Texas had 271, while Vice President Gore had 266.

Clearly, some of the uniqueness of *Bush* v. *Gore* derives from the fact that it involved the presidency, that singularly visible and powerful political office. Some critics go so far as to accuse the Supreme Court of having, in effect, determined who would occupy that office for the next four years. Such a charge, however, presupposes that the manual recount ordered by the Florida court would have produced a popular victory for Gore in Florida, and the factual basis of that assumption, though held by many at the time of the Supreme Court's decisions, is far from clear.

The Florida Supreme Court's decision ordered that "undervotes" be recounted. Undervotes are ballots on which an intention to vote for one candidate has been indicated, but which fail to register a vote on a voting machine. An extensive study conducted for the *New York Times* and the *Washington Post* found that George W. Bush would almost certainly have won a recount of the Florida undervotes. The papers found, therefore, that the United States Supreme Court's decision did not determine the outcome of the election. The same study noted, however, that if "overvotes" (ballots that registered a vote for two presidential candidates but on which a clear preference was indicated for only one) were included in a recount, Gore would have won. Although the Florida court's order required only the recount of undervotes, some have speculated that Florida election officials would have interpreted the court's decision to require them to count overvotes as well; on this assumption, the recount might have gone to Gore, though there is no way of validating such an assumption. In the face of such uncertainty, it seems improper to accuse the Supreme Court of determining the outcome of Election 2000 and, on that basis, to argue that *Bush* v. *Gore* represents a special kind of judicial failing.

Although the presidency is a unique office and is at the center of democratic politics in America, it has often been the subject of constitutional decisions. Consider *Youngstown Steel,* setting aside the order of the president to seize the steel mills during the Korean War; or the Pentagon Papers case, refusing the president an injunction that would have prevented the publication of a Department of Defense study, classified as "top secret," of United States military involvement in Vietnam; or *United States* v. *Nixon,* denying the president the right to maintain the confidentiality of recordings of conversations in his office. All these decisions, and many others, have involved the presidency in dramatic ways.

Some of the decisions mentioned may have had even greater consequences for the presidency than *Bush* v. *Gore,* particularly once we take account of its indeterminate practical consequences. One example is the Supreme Court's rejection of the claim of executive privilege in *United States* v. *Nixon* and its insistence upon the disclosure of previously suppressed recordings. That decision made impeachment of President Nixon and his removal from office a near certainty. It almost immediately led to his resignation. No one would say, however, that merely because the Supreme Court's decision affected the presidency in such a decisive way that it caused an intellectual crisis in the law or threw the legitimacy of the entire enterprise into question. Whatever affront to the law *Bush* v. *Gore* might present must stem not from the consequences of the decision or the fact that it involved the presidency, but rather from the content of the decision itself.

The Court barred the manual recount on the ground that it violated the equal protection clause of the Fourteenth Amendment. The

Florida Supreme Court had directed those responsible for the manual recount to ascertain the intent of each voter, but a majority of the justices of the United States Supreme Court thought that the risk of inconsistency in applying that standard among and within different counties offended the constitutional principle guaranteeing the equal treatment of voters. Immediately after stating that conclusion, the Court added, "Our consideration is limited to the present circumstances, for the problem of equal protection in election processes generally presents many complexities."

Some critics, most notably Judge Calabresi in Chapter Four of this book, see this sentence as a willful refusal by the Court to abide by principle. By restricting the application of its reasoning to the case before it, the justices sought, according to these critics, to avoid the discipline that inevitably comes from treating a decision as binding precedent—that is, from having to apply the rule announced in one case to the next. This, the critics charge, distinguishes *Bush* v. *Gore* from other controversial decisions, such as those involving affirmative action or the death penalty, and contradicts the most elemental understanding of the rule of law.

Such a reading of the decision seems overwrought. The opinion in *Bush* v. *Gore* constitutes a sustained attempt by the majority to defend the result on the basis of equal protection jurisprudence. The offending sentence does not repudiate that effort, but rather acknowledges the Court's understandable concern that the opinion—written, by necessity, with haste—might unwittingly disturb settled bodies of law. Such disclaimers are commonplace in common-law decisions. They do not disavow principle, but rather warn against overreading the principle articulated.

There is a question in my mind, moreover, of whether the Court even possesses the capacity to free itself from the disciplining force of precedent, which arises not from what the Court wills but from the structure of the law itself. In the very act of giving a reason for its decision—that hand-counts threaten equal protection—the Court established a principle that it and other courts will have to confront. It cannot escape from its own ruling. Indeed, immediately after the decision was handed down, lawyers began laying the foundation for lawsuits resting on the equal protection theory articulated in *Bush v. Gore*. Granted, in future cases the Court might seek to constrain the application of the theory and treat *Bush v. Gore* as truly exceptional, almost idiosyncratic. Whether the Court will in fact seek to cabin the principle remains to be seen. Pursuit of such a policy will, moreover, reflect more adversely on the new decisions than on *Bush v. Gore*, for it is they that will contravene established law.

Although I disagree with those who read *Bush v. Gore* as a disavowal of principle, I join those who criticize the Court for the principle it did apply. Its equal protection holding has no constitutional warrant. Undoubtedly, hand-counts introduce a risk of treating voters inconsistently, but that kind of disparate treatment has never been nor should be deemed a violation of the equal protection clause. That provision has been primarily construed to guard against classifications, such as those based on race, ethnicity, or gender, that systematically disadvantage various social groups. Hand-counting neither employs such a forbidden classification nor threatens to disadvantage in a systematic or predictable way any cognizable social group.

Admittedly, the "one person, one vote" rule of *Reynolds v. Sims* might seem to provide support for the Court's decision. That case affirms the moral equality of citizens, which might seem to be offended by the risk of disparate treatment invariably entailed in hand-counts. One person's vote may be counted while another's is not, even though there is no morally relevant difference between the two, only a difference of who happened to be doing the counting.

Such a theory might be thought to offend the principle of "fundamental fairness," more than that of "equal protection," but in the context of *Bush v. Gore* that distinction is of little moment because the Court invokes both phrases, at times almost interchangeably. The theory fails, however, to account for the fact that every method of tabulation—even one employing machines—has a certain incidence of error built into it, and thus cannot avoid the arbitrariness that offended the Court. In contrast, the arbitrariness of the electoral practice condemned by *Reynolds* v. *Sims*—aggregating more voters in one electoral district than another—had no quality of inevitability. The moral equality of citizens that it affirmed could be achieved by establishing electoral districts that contained equal number of persons.

The rule of *Bush* v. *Gore* favors the exclusive use of machines, but there is no indication that the risk of error in hand-counting is any greater than that introduced by the use of different types of machines in different counties or different precincts. In fact, it might even be less. Modern electronic systems—optical scanning of paper ballots (as used for SAT exams) or touch screen voting (as used in ATMs)—are better than the much maligned punch-card ballots, but even they have considerable incidence of errors. As Justice Stevens complained in dissent, "The percentage of nonvotes in this election in counties using a punch card system was 3.92%; in contrast, the rate of error under the more modern optical-scan system was only 1.43%."

Although the Florida court conceived of a hand-count as a way of correcting for the errors of machine counting, the risk of error it introduced might nevertheless be of a different order than those associated with machine counting. Hand-counting entails the risk of partisan bias. The appropriate remedy for this danger, however, is not to bar hand-counting altogether, as the Court did, but rather to establish procedural rules that would minimize that risk. For example, it might have been stipulated that the hand-counting was to be done by a committee of persons that included representatives of all parties.

Construction of such safeguards would have required a remand to the Florida Supreme Court. Like Justices Rehnquist, Scalia, Thomas, Kennedy, and O'Connor, Justices Souter and Breyer believed inconsistency in recounting threatened to deprive voters of equal protection. Souter and Breyer sought a remand so the Florida court could construct procedural rules that would prevent or minimize such inconsistency, but, citing insufficient time, the other five refused to allow a remand. In this action the majority of five also erred; indeed, they compounded their initial error of staying the Florida Supreme Court's order.

The stay issued on Saturday, December 9, was improperly granted because the applicant—Governor Bush—did not show, as was legally required, that absent the stay he would have suffered irreparable harm. Justice Scalia defended the stay on the theory that if on completion the hand-count gave Gore an edge and was later, on consideration of the merits, declared illegal, it might cast a "cloud" over the legitimacy of the election. Although such a cloud might have some relevance for politics, it had none for the law, for whatever cloud might have been created would have disappeared if the Supreme Court had eventually ruled that the method that had given Gore the edge was unconstitutional. The Court also erred in failing to take account of the harm that the stay itself would cause by rendering it more difficult for Florida to take advantage of the safe-harbor created by federal statute if, in the Court's final decision on the merits, the hand-recount were held permissible. The safe-harbor statute provides that the electors chosen by December 18 would be binding on Congress.

The Court justified its refusal to remand on the ground that when the Florida court ordered the recount on December 8, it had indicated its desire to take advantage of the safe-harbor provision. In truth, the Florida court expressed that view only indirectly, by way of explaining why the recount had to begin immediately. Once the Supreme Court's stay made the commencement of the hand-count impossible, the Constitution's allocation of power required the Supreme Court, after its final decision on the merits, to remand the case to the Florida court. This remand would have enabled the Florida court not only to devise mechanisms for curbing the risk of partisan bias, but also to decide whether it wished a more fully standardized hand-recount to go forward even if that meant Florida would not be able to take advantage of the safe-harbor provision. Quite often, states are unable to take advantage of the safe-harbor provision, as was the case in Election 2000.

I thus heartily subscribe to the view that the Court in *Bush* v. *Gore* erred in issuing the stay on December 9, in deeming the hand-count a violation of equal protection, and in refusing to remand the case to the Florida Supreme Court on December 12 to minimize the danger of arbitrariness. These errors make *Bush* v. *Gore* wrong as a matter of law, but they do not place it on a moral plane different from that of recent decisions regarding, for example, affirmative action or the Violence Against Women Act. Those cases, too, involve gross errors. Although some may perceive the errors in *Bush* v. *Gore* with an exceptional clarity, those errors are not qualitatively different from those in many other recent controversial decisions. In all such cases, the errors stem from the fact that the Court's decision lacks adequate basis in defensible principles of law, rooted in either the Constitution, statutes, or consistent and wise practice governing such lesser matters as the issuance of stays.

Some contend, however, that *Bush* v. *Gore* is especially destructive of the authority of the law not only because its errors are so stark, but also because they are a product of bad faith. This charge, voiced by Professor Levinson in particular, assumes that some members of the majority, maybe all of them, were moved by a desire to make certain that Governor Bush would win the election. Although Justices Stevens and Souter, both appointed by Republican presidents, had dissented, all of the majority had been appointed by Republican presidents and had taken positions on the bench that were closely identified with policies advanced by Governor Bush.

This charge of vulgar partisanship is fueled by many factors. Some are rank gossip—for example, news stories based on some off-hand comment made by Justice O'Connor's husband at a social gathering. He allegedly said that Justice O'Connor was anxious to retire and would not feel comfortable doing so if Gore were elected. Months later, the press officer of the Supreme Court had to issue a most bizarre public announcement, denying that Justice O'Connor had any plans to retire in the immediate future.

More substantial factors, however, do lend credence to the charge of partisanship. One is that some of the dissenting opinions scolded the majority for their lack of impartiality and complained of the damage they were doing to the prestige of the Court. Another is that the justices who constituted the majority had to contravene a principle they had affirmed on many other occasions—that of strengthening the power of the states at the expense of the federal government. Indeed, the support within the Court for this principle had grown so in recent years that at the outset of the litigation, it was inconceivable to most law professors that the Court would perceive any merit to federal constitutional challenges to the Florida Supreme Court's interpretation and implementation of Florida law. The lower federal courts had confirmed this speculation when they summarily dismissed Bush's challenges.

Although I acknowledge some basis for a charge of rank partisanship, that charge can never rise beyond the level of suspicion. We may never shake ourselves free of that suspicion, but neither can we validate it. Nor can we preclude a more benign and much less condemnatory understanding of what moved some or all of the majority—a desire to provide closure to the 2000 election. The majority may have feared, for example, that remanding to the Florida court would have only prolonged the uncertainty of the outcome or, even worse, led to an impasse. The justices might have feared that the recount following a remand could result in the Florida court ordering the governor to certify a Democratic slate of electors, with the governor, acting in concurrence with the Republican-controlled state legislature, refusing to acquiesce and adhering to his earlier certification of the Republican slate of electors.

In our system, the Supreme Court sits to apply the Constitution and other laws of the United States. It is not charged with managing elections, even national ones, or avoiding impasses in the electoral process. The Constitution and federal statute provide the necessary mechanisms for resolving such disputes. They require the Senate and

House of Representatives to meet in Washington on January 6, to receive the ballots from the states. If there are conflicting slates of electors for any state and the two chambers cannot agree on which one to accept, the president of the Senate is directed by the statute to accept the slate of electors certified under seal by "the executive" of the state.

Admittedly, some difficulties or awkwardness may have arisen in applying these statutory directives—for example, the president of the Senate was Vice President Gore, the Democratic candidate, and the attorney general of Florida, a Democrat who supported the Florida court's recount order, arguably could be considered part of the executive of Florida. In the face of such conflicts, recourse would have had to be made to the imagination of political actors and their willingness to improvise and bargain; it was no part of the job of the Supreme Court to speculate about the difficulties that might be encountered in such a process and to end Election 2000 at the time and in the way that five justices thought appropriate. The desire to achieve an orderly closure to Election 2000 cannot justify the decision in *Bush* v. *Gore*. Yet, it might stand as a plausible explanation of what moved the justices, or at least some of the five.

Although we will never know what moved the members of the majority (indeed, perhaps they themselves are not fully aware of their motivation), the more fundamental point is that from the law's perspective it doesn't really matter. The motives of the majority are irrelevant. They do not change the character of the Court's errors or magnify their significance. The strength of a decision, its authoritative character, and its claim for respect stem not from the motives of the justices but from their capacity to justify the decision on the basis of publicly articulated reasons.

Judges are the persons through whom the law fulfills its purposes. Although motivation has no bearing on the justifiability of a decision —an error is an error—it may reflect on character. To say, as Levinson and some others do, that the majority was moved by vulgar partisanship is to assail the character of those who sit on the bench. It is to say that those justices were moved by considerations that should have no place in judicial decisions. Such an accusation implies a corruption of office almost akin to accepting bribes. Such a charge, if it could ever be substantiated, which of course seems unlikely, would clearly undermine the authority of these judges and, by extension, the institution they control. But it would not undermine the authority of the law, or cause "an intellectual crisis in the law." Law belongs not to any judge or even the Supreme Court, but to history or society in general.

Law is an idea. It seeks to vindicate public values through a process of reasoned elaboration known as adjudication. It may sometimes be faulted because the process on which it depends cannot prevent partisan manipulation or corruption of the type some suspect was at work in *Bush* v. *Gore*. Public reason, like all things human, is imperfect, but no more so than any other institution. We have turned to the law, and to its handmaiden, adjudication, because it reflects our collective wisdom as to how best to pursue justice and to give concrete meaning to our constitutional values. We will continue to do so, with almost undiminished confidence, even after *Bush* v. *Gore*.

ROBERT POST **6**

Sustaining the Premise of Legality: Learning to Live with *Bush* v. *Gore*

Bush v. *Gore* unfolded with the inevitability of a Greek tragedy. At every step, the Court could have decided otherwise. It could have refused the case, or sidestepped substantive issues by embracing the political question doctrine, or declined to stay the recount. But character was fate, and the Court seemed determined to embrace its destiny as the first tribunal to select a United States president.

The Court enacted its performance in the full glare of public attention. Supreme Court decisions normally involve obscure facts and personae; they limp along for years, complex and intractable, incapable of definitive resolution. In contrast, *Bush* v. *Gore* displayed virtually perfect dramatic form. It was compressed in time, taking six weeks from beginning to end. Each constituent judgment, each tactical maneuver, each argument was the subject of enthralled national attention and analysis. The Court's final decision, issued just two hours before the expiration of its self-imposed deadline of December 12, brought down the curtain with resounding éclat.

The aesthetic impact of these events was bound to be considerable. Aristotle could well have predicted the consequent national catharsis, a catharsis those seeking to unsettle the decision's result have since found exceedingly difficult to undo. But for many, including myself, the drama of the case has not been so easily contained. Its implications continue to leak corrosively into our professional lives.

For the past eighteen years, I have taught American constitutional law at a major law school. I seek primarily to understand and improve the practice of constitutional adjudication. I teach all kinds of contemporary constitutional opinions—those that are splendid, those that fumble for support, those that reach admirable conclusions for inadequate reasons, those that express ugly visions of the American polity. But until *Bush* v. *Gore* I had never been embarrassed to teach a decision of the United States Supreme Court. Never.

Immediately after *Bush* v. *Gore*, however, I found myself apprehensive about entering the classroom, afraid that the opinion would undermine what I aspired to offer my students. Talking with my colleagues, I found that my qualms were far from idiosyncratic. This chapter is about the distress I suffered. It explores why *Bush* v. *Gore* affected me differently from other (equally poor) decisions, and it suggests that my fears may reveal a good deal about the essential nature of constitutional adjudication.

All professors of American constitutional law must face the fierce nihilism of their students. "It is all politics," they say to us. "Your job is simply to spread the sanctimonious oil of rationalization." What lends force to the accusation is the kernel of truth at its passionate core.

It makes no sense to imagine constitutional law as an enterprise distinct from politics. Constitutional law concerns the deepest principles and vision of our nation. It is "the basis," as Chief Justice Marshall observed in *Marbury* v. *Madison*, "on which the whole American fabric has been erected." It would be monstrous to imagine such law as wholly divorced from the political perspectives of the American people. But—and here's the trick—it would also be quite catastrophic to reduce constitutional law merely to the intense conflicts, the everyday strategy and contestation, that make up ordinary American politics.

Constitutional law aspires to abstract from the turmoil of daily politics more stable political principles, principles that are more widely shared and more likely to endure. (Searching for these principles, the Court has been known to gamble on what it perceives to be the future development of American political vision, and it has been known both to inspire and to misjudge the nation.) Constitutional law also aspires to embed these principles within the discipline of a functioning legal system. The principles must be given workable doctrinal formulation; they must be rendered consistent with the unfurling of legal precedent.

If constitutional law were nothing more than the prosecution of politics by other means, I would have precious little to teach my students. I am no student of positive political science; I don't purport to offer a "scientific" perspective on how government actually functions. Nor am I a guardian angel, able to trumpet normative political truths. I have my own viewpoint, of course, but I offer it primarily to prompt my students to think for themselves. I do not seek to make my students into Democrats or Republicans. Instead, like some ancient alchemist, I offer guidance on spinning straw into gold, on the endlessly strange and magical transmutation of politics into constitutional law.

Bush v. *Gore* is certainly a difficult case to spin. It has little or no precedential support. Its equal protection holding seems profoundly inconsistent with the radical disparities in vote tabulation procedures that characterize virtually all contemporary elections. Its conclusion that Florida could not extend its election contest past December 12 seems outright willful. The peculiarity of the case was so extraordinary as to raise suspicions about the elemental good faith of the Court. I do not know a single person who believes that if the parties were reversed, if Gore were challenging a recount ordered by a Republican Florida Supreme Court, the five members of the United States Supreme Court who coalesced to issue the per curiam opinion in *Bush* v. *Gore* would have reached for a startling and innovative principle of equal protection to hand Gore the victory. To make matters worse, the Court seemed deliberately to craft its doctrinal foray into equal protection so as to minimize its future influence, confining its application to "the special instance of a statewide recount under the authority of a single state judicial officer." "Our consideration," the Court announced with conviction, "is limited to the present circumstances."

It is unusual for the Court to act in a way that arouses serious and pointed doubts about the legitimacy of its intent. But even if, as seems likely, the Court was at some level influenced by its conservative attraction to Bush, psychological motives of this kind are ultimately private and opaque, and, more important, it is not plausible to imagine that the Court would have reached out to make Bush president unless it also had in mind what it regarded as a defensible justification for so doing. If *Bush* v. *Gore* is to be assessed as an instance of constitutional adjudication, it is the decision's public implications, which is to say the nature and quality of its holding and justifications, that must be appraised. Illicit scienter is a matter for impeachment, not constitutional law.

Law professors spend a good deal of energy evaluating potential justifications for judicial opinions. The ability both to criticize and to rehabilitate otherwise impossible decisions is sometimes taken as a sign of virtuosity. One could quite possibly recuperate aspects of *Bush* v. *Gore* in this way. One could argue, for example, that its evocation of equal protection was misplaced, and that its reiterated focus on "arbitrary and disparate treatment" of voters, its concern that "the standards for accepting or rejecting contested ballots might vary . . . within a single county from one recount team to another," would better have been expressed as a preoccupation with the procedures required by due process of law for safeguarding "the fundamental right" to vote. A focus on due process would not have put the Court in the position of frantically waving off obvious but undesired implications of the equal protection principle it found itself announcing, while simultaneously allowing the Court to expatiate on the procedural defects it found so deplorable in the Florida recount.

From the perspective of this explicatory project, the capacity of a case to be integrated into the dense web of explanation and justifica-tion that constitutes constitutional law seems less a matter of the actual substance of a case than a matter of the pressing need of legal scholars and professionals ceaselessly to maintain and repair the weave of constitutional law. Even a decision like *Brown* v. *Board of Education,* which self-consciously breaks with precedent, can, by dint of this endless renovation, be prospectively transformed into a foun-tainhead of perfectly legitimate doctrine.

The strange fact about *Bush* v. *Gore,* however, is that I didn't *want* to explain the decision in this manner. In the past, poorly reasoned opinions have sometimes made me agitated and even irate, but *Bush* v. *Gore* was different, because it made me ashamed. My particular embar-rassment with the case did not rest on a technical incapacity to perform the perennial law professor's job of domesticating willful cases into the domain of constitutional law. Instead I had no desire to perform my accustomed professional task of rehabilitation. In part I was simply stung by distrust of the Court's good faith. But no doubt a significant source of my paralysis was also due to the way that *Bush* v. *Gore* seemed to undermine the very practice of constitutional adjudication.

I strongly suspect that the uniquely visceral impact of *Bush* v. *Gore* is connected to the sudden and unexpected reappearance of the category of the "political." And by this category I mean not the lawless, but rather those dimensions of social life that are precisely to be kept immune from law because they represent, in Hannah Arendt's mov-ing account, "the joy and the gratification that arise out of being in company with our peers, out of acting together and appearing in public, out of inserting ourselves into the world by word and deed, thus acquiring and sustaining our personal identity and beginning something entirely new."[1]

1. Hannah Arendt, "Truth and Politics," in Between Past and Future 263 (1968).

Like most law professors who came of age in the afterglow of the Warren Court, I had always celebrated the imperial reach of "law's empire." I admired the progressive expansion of legal reason and justification. I approved the Court's effort in *Baker* v. *Carr* to redefine the political question doctrine so as to enable judicial vindication of the principle of "one man, one vote." I had a robust appreciation of the value of law, but no equivalent appreciation of the value of politics.

This perspective has recently begun to evolve, pushed by the increasingly intolerant juricentricism of the contemporary Court, most notably manifested in its sharp restrictions on congressional authority under Section 5 of the Fourteenth Amendment. The Court's disdain for the political branches of government has prompted me, as well as many others, to reconsider the positive value of politics. *Bush* v. *Gore* landed squarely in the midst of this reconsideration.

Politics is not war. We can have joy and gratification in acting together with our peers to fashion new political identities only if the structure of our exchange is peaceful and orderly. Elections could not exist without just and impartial procedures. Law is thus necessary to sustain politics. It follows that there can be no simple or decisive distinction between politics and law. Courts must on occasion enter what Justice Frankfurter memorably called the "political thicket."[2]

In the past half-century, the Supreme Court has typically addressed issues of politics in terms of the standards by which elections should be held. It has sought to bring constitutional norms to bear on the rules of apportionment, qualifications for the ballot, and so forth. But there is a large and consequential difference between such structural interventions, which set the terms on which elections can be conducted, and a judicial decision that effectively decides the winner of a partisan election. The significance of this difference is most salient in an election to determine the president of the United States.

Bush v. *Gore* is in this respect plainly unique, and its singularity

2. *Colegrove* v. *Green* 328 US. 549, 566 (1946).

raises two distinct questions. The first concerns the institutional relationship between the Court and the presidency. The president nominates justices of the Supreme Court. Inherent in the Court's determination of the outcome of a presidential election, therefore, is the potential for grave conflict of interest. This potential is greatly magnified if the Court is bitterly divided along ideological lines, if the composition of the Court has been a matter of political contention in the campaign, and if the candidate for president selected by the Court vigorously agrees with the ideological perspective of the five-member majority that has chosen him. Regardless of the actual good faith of the Court, there is in such circumstances an inevitable and powerful appearance of impropriety.

Second, and equally disturbing, the Court's selection of a president preempts the outcome of political deliberation and contest. The election of a president is the quadrennial defining moment of American political life. By choosing a president, Americans nationally come as close as they can to fulfilling Arendt's account of the political: they insert themselves, by word and deed, into the world, in an effort to construct a common identity and to begin something entirely new. By specifying that the president shall appoint justices, rather than the reverse, the Constitution signifies that the political choice collectively made by the American people should inform the Court's vision of law. By intervening in *Bush* v. *Gore* to determine the content of this choice, the Court in effect inverted the priority that the Constitution accords to the political. It used law to foreclose, rather than to sustain, the arena of political contest.

Although our actual experience of the 2000 election might have been disappointing, although its controversies might have seemed muddled and its debates banal, they were nevertheless *our* controversies and debates. They expressed the nature of *our* participation and commitments, however impoverished. It was shocking for the Court simply to sweep these aside. Only fifteen years previously Justice

O'Connor herself had pronounced in *Davis* v. *Bandemer* that "the risks . . . to our political institutions" posed by "judicial intervention on behalf of mainstream political parties" are "unacceptable."

But in any particular case, of course, the risks of such intervention in fact may be worth facing. If the legal principle to be vindicated were important enough, or if the consequences of judicial inaction were intolerable enough, a Court might well have no alternative but to decide the outcome of an election. In circumstances where the United States Supreme Court intervenes to select the president of the United States, the pressure for such justification is at its most extreme.

Bush v. *Gore* handles this pressure very badly. It never directly addresses the singular circumstances of its own production. Instead it struggles to characterize itself as a simple and straightforward legal opinion, deflecting any acknowledgment of its own special political context until its conclusion, where it briefly expresses "admiration" for "the Constitution's design to leave the selection of the President to the people" but excuses its own intervention on the breathtakingly disingenuous grounds that "when contending parties invoke the process of the courts . . . it becomes our unsought responsibility to resolve the federal and constitutional issues the judicial system has been forced to confront."

It is evident that at every stage the Court deliberately chose to intervene in the Florida election, and the question is why. In no way does *Bush* v. *Gore* read like a decision driven by the need to articulate and institutionalize a pressing principle of constitutional law. The equal protection rationale of the opinion is weakly and obscurely articulated, and it is in any event so hedged against future application as to deprive it of convincing constitutional force. The Court's declared concern with the unequal treatment of punched ballots loses all conviction in the face of the Court's manifest indifference to the much larger disparities in the treatment of ballots as between different Florida counties. It should not be forgotten that the Court declined even to consider the equal protection argument when Bush originally raised it in his first certiorari petition.

If *Bush* v. *Gore*'s intervention is to be justified, therefore, it must be on consequentialist grounds. The Court might have believed that decisive action was necessary to prevent the Florida Supreme Court from stealing the election for Gore. But assuming that this characterization of the Florida Supreme Court were accurate, which I find doubtful on the facts, the ultimate constitutional remedy for the Florida court's impropriety lay in congressional oversight of Florida's selection of presidential electors. There was no need for the United States Supreme Court to endanger its own integrity in order to discipline the Florida court system. Even if such discipline were truly the concern of the United States Supreme Court, moreover, the proper resolution would have been to remand the case to Florida with an order fashioned to prevent the election from being stolen by anybody. The Court, however, chose not to adopt this option, despite the vigorous objections of Justices Souter and Breyer, who agreed in principle that the Florida recount suffered from deficiencies of equal protection.

Instead the Court decided to shut down the Florida election, which effectively declared victory for Bush. The Court's refusal to permit Florida to recount ballots after the December 12 deadline, a deadline the Court's own December 9th stay guaranteed Florida could not meet, is by consensus the most extreme and least defensible aspect of *Bush* v. *Gore*. For this very reason, it also most starkly reveals the Court's driving purposes. It strongly suggests that the Court's greatest priority was to end all uncertainty by definitively resolving the election.

Recall that as early as November 30, the Republican-controlled Florida legislature had threatened to involve itself in the controversy by naming its own slate of presidential electors. There was a good chance, therefore, that the election would be thrown to Congress for the first time in modern American history. Although federal legislation enacted in 1887 contemplated exactly this possibility, and created procedures for its administration, no one knew for sure exactly how Congress or the nation would respond to such uncertain events. There was apprehension about whether Congress would be adequate to the political challenge of selecting the president. There was anxiety about the effect of protracted and intractable congressional decision-making on the international and economic security of the nation. There was concern about how novel institutional procedures would affect the legitimacy of the incoming president.

Of course not a word about this appears in the opinion itself. But less than a month after the decision, on January 7, Chief Justice Rehnquist issued the text of a speech about the resolution of the 1876 Hayes-Tilden election, which in terms of an uncertain stalemate in the context of potentially miscounted ballots presents a striking and well-recognized parallel to the 2000 election. The 1876 election was ultimately settled by an electoral commission, on which the deciding vote was cast by Supreme Court Justice Joseph Bradley. Rehnquist praised Bradley's decision to join the commission, at the cost of his own "reputation" as "an honest jurist" (as distinct from "a party hack"), because there was "a national crisis" and "only" he could "avert it." In such circumstances, "[i]t may be very hard to say 'no.'" As a result of Bradley's decision, "the nation as a whole settled down to a more normal existence."

If *Bush* v. *Gore* were in fact concerned swiftly and effectively to end the looming crisis caused by the stalemate of the 2000 presidential election, it was an opinion whose raison d'être flowed from a deep distrust of politics. The Court was prepared to abide by elections that were orderly, that followed predictable procedures and clear rules. But it was not willing to allow the nation to venture into the political unknown, the open space of political confrontation unbound by traditional forms, where something "entirely new" might transpire. It conceived the uncertainty of that space as a threat to be averted. The Court thus acted decisively to terminate the 2000 election, though it could barely summon even the fig leaf of a constitutional principle by which to justify its decision. The Court sought to save the nation from its political demons.

If this is correct, and it seems to me the most convincing explanation for the decision, the Court acted not as a champion of constitutional law but instead as a knight of stability. In recent decisions, like *Timmons* v. *Twin Cities Area New Party,* the same five justices who authored *Bush* v. *Gore* have forcefully reaffirmed the proposition that "States . . . have a strong interest in the stability of their political systems." Stability, however, is at root a political virtue. In effect the Court seized the high prerogative of constitutional law in order to impose a decision that rested entirely on an extralegal and practical judgment about whether the politics of the 2000 presidential election needed to be contained so that the nation could get on with its "normal existence."

It is not unusual for the Court to deploy practical judgments of this kind. Constitutional law is not immaculately segregated from pragmatic political virtues. Like any institution that wields political authority, the Court must pursue its objectives in ways that are both prudent and strategic. Moreover, as legal realism has taught us, practical policy judgments perennially lurk behind and propel the development of constitutional doctrine. Without such judgments, constitutional law would quickly turn arbitrary or oppressive.

Although it may be commonplace for the Court to pursue its mission of designing and implementing constitutional norms in a manner that incorporates pragmatic political values, it would seem a rather different matter for the Court to use this mission as a pretext for the imposition of ad hoc political judgments. *Bush* v. *Gore* comes very close to this latter circumstance. The most plausible consequentialist justification for the opinion, the need to ensure political stability, will not bear scrutiny as a constitutional principle capable of legal generalization and application, while the putative equal protection rationale of the opinion is hedged about with reiterated warnings that it should not be mistaken for a robust and generative source of future constitutional law. In fact the *ratio decidendi* of the opinion reads like a kind of desperate last resort, deployed without conviction only when every other legal justification had proved unacceptable.

If the legitimacy of the Court's intervention is to be defended, therefore, it must be on the unique and particular ground that it was necessary to save American democracy from itself. I disagree with the Court on this question. Although in December 2000 Americans were far more politically alert and attentive than is their custom, there were no mobs in the streets, no crisis of the established political order. Events were unfolding that had been specifically anticipated and ordered by venerable federal statutes.

Even if I am right on this point, however, I have not yet explained the fierce and strange nature of my reaction to the decision. For on the assumption that *Bush* v. *Gore* was wrongly decided, that the Court had abused its authority by trading on the trappings of judicial power unnecessarily to impose extralegal values, the appropriate response would have been anger rather than apprehension; outrage rather than shame. Why, then, did the case inspire in me such fear and embarrassment? The answer, I believe, lies in the nature of constitutional law itself.

Law carries within it high prerogatives. It differs from politics because it commands, as well as persuades. That is why *Bush* v. *Gore* could so effectively shut down the 2000 election. The price for these prerogatives, however, is that law must hold itself answerable to the appraisal of reason and of craft. My task as a professor of law is to inculcate the responsibility and techniques for such appraisal. To teach *Bush* v. *Gore* in a law school classroom, therefore, is to presuppose that the decision is amenable to the usual forms of legal evaluation. It means approaching the case on the premise of its claim to legality.

Law students tend to be skeptical of this premise, and nowhere more so than in the arena of constitutional adjudication. No legal domain changes as rapidly or as controversially as constitutional law. Constitutional doctrine continuously evolves as the Court's political perspective alters. Because constitutional law and political vision are necessarily and properly intertwined in this way, students frequently find it difficult to see the point of evaluating judicial decisions according to the usual standards of legal reason and craft. They attribute to such decisions a curiously amorphous, empty quality. The decisions are not law, because they are not answerable to legal norms. But neither are they politics because, carrying the force of law, they hold the power to shut down the realm of political contestation. Judicial opinions thus appear as weirdly sui generis, as bizarrely monologic acts of will.

Bush v. *Gore* is wickedly calculated to reinforce this cynicism. It is true that I could have approached the decision as I teach all constitutional cases, as an example of the ongoing process of constitutional lawmaking. This would not have prevented me from challenging the opinion; I would have been free to criticize the Court's reasoning and its conclusions, and even to express outrage at its abuse of judicial power. Approaching the case in this way might also have defused the skepticism of my students, because it would have required them to *assume* that *Bush* v. *Gore* is to be incorporated into the warp and woof of ordinary constitutional adjudication. But this approach also would have required me to maintain, by sheer force of will, the premise of legality, which holds that no matter what the Court has actually done, its decisions always remain accountable to the values and standards of constitutional law.

The extraordinary circumstances of *Bush* v. *Gore,* however, made it feel false to address the case in this way. For all the many reasons I have suggested, the decision did not seem a normal example of constitutional adjudication. At the very moment when it was most urgent that the Court invoke the legitimacy of legal justification, it disavowed its own doctrinal formulations, strongly hinting that they were not to be taken seriously as legal principles. Despite the possibility of gravely compromising the appearance of its own judicial neutrality, the Court seemed bent on achieving a blatantly extralegal objective, even at the cost of shutting down a presidential election. Because the Court itself sent such obvious and repeated signals that it would not be bound by the usual standards and values of constitutional law, it seemed merely naïve and credulous to express concern or outrage at their violation.

It is striking how the sting of this dilemma has diminished in the passing months. As *Bush* v. *Gore* recedes in time, as it merges with the great mass of Supreme Court opinions, I can recognize the resurrection of old habits and proclivities, well described by Owen Fiss in Chapter Five of this book. I find it easier to conceive the decision as merely an aberration, an important but temporary lapse in the nation's ongoing and encompassing commitment to constitutional law. Although I still feel slightly gullible in doing so, I can now even wax indignant at the opinion's many departures from received norms of judicial craft. I take this to signify that the singularity of the decision is no longer quite so threatening to my capacity to sustain the premise of legality.

But the drama and circumstances of *Bush* v. *Gore,* when it was first announced, conspired to inflict a searing and disorienting vision of a world without law, a nation subject to courts who command without accountability. The decision exposed the molten core of constitutional lawmaking, where law and will wrestle in perpetual indeterminacy, and where the triumph of legality depends upon nothing more efficacious than our continuing determination to make it so. I am reminded of Walter Benjamin's description of El Greco, who "tears open the sky behind every gesture." *Bush* v. *Gore* tore open the very fabric of constitutional law, and by so doing forced a choice: either to repair that fabric, at the risk of perpetuating a falsehood and a myth, or to suspend allegiance to the premise of legality, at the risk of losing hold on the possibility of constitutional law. Only a fool would confront such a choice without embarrassment or fear.

MARGARET JANE RADIN

7

Can the Rule of Law Survive *Bush* v. *Gore?*

What Is the "Rule of Law"?

These days you often hear proponents of international trade talk about the rule of law. They mean we should persuade or force other countries to promulgate and enforce legal rules of property and contract. They are talking about Russia or China, not the United States. They are worried about a Kafkaesque picture. Market exchange won't work when people do not know what entitlements will be respected as theirs, so that they can trade them. Market exchange won't work when no rules exist (or will be enforced) against theft and fraud; when contracts change after you sign them; when your trading partner feels it has no obligation to perform and there is no court system that can be trusted to make it do so; when judges take bribes or take dictation from powerful groups or decide cases arbitrarily in favor of their monetary or political interests and against disfavored groups (such as foreigners).

But there is much more to the ideal of the rule of law than the call for stable and enforceable rules of property and contract in other countries. The ideal has a long and central history in Western political thought. It is the backdrop of the legal system as we know it—at least as we conceive of it, whether or not the system lives up to it in practice.

It is not just something we need to worry about in other countries; not something that we can take for granted at home. The traditional premises of the rule of law have been intellectually challenged by contemporary approaches to knowledge and politics, and these critiques I believe should be taken seriously. Nevertheless, when push comes to shove as it did in *Bush* v. *Gore,* we remain committed to the rule of law. We must now recognize that it is in trouble and in need of our most serious attention.

The ideal of "the rule of law, not of men" expresses the norm that law itself should govern us, not the wishes of powerful individuals or groups. In a statement that goes back to John Locke, government should be by "settled, standing laws," not by "absolute arbitrary power."[1] Modern philosophers of liberal democracy have all included the rule of law in their descriptions of the institutions of a just and properly functioning state. Variously formulated though the ideal has been, its basic characteristics are easy to sum up: rules should exist in advance of the conduct they are supposed to regulate; they should be knowable by those who are supposed to follow them; they should not be impossible to follow or irrational or useless for human well-being. The rules should be enforced fairly and impartially, not capriciously and arbitrarily. The entities that make the rules (such as legislatures) should address them to rationally determined groups or citizens as a whole, and not single out individuals or unfairly target subgroups. The rule-making entity should be separate from the entities (such as courts) that enforce the rules against individuals. The courts should enforce the rules impartially and according to the preexisting law and legal principles, rather than arriving at results arbitrarily and ad hoc. The law on the books should correspond with the law in practice. Judges should be guided by law and legal principles, not by their

---

1. J. Locke, Of the Extent of Legislative Power, in Two Treatises of Government (P. Laslett rev. ed. 1970) (3d ed. 1698).

personal political commitments or monetary interests, and not by arbitrary procedures such as flipping a coin.

Of course, all these principles apply to the legal system as a whole, not just to the rules governing property and contract, which is why the exhortations of businesspeople are incomplete. Under the ideal of the rule of law, everything from fundamental constitutional rights to traffic tickets is supposed to be decided under reasonable principles that can be known in advance and are consistently and impartially applied in practice.

Law Professors as Activists

We law professors are typically conservative in the sense that we don't go around signing petitions or statements that criticize judges; instead, we try to remain polite with them. We keep our arguments to the restrained venue of law reviews, just as practicing lawyers constrain themselves to briefs. Judges are our professional colleagues. They are the people we went to law school with. We normally don't want to offend them, both because they are our friends and colleagues, and because we might appear before them someday or want them to regard our law review articles favorably.

But with *Bush* v. *Gore* something extraordinary happened within the ranks of legal academics. Within two days after the stay order that stopped the Florida recount on December 9, several hundred law professors had come together in an ad hoc group called Law Professors for the Rule of Law to sign a statement in protest. The statement was circulated rather haphazardly through e-mail by an accidental activist (me), pushed over the edge by a sense of outrage. The impetus was a message from one of Stanford Law School's alumni, Mitchell Zimmerman, a veteran of the anti-war and civil rights struggles of the 60s, asking whether anyone was willing to speak truth to power. By the time the statement was published in the *New York Times* on January 13, 2001, 554 law teachers from 120 schools had signed it, and eventually the count reached 673, from 137 schools. The statement criticized the five justices in the majority for being "political partisans, not judges of a court of law." As law teachers, we protested in the name of the rule of law:

By stopping the vote count in Florida, the U.S. Supreme Court used its power to act as political partisans, not judges of a court of law.

We are Professors of Law at 120 American law schools, from every part of our country, of different political beliefs. But we all agree that when a bare majority of the U.S. Supreme Court halted the recount of ballots under Florida law, the five Justices were acting as political proponents for candidate Bush, not as judges.

It is not the job of a Federal Court to stop votes from being counted.

By stopping the recount in the middle, the five Justices acted to suppress the facts. Justice Scalia argued that the justices had to interfere even before the Supreme Court heard the Bush team's arguments because the recount might "cast a cloud upon what [Bush] claims to be the legitimacy of his election." In other words, the conservative justices moved to avoid the "threat" that Americans might learn that in the recount, Gore got more votes than Bush. This is presumably "irreparable" harm because if the recount proceeded and the truth once became known, it would never again be possible to completely obscure the facts. But it is not the job of the courts to polish the image of legitimacy of the Bush presidency by preventing disturbing facts from being confirmed. Suppressing the facts to make the Bush government seem more legitimate is the job of propagandists, not judges.

By taking power from the voters, the Supreme Court has tarnished its own legitimacy. As teachers whose lives have been dedicated to the rule of law, we protest.

What accounted for the wave of outrage among law teachers? Was it Justice Scalia's opinion, which went along with the Five's grant of the stay order to stop the recount? How could he assume that counting votes by hand was casting a cloud on the legitimacy of Bush's election, when the election was a statistical tie and was clearly still in doubt? How could he say that continuing a recount mandated by state law is the kind of irreparable harm that justifies intervening on behalf of one contender before the case has even had a chance to be argued by both sides? How could he assert—nearly two centuries after the concept of seditious libel had supposedly disappeared from American law—that the risk that a politician's image might be damaged is cognizable harm? All this was unimaginable for those of us who believe that judges follow the rule of law, or at least pay lip service to it. Yet it happened. Scalia's opinion will now live forever in the pages of the *U.S. Reports,* where it will embarrass the Court for the rest of its history—assuming that future Courts have more capacity for embarrassment than this one does. The ideal of the rule of law says that judges don't decide cases before the arguments are heard—but this one did. And wrote it down for all to see.

Scalia's ravings aside, what accounted for the wave of outrage among legal professionals was the broad assault on the rule of law signified by *Bush* v. *Gore* as a whole.

Bush v. *Gore* as an Assault on the Rule of Law

So why is *Bush* v. *Gore* so damaging to the rule of law? Put as bluntly as possible, instead of deciding the case in accordance with preexisting legal principles, fairly interpreted or even stretched if need be, five Republican members of the Court decided the case in a way that is recognizably nothing more than a naked expression of these justices' preference for the Republican Party. To be still more direct, as many of the other chapters in this book demonstrate, the Republican justices' "analysis" doesn't pass the laugh test, particularly their decisions to stop the vote count and to forbid the Florida Supreme Court from addressing the constitutional problems the federal Supreme Court purported to find.

Or so it appeared to a very large number of observers. Yet some who defend *Bush v. Gore* say it looks just like other Supreme Court opinions, no worse than and no different from them. After all, there's a written decision, and it has legalese, cites cases, and so on, just like other judicial decisions. Is *Bush v. Gore* simply a decision whose result many law professors lament? What is it about the decision that undermines public confidence in the rule of law in America and makes it more difficult to argue that the rule of law is a viable ideal?

First, the stay. The stay seemed outrageous to law teachers for three reasons. One, its notion of irreparable harm was a travesty of an extraordinary legal process designed for emergencies of the kind where someone's life is in danger. Having one's favored candidate in danger of losing an election is not that kind of emergency. Two, the stay was issued to nullify a state court decision that seemed to law professors like a garden variety state court opinion interpreting state law, like hundreds of opinions we have read in the course of our professional lives. The federal courts are not supposed to interfere with state sovereignty unless the state violates federal law or the constitution. In fact, these particular judges have purported to believe deeply in state sovereignty, so deeply that they have been steadily undercutting federal laws meant to protect against discrimination and other harms. Three, the stay was an egregious interference with the political process.

As other contributors to this book point out, there would have been a way for the Court to redeem itself to some extent, making the stay look somewhat better in retrospect. That way would have been for the Court to send the case back to Florida for the votes to be counted in whatever manner the Court deemed proper. In other words, if the Court wanted to say that it stopped the vote count on an emergency basis because Florida was not doing it correctly, then its opinion on the merits should have sent the case back to Florida with directions for how it should be done. It is a good conjecture, though we will probably never know, that the two justices who endorsed the equal protection rationale in *Bush* v. *Gore* but dissented on the issue of remand thought they had a deal that there would be such a remand if they signed on. If so, they were betrayed.

Next, the opinion on the "merits." After the stay, the decision on the merits stopped the count by saying it was too late. Why was it too late? In part because of the stay. Moreover, as other contributors to this book also point out, it wouldn't have really been too late until January when the Congress met. The deadline of December 12 resulted from the Five's interpretation of the state court's interpretation of a federal statute obviously designed only to give states a safe harbor, in the sense that if that date were met Congress would have to accept the state's certified delegation of electors. There was nothing about that deadline that said Congress couldn't receive delegations certified later than that and rule upon them itself. It was surely ironic, perhaps even Kafkaesque, for what was envisioned as a safe harbor for a state to be used against the state in this way by the Supreme Court.

One of the things we do as law professors is help our students come to situate themselves in the domain of acceptable legal argument. Learning to situate oneself in this way is a process, an assimilation to a social practice. It is learned more by osmosis than by lecture; more by rearguing the past artifacts that the legal system has given us than by laying down a template for all cases. Hence the famous "Socratic method."

Within that domain of acceptable legal argument there is controversy. After each side has given the other side what it believes are completely convincing arguments, the controversy often remains. Yet the community of legal practitioners understands that some arguments are off the charts or out of bounds—not acceptable legal argument. If you argue that the defendant should get a longer sentence because his eyes are blue, no one socialized into this legal system will think your argument results from a "legal" principle, even though it does result from some sort of principle (the principle that blue-eyed people can be treated more harshly than others, for example). Writing something that looks like a legal opinion but decides the case on the basis of eye color is just as offensive to the rule of law as deciding the case with no reason given at all—perhaps more so, because in the case with no opinion given, the audience (the polity) can still hope that an acceptable reason was behind it. How many readers can say with a straight face that if the case had been *Gore* v. *Bush*—that is, if all facts were the same except that Florida was controlled by Democratic officials, Gore were a few hundred votes ahead in the count, and Gore brought a federal case to stop a recount Bush had sought under state law—it would have come out the same? If you cannot say it would have come out the same, then you know that the decision was contrary to the rule of law, because political party affiliation of the plaintiff is no more a valid legal distinguishing principle than is eye color.

Bush v. *Gore* looks like a legal opinion, but it isn't a legal decision, because it is outside the boundaries of acceptable argument. Although I have had a hard time explaining this to lay people, the treatment of equal protection in *Bush* v. *Gore* is so out of touch with the prevailing principles that it is not a decision that follows (or reasonably extends) the law. The version of equal protection doctrine used in *Bush* v. *Gore* is not related to the body of equal protection law as it now stands, nor is it related to a reasonable extension of that body of law, nor is it related to whatever was intended by those who enacted the Fourteenth Amendment. (For elaboration of this point, see Chapter Three of this book, by Laurence Tribe.)

The way the Five treated equal protection law is not their only offense against the rule of law, and perhaps not their main one. If *Bush* v. *Gore* were just a kooky equal protection case, it probably would not have sparked such outrage. Perhaps one could find a plausible legal argument for interpreting equal protection law in this way—and, anyway, every once in awhile there's a kooky case. Kooky cases can be reinterpreted in retrospect. But it is impossible to come up with a plausible argument for why the Five should be entitled to decide the case on equal protection grounds without giving both sides a chance to argue it. They had denied certiorari on Bush's equal protection claim the first time Bush brought his case to the federal courts a few weeks earlier. If cleansing Florida of possible equal protection violations was their real concern, they could have intervened at that point. There would have been time, even before the phony December 12 deadline, to remedy whatever they found to be amiss.

Instead, after finding a violation of equal protection, the Five declared it to be without remedy. Under the rule of law, courts do not find a constitutional wrong and then say to the wronged parties, "Tough luck." Constitutional harm is serious, going to the core of our political values. There are statutes of limitations of course, but under the rule of law, courts do not get to make them up for a particular case while they are deciding that case. Equally deplorable is the way the Court created the very kind of harm it purported to find. When the Court stopped the recount, many voters whose intent would have been clear in the hand recount, and who were supposedly protected by state law providing for such a recount, were deprived by federal judicial fiat of their rights under those provisions.

Worst of all for the rule of law, the Five said in so many words that their decision holds for this case only; it's not based on legal principles applicable to other cases and presumably will not serve as precedent for other cases. The rule of law means nothing if it doesn't mean treating like cases alike, and that means that principles must endure from case to case. If judges are able to say with impunity that what they decide today means nothing for any case to come, the rule of law evaporates.

Polarization in the Aftermath of *Bush* v. *Gore*

One of the troubling aspects of *Bush* v. *Gore* is that it tended to polarize legal observers, in the same way (although not to the same extent) as the election split the country. Yet, of those who voted Republican and therefore welcomed the outcome of *Bush* v. *Gore* in some sense, many think nevertheless that the Court was wrong to halt the political process. (See, for example, Chapter Eight of this book, by Steven Calabresi.) In the aftermath of the decision, there was a loud silence from many conservative scholars. I like to think the silent conservative scholars are as worried about the rule of law as I am. Nevertheless, those who do say the decision was legally legitimate are overwhelmingly confined to a small subset of those who supported the Republicans; non-Republicans have not been heard to say this.

Polarization is troubling for the rule of law because it breaks down the distinction between political partisanship and impartial decision-making in accordance with nonpartisan principles. I am grateful, therefore, to people like former Dean Terrence Sandalow of the University of Michigan Law School, who identify themselves as Republicans and yet can see the damage done to the rule of law by *Bush* v. *Gore*. I hope, were the situation reversed, that I would have the courage and clarity of mind to do the same.

Recognizing the polarization of perceptions, I am going to spend the rest of this chapter talking about the reactions of non-Republicans, both liberal and not so liberal.

The Three-Way Split Among Liberals and Moderates   In the aftermath of *Bush* v. *Gore,* liberal and moderate legal observers who did not support the Republicans split into three groups. One group thinks the ideal of the rule of law was deeply damaged by *Bush* v. *Gore*—people like me who were outraged and energized to protest, as we were not when the Five struck down the Violence Against Women Act, gutted the Americans with Disabilities Act, overturned a federal gun control measure, and so on. What fueled the outrage, as I have said, is that we found *Bush* v. *Gore* different in kind; not just misguided or ideologically twisted, but a naked affront to the rule of law.

These champions of legality have been criticized from two different perspectives. One group thinks the rule of law is simply a mythological fig leaf, an artifact of conservative ideology, useful only for the purpose of covering over with rhetoric the reality of how the judicial system operates. A second group faults Law Professors for the Rule of Law for disrespecting the Five by naming what they did as a naked power grab instead of talking politely in normal legal discourse.

The first critical position is a hard-nosed version of "legal realism" (its name during the Progressive Era) or "critical legal studies" (its name over the past few decades). For these skeptics, every decision is an exercise of naked power. Judges manipulate the system—constructing verbal formulations that are mere propaganda—to reach results they want for themselves and their class; that is, results that are almost always for the benefit of rich white men. To these skeptics, *Bush* v. *Gore* isn't exceptional, but run-of-the-mill, business as usual. The only difference is that instead of deciding on a gun control issue or the rights of poor women, in this case the Court decided who would be president.

On this skeptical view, there's no such thing as compelling reasoning or consistent principle or legal integrity; no such thing as better or worse reasoned decisions; no such thing as reaching the right answer for the wrong reasons; and so on. All that matters is the vote, and the bottom line.

This is the way the media reported the legal struggle over *Bush* v. *Gore*. Each time a court decided, what mattered was the bottom line (who won, who lost). The political party of the judges was considered relevant too, much more relevant than the reasoning and whether it was good. Just recall how the decisions of the Florida Supreme Court were reported. The assumption was that the judges would vote their political party. The separation of powers doesn't exist for the media, nor does the notion that the judicial role is one of impartial principle. The media deny the rule of law. And they got what they expected in *Bush* v. *Gore*.

The media have much more power to affect public opinion than do skeptical legal professionals. They may be bringing about the very situation they purport to observe. If the media keep telling us that judicial decisions are no more than naked votes for one's favored political positions, to be reported as outcomes like a sporting event, does that mean that the skeptics are correct and the rule of law is mythological? Or, if not mythological, at any rate pretty dead?

Now turn to the second group of critics—the ones who found it impolite (or impolitic) to speak the truth. From their perspective, there should be an irrebuttable presumption that the Supreme Court is acting in good faith as a legal institution. No doubt some of these people plan to use the equal protection rationale in *Bush* v. *Gore* to litigate voting rights cases in the future, in spite of the Five's warning that the case isn't precedent for anything. It would be possible, of course, to criticize the Court in the public arena for being outside the purview of the law while at the same time citing *Bush* v. *Gore* to a district judge in a voting rights case; but some may find this disjunction too difficult to navigate. Their position amounts to this: however absurd the case seems, we must take it seriously as law. If we are given lemons, we'll make lemonade.

This is "normal science" for lawyers. Once a decision comes down, it becomes grist for the mill of legal argument. Legal briefs don't cite only those cases the lawyers agree with. Instead, lawyers construe past cases to support their position, whatever those cases meant originally in context. Legal "normal science" is a process of continuous reinterpretation. Arguing bad decisions against their authors in the next case—trying to turn the tables on judges who are one's ideological opponents—is a time-honored tradition of good lawyering.

For this strategy to work, one's ideological opponents in the judiciary have to adhere to the rule of law. They have to treat the law as if it consists of principles that have broader application than to just one case. They have to feel bound by precedent, at least to some extent, so they are not free to decide each case in a vacuum. If judges feel no obligation to be consistent, this time-honored strategy of legal argument is doomed to failure.

Perhaps some people believe that it's worth a shot: even if there's very little chance the rule of *Bush* v. *Gore* (whatever they want to claim its rule is) will advance any civil rights or voting rights agenda, there's no harm in trying. They might think there's no harm in pretending that something is "normal science" for the rule of law, when actually it isn't. The pretense creates a sort of "as if" rule of law—maybe if we treat these judges as if they were following the rule of law, they will actually follow it.

But I think this sort of pretense is not without its cost. The cost is hypocrisy. There's enough doublethink and newspeak in this society already. Clarence Thomas was the most qualified person for the job, and his race did not play any role at all in his selection. George W. Bush was a uniter, not a divider. We cannot now afford, I think, to pretend that we see the rule of law when we know that we are seeing the opposite. That is why I refer here to Republican justices rather than simply justices; they have forfeited the presumption of impartiality that goes with the judicial role. The rule of law is in trouble, and pretending that it isn't makes the trouble worse. Legal professionals should tell the truth about the Supreme Court.

The Intellectual Critique of the Rule of Law

The skeptics give me more pause than those who want to pretend there has been no transgression. What gives me pause is not the reductionism that some skeptics ironically share with the media; not the simplistic notion that there's just no difference between law and politics (or, more accurately, between law and naked arbitrary power, because politics, too, can be reasoned and principled). But there is a more complex and nuanced critique that at least has intellectual appeal. On this view, the ideal of the rule of law reflects a formalist notion of rules and rule-governed behavior. Starting with Wittgenstein, philosophical thought has undercut this notion of rules, and with it undercut the notion that formalistic decision-making is possible.

The traditional understanding of formal applicability as the crucial property of rules correlates with the traditional conviction that the rule of law demands that judges "apply" rather than "make" the law. If rules do not tie judges' hands with their logical or analytic application, says the traditional view, judges will have personal discretion in how to apply the law. This will undermine the correlation between the law on the books and the law in practice and will confuse those who are supposed to follow the rules; and it will confer on judges a realm of arbitrary power and undermine democracy. Yet the modern critique says, and I agree, that the dichotomy between formalist application and personal discretion is a false one.

Once we admit that rules are mutable and inextricable from material social practice, we can see that whenever we follow a rule, we are also making it, and whenever we fail to follow it, we are also unmaking it. Many rules and principles interact in every legal case, and sometimes, but not always, thought and argument can change our perception of the legal complex that bears on any given dispute. That is, we can't know what the rules say until we work on them; and in the process of working on them and finding out what they say, we—as participants in the social practice called law—are also changing them. If we come to have conscious awareness of the malleability of the legal field in response to work—the non-preexistingness of the law—then we can't maintain the prevailing rhetoric about decisions predetermined by the plain meaning of rules. The traditional ideal of the rule of law turns out to be conservative and mythological in at least this sense: it rests on an outmoded and overanalytic conception of rules, one that does not understand rules as a social practice, malleable as social practices are.

Overemphasis on ruleness is part of a complex of ideological assumptions about the rule of law that must be reconceptualized. The traditional ideal of the rule of law, in all its various formulations, assumes (1) that law consists of rules; (2) that rules are prior to particular cases, more general than particular cases, and applied to particular cases; (3) that law is instrumental (the rules are applied to achieve ends); (4) that the person is a rational chooser ordering her affairs instrumentally in response to rules; and (5) that there is a radical separation between government and citizens—there are rule-givers and appliers (legislatures and judges) versus rule-compliers (citizens).

All these assumptions are part of a worldview that has been undercut by thinkers from Kant to Habermas. Law consists not merely of rules but of general principles and underlying cultural value commitments. The relationship between law and particular cases is dialectical, not a version of strict entailment. People don't order their affairs primarily in response to rules (whether enforced by carrots or sticks). Family and group ties, philosophical and religious commitments are also important to us. Legal rules are enacted not only to achieve ends in a narrow sense, but also to make text of our commitments—to teach us who we are as citizens, to exhort us to live up to the values we profess, to express who we are and what we value.

In our democracy the relationship between government and citizens is not just the "we–they" relationship embodied in the traditional rule of law. Rather "we"—in some sense that we don't want to lose—are still "We the People," the governors as well as the governed.

I accept this critique, but it requires us to reinterpret, not abandon, the rule of law.[2] The hard and fast distinction between "making" law and "applying" law, if one is a judge, is implausible, at least some of the time. But there are ways for judges to "make" law that are in accord with general commitments of democracy and consistency, and ways that are clearly out of bounds. There are ways to "make" law (in light of the past and looking toward the future) that can be distinguished from arbitrary individual decisions taken to further the judges' goals of the moment. Rules do not apply self-evidently to the complex particulars that we call a case, nor do they entirely preexist the outcome of the case, because the outcome will remake the rule.

2. See my Reconsidering the Rule of Law, 69 B.U. L. Rev. 781 (1989).

That is why law is not fundamentally a set of rules laid down, but rather a process of continuous reinterpretation. Nevertheless, some rules are so well-entrenched that whoever goes against them is seen as outside the social practice that we call "rules"—if it is a person, her behavior is seen as unbalanced; if it is a legislature, as undemocratic; if it is a judge, as unjudicial. The behavior of the Five in *Bush* v. *Gore* was unjudicial.

What Now?

Bush v. *Gore* brought me down from the intellectual heights of debates about legal theory, including the debate about where the rule of law stands in the modern understandings of knowledge and practice. When I was faced with a gross, bald-faced violation of the rule of law, I didn't want to argue Wittgensteinian theory—I wanted to protest in the streets. I think many other legal professionals had the same experience. We had more of a commitment to the rule of law than we knew. We hadn't dreamed that such a decision could have five adherents. We had no idea our Court was so far gone.

An organization called Law Professors for the Rule of Law was born of shock and outrage. Were we naïve? Had the rule of law been dead for some time? Is the rule of law really impossible anyway, as the skeptics say and the media daily imply? Or is it, in fact and not just in ideology, the backbone of our system of government by settled laws rather than arbitrary power, a sine qua non of constitutional democracy? If so, it's past time to start speaking truth to power. If *Bush* v. *Gore* pushes us to do that, the decision will turn out to be not only the downfall of the rule of law, but the beginning of its reconstruction.

PART TWO

Political Questions

STEVEN G. CALABRESI 8

A Political Question

To a startling degree, both state and federal judges played a decisive part in resolving the recent presidential election controversy. The United States prides itself on being the world's oldest democracy. We fought two world wars and one cold war in the past century to make sure, in Lincoln's words, that "Government of the people, by the people, and for the people would not perish from the earth." Yet, in the 2000 presidential election, we the American people were content to let unelected state and federal judges decide who should hold the most powerful office in our federal government. How did a nation committed to democratic rule come to have such faith in the role courts could play as umpires of the political process? Were there no elected officials who could have legitimately umpired the election dispute in place of the U.S. and Florida Supreme Courts?

There were several groups of elected officials who, according to our laws and traditions, would have been more legitimate arbiters of the 2000 presidential election than the judges. All these officials had their reputations tarnished early on in the dispute. At every stage in the process, elected officials were given too little deference in the court of public opinion, while unelected judges were given too much. The 2000 presidential election was in all important respects a tie. The crucial question was who should serve as the tiebreaker. The second section of this chapter reviews the degree of deference given to six actors in the election controversy who were potential tiebreakers, documenting how elected politicians were treated badly and judges were treated too generously. The third portion of this chapter speculates on how a nation committed to democracy has become a nation of court worshipers. The chapter concludes with a consideration of the likely legacy of *Bush* v. *Gore*.

Nobody had any interest in conceding the key fact: the presidential election of 2000 was a tie. Six million Floridians went to the polls on election day, and they produced an outcome under which either Bush or Gore could plausibly claim to be the winner of Florida's twenty-five electoral votes. The system of punch-card voting used in a number of key Florida counties was simply not designed for elections as close as the 2000 presidential contest. For ordinary elections, even for an elections in which the victory is, say, as narrow as 51 percent to 49 percent, punch-card voting works just fine. But, the 2000 presidential election was closer than that. It produced an outcome that was literally within the margin of error of the punch card voting system itself. Depending on what post hoc theory one used to deal with the undervotes, one could make a plausible claim that either George W. Bush or Albert Gore had won. By the way, I say this as a staunch supporter of George W. Bush, whose candidacy I endorsed in May 1999, when I signed on as one of his campaign's policy advisors.

In politics, as in all walks of life, it is sometimes necessary to have rules for breaking ties. *Robert's Rules of Order* specifies that a motion that receives a tie vote fails for lack of a majority. The electoral college itself functions as a kind of crude tiebreaking rule. Whenever the popular vote is reasonably close, the electoral college steers the victory to the person whose margin is best distributed nationwide. This guarantees that only candidates with truly national support will win the presidency. Bush carried one northeastern state, New Hampshire, and two midwestern states, Ohio and Indiana, and so if Gore had no southern States like Florida in his column, then Bush would win.

The key questions raised by *Bush* v. *Gore* was: What was the tie-breaking rule going to be for this election and what institutional actor or actors would break the tie?

In the five weeks between election day and December 12 it gradually became clear that there were two judicial actors, and at least four political actors, who could resolve the dispute. At every turn along the way, elected officials were given too little deference and judges were given too much. I begin with the four elected officials who were potential tiebreakers.

The first elected official was Katherine Harris, the Republican secretary of state. As in many other states, Florida's secretaryship of state is a minor partisan affiliated office that is important mainly as a stepping-stone to higher office and for arbitration of close elections like the 2000 presidential election. Thus, the first question that went through my head at 5 AM on election night when I learned that Florida was too close to call was: Who is Florida's secretary of state? Surely that person, whether Democrat or Republican, would be able to make crucial policy judgment calls that would, in essence, break the tie of this election. This would not be an unjust outcome, I thought. This is practically the only reason Democrats and Republicans contest each other over an office like secretary of state!

My hunch about the role of Florida's secretary of state turned out to be essentially correct, although I was quite wrong in assuming that the official would be accepted as the tiebreaker. Under Florida law and precedent, Secretary of State Katherine Harris was indeed charged with supervising and overseeing the state's 2000 presidential election. And she was the one state official with the jurisdiction to coordinate the actions of the numerous county canvassing boards. In recognition of the special role the Florida legislature had carved out for Ms. Harris, the Florida Supreme Court had previously held that, like all state and federal administrative officials, her interpretations of state law were entitled to substantial deference.

But as we all know, Ms. Harris's reasonable interpretations of state election law were given essentially no deference by the Florida Supreme Court. There are many reasons for this. Most damaging was Ms. Harris's foolish pre–election day decision to sign on as a campaign official in George W. Bush's presidential campaign. This open Bush affiliation, on top of her connection to the Republican Party, greatly damaged her credibility as a tiebreaker from the outset. A biting media campaign—supported in part by Vice President Gore—was also damaging. Ms. Harris was ridiculed on national television as being a Bush partisan because of her ties to Governor Jeb Bush, the candidate's brother; she was made fun of for wearing too much makeup; and she was even compared by some with Cruella De Vil—the villain in the movie *101 Dalmatians.* In the first week after November 7 Ms. Harris was so vilified that few Americans would be likely to believe her interpretations of Florida election law even though she was the highest elected election official in the state.

I think in retrospect that the quick dismissal of Katherine Harris as a potential tiebreaker was a mistake. The secretary of state's office in most U.S. states is designed to deal with precisely the sort of contest that the Florida 2000 presidential election became. Harris was elected by the people of Florida, wisely or not, to hold this office and to play precisely this role—which is more than can be said of Anthony Kennedy or Sandra Day O'Connor. Indeed, Harris was no less or more of a Republican loyalist than those two justices turned out to be. It was a mistake to write off Katherine Harris so quickly.

The next group of democratic tiebreakers were the county canvassing boards. Under Florida law, these Boards had important authority under Florida law over requests for manual recounts and over the conduct of these recounts. Most of these boards were controlled by the Democrats 2 to 1, and at first received favorable treatment in the media. The members of the boards did not seem to have the partisan edge that bedeviled Katherine Harris's efforts to break the tie. But when the Miami–Dade County Canvassing Board decided to abandon the manual recount and not to count some ballots for Al Gore that had turned up in selected precincts, the tide turned. Suddenly, the national media portrayed the Miami Dade board as the victim of intimidation by Republican demonstrators. And the Florida Supreme Court, which in its first rulings after November 7 gave great deference to the county canvassing boards, surprisingly turned on a dime. And in its critical 4–3 decision on December 8 it accorded the county canvassing boards no deference at all.

This, too, was a mistake. The commissioners of the county canvassing boards had been chosen to make judgment calls about manual recounts, which is precisely what they were being asked to do in *Bush v. Gore*. Because a majority of the commissioners were Democrats, they seemed an eminently fair and well-qualified tiebreaking entity. Al Gore's refusal to accept their rulings on manual vote recounts and his decision to challenge those rulings in court was a precipitating condition of the judicial calamity that ensued. Just as Gore was wrong to deprecate Katherine Harris, he was wrong to challenge in court the rulings of the county canvassing boards.

Gore's continuing challenge raised the specter of a third potential tiebreaker. This third group was the Florida state legislature whose members I spoke with when I visited Tallahassee in early December of 2000. They, too, were given no deference in the court of public opinion.

These legislators were preparing to pick a slate of electors pledged to George W. Bush if the court struggle dragged on past December 18—the day on which the members of the electoral college had to cast their votes. This action was portrayed by pro-Gore forces in the media as a wholly illegitimate partisan move. And yet it is crystal clear that the U.S. Constitution gives state legislatures plenary power over the picking of presidential electors. In fact, before the Civil War in many states, the state legislature picked presidential electors directly without any popular vote.

Moreover, federal statutory law specifically says, "Whenever any State has held an election for the purpose of picking [presidential] electors and has failed to make a choice . . . the electors may be appointed on a subsequent day in such a manner as the legislature of such State may direct." Arguably that is what happened in Florida—because the November 7 election had resulted in an outcome that could not be resolved by the punch-card voting system in place in many Florida counties. Because Florida had arguably failed to make a choice on November 7, federal constitutional and statutory law suggested, its legislature was the legitimate tiebreaker.

The pro-Gore forces in the national media would hear none of this. Because the Florida legislature was controlled by Republicans, it was presumptively biased—just like Katherine Harris. Tremendous pressure was brought to bear on the state legislature to abstain from its constitutional responsibility to make sure that Florida was represented in the electoral college, and in the end the state legislature held off until the U.S. Supreme Court made action unnecessary.

There was a fourth and final democratic tiebreaker, and that was the newly elected Congress of the United States. Under federal constitutional and statutory law, Congress was set to meet in a joint session on January 6, 2001, so Vice President Gore, president of the Senate, could count the electoral votes in the presence of the House of Representatives and the Senate as the Twelfth Amendment requires. Title III of the U.S. Code provides an elaborate set of rules for challenging a state's electoral votes before this joint session. Conceivably, Congress could have acted as the tiebreaking entity and decided whether Bush or Gore was the proper winner of Florida's twenty-five electoral votes.

The prospect of congressional tiebreaking was discussed in apocalyptic terms during the frenzied final weeks of the election crisis, and similar predictions of imminent chaos and doom have been made recently by Judge Richard Posner. The general assumption, and the assumption made by Posner, is that Congress would be unable to arbitrate the dispute because the two Houses would be split between the Republicans and the Democrats. And the Democrats would control the 50–50 split Senate because of Vice President Gore's tiebreaking vote. Public opinion seemed to assume that if the election was thrown into Congress, it might never be resolved, and chaos would result. Few commentators considered the possibility that Congress might appoint an electoral commission to resolve the dispute as it had done during the contested presidential election of 1876. Moreover, as long as the Houses were deadlocked, Denis Hastert, the Republican Speaker of the House of Representatives, was in line to assume the presidency as acting president come January 20, when Bill Clinton's term came to an end. This probably would have given the GOP a clear upper hand in resolving the impasse, because an impasse would only result in a different Republican occupying the Oval Office.

The failure of commentators to consider Congress's constructive role was a mistake. It is, after all, the elected representative of the American people. A congressional effort to thrash out the election dispute would have been more democratic, more satisfying, and more legitimate than leaving it to the courts. Moreover, had Congress been forced to resolve the election, much needed reforms of our presidential election system would have been far more likely to emerge. Reform of the way people vote in this country, or even electoral college reform itself, would have received far more consideration following a congressional arbitration of the 2000 presidential election. By shutting down the democratic process and arbitrating the election dispute themselves, the state and federal courts may have stymied necessary reforms from emerging. Congress would have been a far more legitimate tiebreaking entity than the five justices of the Supreme Court majority in *Bush* v. *Gore*.

While public opinion gave essentially no deference to Katherine Harris, the county canvassing boards, the members of the state legislature, or the national Congress, it gave great deference to the seven-member Florida Supreme Court, six of whose justices were Democratic appointees. That Court eventually ruled 4–3 over the dissent of its chief justice that statewide manual recounts of thousands of improperly marked ballots should be held in the four days between December 8 and December 12. Moreover, the Florida Supreme Court also behaved outrageously by granting stays that were not sought by the litigants and by imposing wholly novel forms of relief that had not been sought by the litigants.

Were I ruling on the Florida Supreme Court's behavior as a member of the state or federal legislature, and not as a U.S. Supreme Court justice, I would hold that the Florida Supreme Court's erratic behavior clearly violated Article II of the U.S. Constitution by changing Florida election law from what it had been on November 7. Never before in Florida's history had manual recounts of undervotes from improperly marked punch-card ballots been held. Moreover, Florida had no standards in place to guide those manual recounts—unlike Indiana and Texas, two states where manual recounts of undervotes are commonplace and where the state legislature had accordingly provided standards to govern the counting of hanging chads. Before November 7 Florida did not allow for manual recounts of improperly marked punch-card ballots, because voters were explicitly instructed to punch out the ballot cleanly. The voting instructions in at least Palm Beach County specifically said: "AFTER VOTING, CHECK YOUR BALLOT CARD TO BE SURE YOUR VOTING SELECTIONS ARE CLEARLY AND CLEANLY PUNCHED AND THERE ARE NO CHIPS HANGING ON THE BACK OF THE CARD." While the Broward County instructions were less clear, I nonetheless find it surprising that the Florida Supreme Court treated as legal votes hundreds of improperly marked ballots with dimples and hanging chads. And they did this in their December 8 opinion while continuing to cite and rely upon their November 21 decision without mentioning that it had been unanimously vacated by the U.S. Supreme Court!

The Florida Supreme Court's decision on December 8 unconstitutionally changed Florida election law in violation of Article II of the U.S. Constitution for the reasons stated by Justices Rehnquist, Scalia, and Thomas in their separate concurrence in *Bush* v. *Gore*. In particular, the Florida court decision changed Florida law unconstitutionally in at least five ways:

1. It probably defined legal votes too broadly by allowing punch-card ballots with dimples and hanging chads to be counted as legal votes when they had never before been counted that way in Florida history.
2. It clearly showed no deference in a contest action to the county canvassing boards or to the secretary of state as was required by Florida law, including the court's own prior case law.
3. It improperly relied on its vacated November 21 ruling, which had extended the one-week statutory certification deadline imposed by Florida law, thereby impermissibly lengthening the protest period and shortening the contest period.
4. It wrongly allowed a contest to proceed in the absence of evidence of actual fraud or miscounting of legally cast votes.
5. It ordered a remedy on December 8 that was wholly inappropriate in requiring a massive, standardless recount of ballots with insufficient time for this to be done properly.

The final actor in the drama was the U.S. Supreme Court, which correctly gave no deference to a Florida Supreme Court that had itself given no deference to Secretary of State Katherine Harris or to the Miami–Dade County Canvassing Board. Three justices of the U.S. Supreme Court correctly found that Florida had violated Article II of the U.S. Constitution, and seven justices correctly found an equal protection violation with the standardless recount. But the U.S. Supreme Court failed to address an absolutely vital argument against its taking jurisdiction over *Bush* v. *Gore*. The problem with *Bush* v. *Gore* is that the case raised a political question that ought to have been decided by Congress on January 6 when it counted the votes in the electoral college. The Court quite simply lacked jurisdiction to decide *Bush* v. *Gore*, as Professors Charles Fried and Einer Elhauge of the Harvard Law School explicitly pointed out in an early amicus brief they filed on behalf of the Florida legislature.

The case that *Bush* v. *Gore* raised a political question is quite clear-cut. In *Walter Nixon* v. *United States*, the Supreme Court said a controversy raises a nonjusticiable political question "where there is 'a textually demonstrable constitutional commitment of the issue to a coordinate political department; or a lack of judicially discoverable and manageable standards for resolving it.' " In *Baker* v. *Carr*, the Court identified four other attributes of political questions:

> The impossibility of deciding [the case] without an initial policy determination of a kind clearly for nonjudicial discretion; or the impossibility of a court's undertaking independent resolution without expressing lack of the respect due co-ordinate branches of government; or an unusual need for unquestioning adherence to a political decision already made; or the potentiality of embarrassment from multifarious pronouncements by various departments on one question.

All six of these characteristics suggest that the Court should have stayed its hand.

The first characteristic is a demonstrable textual commitment to another coordinate branch of the government. The Twelfth Amendment to the Constitution commits the counting of electoral votes to "The President of the Senate," who "shall, in the presence of the Senate and House of Representatives, open all the certificates and the votes shall then be counted." Title III of the U.S. Code regulates this process in great statutory detail and provides that Congress, *and not the Supreme Court*, is the entity charged with resolving disputes about who really won a state's electoral votes. The theory underlying Title III clearly suggests that the enacting Congress believed that future Congresses would resolve disputed presidential elections. Indeed, in our only real precedent—the contested presidential election of 1876—it was Congress and not the Supreme Court that decided the controversy. One reason *Bush* v. *Gore* is unprecedented is that for most of our constitutional history it would have been considered obvious that the question was one that the political branches of government should decide and not the courts.

One may object that many constitutional questions seem textually committed to another branch and yet are susceptible to judicial review. This is true of cases arising under the commerce clause or Section 5 of the Fourteenth Amendment—both of which involve textual commitments of power to Congress. But in contrast to these areas, the Court's intervention in *Bush* v. *Gore* guarantees that the constitutional issues will never, under any circumstances, get determined by Congress because the Court will always arrive there first. Moreover, the textual commitment of the Twelfth Amendment is unusually specific and is uniquely backed up by the congressional opinion that underlies Title III. In sum, there is a strong case that the question decided by the Court in *Bush* v. *Gore* was textually committed to the president of the Senate and the Congress and was hence nonjusticiable.

The second criterion for determining the existence of a political question is whether there was a lack of judicially discoverable and manageable standards for resolving the case. On this score, I would submit that *Bush* v. *Gore* also exhibited the classic attributes of a political question. The issue was fundamentally nonlegal because the case depended on making a value judgment about whether or not to hand-count thousands of undervotes—votes Florida had not hand-counted in past elections. Any decision on that question is ultimately value-laden, and it really cannot be said that there is a clearly right legal answer. My personal view is that the undervotes were spoiled ballots and should not be counted, but there are enough indicators that others held a different view to make me uncomfortable with a court imposing this as the legally right answer. A better resolution would have been to leave the question in the political arena because the question at bottom is more political than it is legal.

The third characteristic of a political question is the impossibility of a court deciding the case without an initial policy determination requiring nonjudicial discretion. Here again, the question of whether to hand-count undervotes for the first time in Florida in a U.S. presidential election is a policy decision that ought not be made by a court. It would have been better made by a politically accountable tiebreaking entity like Katherine Harris, the county canvassing boards, the Florida legislature, or the U.S. Congress.

The fourth characteristic is the impossibility of a court's undertaking independent resolution without expressing lack of the respect due coordinate branches of government. Given the existence of Title III, and the implicit congressional determination that Congress and not the Court was to arbitrate presidential elections, I think the Court did fail to give Congress the respect it was due. Presidential elections are defining and critical events in our American system of democracy. It is not appropriate that they be decided by judges or justices, even in circumstances as unusual as this. The only proper entities to adjudicate a tied presidential election are political bodies.

The fifth characteristic is an unusual need for unquestioning adherence to a political decision already made. In this respect, it is worth noting that Secretary of State Katherine Harris had already certified Bush as the winner of the election and the Florida legislature was well on its way to passing a resolution that would back up Bush's certified victor status in the face of the judicial activism exhibited by the Florida Supreme Court. Instead of jumping into the fray itself by granting certiorari unasked and by setting absolutely extraordinary expedited briefing and argument deadlines, the Court ought to have let the political process take its course. It was unseemly for the U.S. Supreme Court to rush in breathlessly to take action when the Florida legislature already was playing its constitutionally ordained tiebreaking role.

The Court itself said in the *Walter Nixon* case that judicial review of a Senate impeachment conviction was most unthinkable in the case of a conviction of a president of the United States. The Court should have remembered that warning and avoided the adjudication of a presidential election.

The final characteristic of political question cases is that they may exhibit the potentiality of embarrassment from multifarious pronouncements by various departments on one question. This risk, too, was present in *Bush* v. *Gore* although it did not materialize because Al Gore chose to drop his appeals rather than pursue a challenge to Florida's electoral votes before the U.S. Congress. Had Gore not dropped his appeals, there was a real possibility that the Senate and House of Representatives would have split along partisan lines on whether *Bush* v. *Gore* was correct—with the Democratic Senate denouncing the opinion even as the Republican House followed it. A more embarrassing scenario of multifarious pronouncements by various departments on one question would be difficult to conjure up.

At this point a skeptic might ask whether my Frankfurterian impulses run so deep that I think *Baker* v. *Carr* was wrongly decided, the implication being that my view of the political question doctrine is an unorthodox outlier. I do not think *Baker* v. *Carr* itself was wrongly decided, although I do have trouble with the rigidity with which the Court has enforced the "one person, one vote" rule and with the Court's activist intervention in many recent racial gerrymandering cases. *Baker* v. *Carr* was a truly egregious injustice that had gone unaddressed for decades by the political branches and that was unlikely ever to be addressed by the political "in group" that benefited from gerrymandered districts. In contrast, in *Bush* v. *Gore* the political branches of Florida's state government were diligently acting on all the key questions until a frantic U.S. Supreme Court, tossing all its standard briefing and argument deadlines out the window, rushed in and resolved the case. In sum, I think it is quite clear that *Bush* v. *Gore* improperly resolved a political question.

Notwithstanding this glaring defect, the opinion succeeded in quieting the fervor of the election dispute to an alarming degree. Once the *New York Times* editorial page and Al Gore accepted the Supreme Court's very problematic ruling, the whole controversy that had consumed the nation for five weeks suddenly melted away. To a frightening extent, the country accepted the right outcome from a constitutionally problematic source. Today, Bush's claim on the presidency remains largely uncontested—a reaction that was virtually unthinkable in the weeks after November 7.

I return, then, to the critical question: Why did public opinion treat the possible democratically selected umpires of this dispute so rudely, while it was highly solicitous of the state and federal courts playing umpire even though those courts were doing a bad job? The answer, I think, can be found in the events of the past forty years, which have turned the Supreme Court into an umpire of the democratic process. In particular, I think the "one person, vote" decisions of the 1960s were a major triumph for the judiciary in that they transformed public expectations about the umpiring role of courts. Since those decisions came down, we have become very used to judges supervising in minute detail the drawing and redrawing of election district lines. The impression has grown in the public's mind that this is what judges should do. They have become the umpires or tiebreakers in our system of government in place of democratically elected officials.

This umpiring role of the Supreme Court received enhanced legitimacy during the case involving the Nixon tapes in the Watergate era, when the Court for the first time issued a ruling that led to a change in presidents. Even though the Court lacked jurisdiction to hear the Nixon tapes case, which was an internal executive branch dispute, its decision was a triumph for the judiciary, and the decision was very well received by the general public.

One anecdote from a colleague reveals how far our public culture has slipped in the direction of assuming the Supreme Court should play umpire in our political process. On election night, former Senator Alan Simpson appeared on television and said something like, "The Supreme Court will have to decide this election." My colleague reports that he was astonished by this statement, even though of course it was prophetic. What does it say about our political culture that a former U.S. Senator would immediately assume that an election too close to call would end up being decided by the Supreme Court, before anyone had even identified any legal issues that might be presented to the Court? Does not this comment reveal the extent to which belief in democracy has waned in this country, while belief in the legitimacy of government by the judiciary has grown?

There is great danger to the courts and to our political process from judges immersing themselves in political thickets. In future elections, low expectations about the role played by secretaries of state and county canvassing boards may cause these officeholders to behave in a more partisan and lawless way. Low expectations for politically accountable officials could turn out to be self-fulfilling. Lawsuits like *Bush* v. *Gore* may become more common, and the public's confidence in the impartiality even of the U.S. Supreme Court will certainly be damaged. A Gallup poll taken in the aftermath of *Bush* v. *Gore* reveals that public approval of the Court has slipped only a little bit, but Gallup found that this is masking a startling shift in the rates at which self-identified Democrats and Republicans approve of the Court. As Jeff Rosen reports, "Among Republicans, approval of the court between August and January jumped from 60 percent to 80 percent, but among Democrats, it fell from 70 percent to 42 percent." This high degree of politicization cannot be good for the institution.

The nomination and confirmation process for future Supreme Court vacancies, which is already under tremendous strain, is now probably going to be incomparably more difficult. Democratic senators are unlikely to give George W. Bush's judicial nominees a pass now that they know those nominees, once confirmed, may be deciding future presidential elections. With the outcry over the John

Ashcroft nomination and confirmation, we are already experiencing a foretaste of the many bitter struggles that are probably to come.

It should be noted that many law professors have pronounced themselves stunned and horrified by the Court's decision in *Bush* v. *Gore*. But for forty years it has been the legal academy, led by John Hart Ely in *Democracy and Distrust*, that has urged judges to play the role of umpire in our political process. On December 12, 2000, the Supreme Court in *Bush* v. *Gore* simply fulfilled these professorial expectations. Unfortunately, what the Court should have done was to abide by the limits of the political question doctrine and stay its hand. We would all be much better off today if that horrible partisan Katherine Harris had prevailed without being challenged in litigation way back on November 14 when she first attempted to certify this election.

The legacy of *Bush* v. *Gore* is likely to depend mainly on how George W. Bush's presidency comes to be viewed. If he is successful in office, then the case may come to be viewed in the same way the Nixon tapes case was regarded: as a good result in a case where the Court regrettably lacked jurisdiction. If Bush fails in office, history's judgment may be a little less forgiving. Ultimately, the case will cease to be terribly important after 2004—by then, Bush will either be vindicated by being reelected or repudiated by losing. After 2004, *Bush* v. *Gore* will be chiefly remembered as being like the Nixon tapes case in that it is one of two erroneous Supreme Court decisions in American history that have led to a change in who holds the presidency. Unlike the Nixon tapes case, the Court was not unanimous but was split 5–4—which makes the erroneous decision and the speed with which it was reached all the more regrettable.

Political Questions and
the Hazards of Pragmatism

The most striking aspect of *Bush* v. *Gore* is how politically polarizing it is. Many Supreme Court decisions are controversial, but *Bush* v. *Gore* has a unique ability to unbalance the judgment and inflame the partisanship of everyone who confronts it. During the case and afterward, justices and commentators didn't merely disagree; they impugned each others' motives, accusing each other of allowing their legal judgment to be distorted by their partisan allegiances. And although members of both camps insisted their motives were pure, reaction to the decision divided along predictably partisan lines. With a few notable exceptions in this book, Republicans tend to approve of the pragmatic result (if not the legal reasoning) of the decision, while Democrats find both transparently unconvincing. Among Republicans, approval of the Court between August 2000 and January 2001 jumped from 60 percent to 80 percent, according to a Gallup poll, but among Democrats it fell from 70 percent to 42 percent.

The starkness of the partisan division has led many liberals and moderates to despair about the possibility of separating law and politics. We're all "crits" now, the lament goes. But this despair is premature. *Bush* v. *Gore* is unusual, rather than typical, because it is part of a narrow category of cases that judges should resist the temptation to decide at all costs. These cases are political questions, and *Bush* v. *Gore* helps us to understand the political question doctrine in a new light. It suggests that judges should restrain themselves from deciding political questions not only when the decision is textually committed to another branch of government or when pragmatic considerations— such as the legitimacy of the Court or the good of the country—point in favor of judicial abstention. *Bush* v. *Gore* suggests that judges should allow pragmatic considerations that take the form of political predictions to play little or no role in their deliberations about whether to hear cases involving political questions. These cases, by definition, are so likely to distort their judgment and inflame their passions that judges can't trust themselves to make reliable evaluations of the pragmatic consequences of a decision to intervene. And even judges who somehow believe that they are acting in the best interest of the country are likely to be perceived by those who disagree with them as political partisans rather than as heroic saviors when they are unable to defend their decision with reference to legal (as opposed to political) arguments. A restrained judge, therefore, would have refused to hear *Bush* v. *Gore,* in other words, not because she didn't trust an ungrateful public to misconstrue her motives but because she had enough humility not to trust herself.

Bush v. *Gore* also suggests that the political question doctrine, which was designed to focus mostly on the question of rights, should also focus on the question of remedies. In reluctantly approving the Court's intervention in *Baker* v. *Carr,* the great malapportionment case, Alexander Bickel stressed that the case could be defended because the Court hadn't imposed a particular political remedy for the obvious political process failure; it had opened up a dialogue with the Tennessee legislature, inviting the political branches to correct the error themselves. Because the underlying equality violation was hard to define, except in political terms, a judicial remedy might have precipitated a political process violation even greater than the one it attempted to correct. By refusing to follow Bickel's counsel, and imposing judicial remedies for equality violations in cases involving political questions, the Rehnquist Court has highlighted the special dangers of allowing judges to entangle themselves in the political thicket.

Bush v. Gore is also a powerful caution against the hazards of judicial pragmatism. The most prominent conservative supporters of the decision, from the members of the Supreme Court majority to Richard Posner, have defended it on purportedly pragmatic grounds, asserting hyperbolically that only the Supreme Court could have saved the nation from the political chaos—which they conflate with a constitutional crisis—that they feel would have been likely to ensue if Florida had sent two competing electoral slates to Congress, in a reprise of the election of 1876. But for purported pragmatists, the conservative defenders of *Bush v. Gore* are remarkably unempirical. They offer only unsupported speculations about the likely political course of events, and their conclusions about the effects of a congressional dispute on the legitimacy of the president seem transparently unconvincing to those who do not share their political allegiances.

The failure of the pragmatic defense of *Bush v. Gore* points toward a revival of Bickel's original conception of the political question doctrine. Although he would later come to focus on the pragmatic effects of a judicial decision to intervene, Bickel initially emphasized the limits of judicial competence in cases where judgment was likely to be unbalanced by the political stakes. "Such is the foundation, in both intellect and instinct, of the political-question doctrine," Bickel wrote in *The Least Dangerous Branch*. "The Court's sense of lack of capacity, compounded in unequal parts of (a) the strangeness of the issue and its intractability to principled resolution; (b) the sheer momentousness of it, which tends to unbalance judicial judgment; (c) the anxiety, not so much that the judicial judgment will be ignored, as that perhaps it should but will not be; (d) finally ('in a mature democracy'), the inner vulnerability, the self-doubt of an institution which is electorally irresponsible and has no earth to draw strength from."[1]

As an example of a political question that unbalanced judgment and tested the limits of judicial competence, Bickel cited Joseph Bradley's service on the electoral commission of 1876, where he cast the tie-breaking vote that gave the election to Hayes. Although widely attacked as a partisan, Bradley insisted that he had not allowed "political, that is, party, considerations to have any weight whatever in forming my conclusions." After giving Bradley the benefit of the doubt, Bickel concluded that Bradley's emphasis on the legal question—that is, whether Congress had authority to go behind the election returns submitted by the Florida canvassing boards—was inevitably lost in the political firestorm: "It was overwhelmed by all that hung in the balance, and it should not have been decisive." Because there had been election fraud on both sides, "the real great question was not fit 'for the wrangling of lawyers.' "[2]

It's true that the legal questions in 2001 were more intricate than those in 1876—largely because of the decision in the 1960s to expand the equal protection clause so that it now regulates political rights—a decision impossible to reconcile with the original understanding of the Fourteenth Amendment, which was limited to civil rights alone.[3] But the progress of the voting rights doctrine that began in the 1960s and culminated in *Bush* v. *Gore* shows that certain kinds of legal questions should be viewed as political questions because they resist principled resolution. Unfortunately, Bickel's emphasis on the tendency of these questions to unbalance judgment was lost in the 1960s and 70s. Instead of counseling self-doubt and encouraging judges to look inward, at the limits of their own authority, the political question doc-

1. Alexander M. Bickel, The Least Dangerous Branch: The Supreme Court at the Bar of Politics (1962).
2. Ibid., p. 185.
3. See, e.g., Akhil Amar, The Bill of Rights: Creation and Reconstruction 217 n. 260–61 (1998).

trine, as it was codified by the Warren Court, encouraged judges to look outward, speculating about the pragmatic consequences of a principled decision on their own authority and legitimacy. In *Baker* v. *Carr*, Justice Brennan identified six characteristics of political questions, ranging from a "textually demonstrable constitutional commitment of the issue to a co-ordinate political department" at one end to a purely prudential concern on the other—"the potentiality of embarrassment from multifarious pronouncements by various departments on one question" on the other. This, of course, invited bullying of the courts, as judges anxiously considered the effects of noncompliance on their own prestige before deciding whether to order a legally appropriate remedy. And the other four factors in Baker also invited judges to balance pragmatic concerns against principle, such as the importance of expressing respect for coordinate branches of government or "an unusual need for unquestioning adherence to a political decision already made." What had begun as a doctrine of judicial humility morphed into one of judicial heroics.

As the Court expanded its supervision of the political process in the 1970s, the political question doctrine went out of fashion, to the point where Louis Henkin at Columbia could argue that no case actually had applied the doctrine and Martin Reddish at N.Y.U. could argue against the wisdom of applying it. In the 1970s and 80s, the Court rejected the claim that political gerrymandering of legislative districts and cases involving the separation of powers presented nonjusticiable political questions. "Although it was not possible in 1988 to conclude that the political question doctrine was entirely gone," Robert Nagel observes, "its significance was small and declining."[4]

In the 1990s, the political question doctrine was transformed into its antithesis: a justification for judicial intervention, rather than a warning for judges to stay out of the political thicket. As conservative

---

4. Robert F. Nagel, Political Law, Legalistic Politics: A Recent History of the Political Question Doctrine, 56 U. Chi. L. Rev. 643, 649–50 (1989).

justices proved themselves no less willing to cast themselves as national saviors than their liberal predecessors, they began to invoke pragmatic considerations to justify judicial supervision of the political process that fulfilled Felix Frankfurter's most dramatic fears about the dangers of mixing law and policy. The most notable example was the expansion of the equal protection clause to regulate racial redistricting, in which Justice Sandra Day O'Connor, the leader of the enterprise, explicitly invoked pragmatic considerations to justify the regulation of oddly shaped districts drawn to protect incumbents and create safe districts for minorities. Although the injury that these districts caused was elusive and the standing of those who objected to them questionable, O'Connor said these districts caused a pragmatic and expressive harm, running the risk of balkanizing the country and reinforcing the perception that blacks and whites vote in polarizing blocks. To save the country from a (speculative) political harm, O'Connor suggested judges should do precisely what Bickel had warned against: striking down some districts, approving others, and redrawing districts lines on their own, rather than engaging in a dialogue with the legislature.

This self-aggrandizing sensibility culminated in *Bush* v. *Gore*. In the most extended defense of the decision, Richard Posner justifies the court's decision to stop the Florida recount by invoking what he calls the "reverse political question doctrine." "Political considerations in a broad, nonpartisan sense sometimes counsel the Court to abstain, but sometimes to intervene," Posner wrote. "What exactly is the Supreme Court good for if it refuses to examine a likely constitutional error that if uncorrected may engender a national crisis?"[5]

Posner's purportedly pragmatic defense of *Bush* v. *Gore*—saving the country is a tough job, but sometimes only the Supreme Court can do

---

5. Richard Posner, Breaking the Deadlock: The 2000 Election, the Constitution, and the Courts 162 (2001).

it—is the same defense that has been offered, in various extrajudicial contexts, by members of the *Bush* v. *Gore* majority. Soon after the decision, in a speech to a Catholic service organization, Chief Justice Rehnquist defended the participation of Supreme Court justices in the Hayes-Tilden commission of 1877. "There is a national crisis, and only you can avert it," he said. "It may be very hard to say no." And in May, Justice Scalia struck a similar note at the Economic Club of Grand Rapids. "The Court's reputation," he said, should not be considered as "some shiny piece of trophy armor" to be mounted over the fireplace. "It's working armor and meant to be used and sometimes dented in the service of the public."

The pragmatic defense of *Bush* v. *Gore* is easy to summarize. The Supreme Court sacrificed its prestige for the good of the nation, Posner argues, and had it failed to do so, it might have been thought selfish. Posner acknowledges a modest role for the political question doctrine, which he understands in entirely pragmatic terms. There is a class of constitutional questions, he says, that "are not amenable to judicial resolution because the relevant considerations are beyond the courts' capacity to gather and weigh; the answers the questions demand simply are not legal answers." He concedes that had Florida sent two competing slates to Congress—one for Bush, endorsed by the Florida legislature, and the other for Gore, produced as a result of the recount ordered by the Florida Supreme Court, then it's arguable that the Supreme Court's jurisdiction would have ceased. (The case would have looked very much like the paradigm case of a political question, *Luther* v. *Borden,* in which the Supreme Court refused to decide which of the competing state governments in Rhode Island was the legitimate one, because there were no intelligible legal concepts to guide the decision.) But Posner uses the fact that the Supreme Court would have been obliged to stay its hand in January as a pragmatic justification for the Court's intervention in December: it might have been accused of "fiddling while Rome burned," he says, by refusing repeated appeals to settle the constitutional questions that could have arisen from the counting of electoral votes.[6]

A pragmatist believes "the decision that has the better consequences for society is the one to be preferred," Posner says. "We only know what *could* have ensued—and what could have ensued is fairly described as chaos, providing a practical argument in defense of the Court's remedy." Because "delay might have dragged on for weeks," and the new president would have started "with an irregular and disputed accession, an abbreviated term of office, and no transition" (Posner twice refers to the horror of having no presidential transition), the Court was justified in stepping in to avoid disorder. "It is a function of law in general . . . to *produce* order," he declares confidently.[7]

Posner's fears of chaos are consistent with his general preference for efficiency above all in his writings about antitrust and law and economics. But they are theoretical and speculative. For a purported pragmatist, he is remarkably uninterested in testing his predictions against the kind of evidence that judges are equipped to evaluate. "That there was a real and disturbing *potential* for disorder and temporary paralysis (I do not want to exaggerate) seems undeniable," he says. "This is why the Supreme Court's intervention was greeted with relief by many people, not all of them Republicans." But in fact, most of those who applauded the decision were Republicans, according to the Gallup poll that I've mentioned. Posner provides no other polls or other data to support his sweeping generalizations about the political reception of the decision, and he offers no data to support his overheated predictions about the potential for disorder. Many outcomes might have prevented two slates from reaching Congress—ranging from Gore's losing the manual recount (a likelihood under the Florida court's standards) to the governor's refusal to certify a slate produced by a Gore victory in the recount. Despite an entire chapter of statistical

6. Ibid., pp. 183, 163.
7. Ibid., pp. 186, 134, 161.

analysis, Posner presents no statistical probabilities about the likelihood of one political outcome over another. Nor does he offer any empirical support for his predictions about legitimacy: he claims, for example, that if Bush had been chosen by Congress rather than the Court, "his 'victory' would have been an empty one; he could not have governed effectively."[8] How does Posner know this? Bush's legitimacy as president has been affected more by the unforeseen attack of September 11 than by anything Posner could have predicted last winter. Like Holmes, whom Posner has accused of being interested in policy analysis in theory but being too lazy to do it properly, Posner is acting more like an armchair pundit than like a rigorous empiricist.[9]

Indeed, the definitive recount sponsored by the media consortium after the decision suggests that predictions of chaos by Posner and the conservative justices were hyperbolic and overwrought. In a manual recount of the undervotes, rather than the overvotes, which is what Gore requested and the Florida court ordered, Bush almost certainly would have won without the Supreme Court's eager assistance. Gore might possibly have eked out a tiny majority based on a recount of the overvotes, in which more than one vote was recorded. But because Gore didn't ask for, and the Florida court didn't order, a recount of the overvotes, the constitutional crisis that Posner predicts was unlikely, rather than likely, to materialize. In his separate statement justifying the Court's initial decision to stay the recount on December 9, Justice Scalia suggested with similar overconfidence that Gore was likely to win the recount ordered by the Florida court and if the recount were later found to be unconstitutional, this would cast a pall over the legitimacy of Bush's election. But Scalia's prediction turned out to be wrong.

In his eagerness to keep Congress out of the picture at all costs, Posner offers no arguments—empirical or constitutional—to support

8. Ibid., pp. 143–44.
9. Richard Posner, The Problems of Jurisprudence 252 (1990).

his bald assertion that the effort to *"produce* order" is important enough to trump the clear intentions of the framers of the Electoral Count Act. They anticipated that there might be dueling electoral slates, and if there were, Congress, not the courts, should choose between them. In his dissenting opinion, Justice Breyer quoted from the legislative history of the act, which makes clear its intention to entrust the power to resolve disputes about presidential elections to Congress rather than the courts. This was in line with the understanding of Madison, who believed that allowing judges to choose presidential electors was "out of the question." Posner may prefer efficiency and order to the vision of democratic dispute resolution endorsed by the framers of the Constitution and the electoral count act, but this is a personal preference.

Posner is full of invective for "shrill" critics of *Bush* v. *Gore* (including me), but surely it is he who is shrill in his hyperbole about the dire consequences of allowing Congress to choose between competing electoral slates, as those who experienced the election of 1876 expected it to do. He calls the possibility of interbranch conflict between the Florida legislature and the Florida courts "a miserable dénouement—not provided for in the Constitution, unreliably provided for in Title III [of the electoral count act], yet imperative to avert," and suggests that the Court's failure to intervene would have precipitated "a potential political and constitutional crisis," even though he offers no evidence that political disorder would have amounted to a constitutional crisis.[10]

In his inability to define the legal injury the Court's intervention averted, Posner reveals that he is skating on very thin ice. In a particularly implausible passage, he says that the political harm to Bush would have been irreparable if the Supreme Court hadn't granted a stay of the recount, and "it is arguable (though a bit of a stretch, and not directly supported by any previous case that I have found) that candidate Bush's participation in the political process would not

10. Posner, Breaking the Deadlock, pp. 155–56, 168.

have been 'full and effective' had a recount at once unlawful and arbitrarily truncated been permitted to cast a shadow over the legitimacy of his election." This fanciful suggestion shows how poorly rooted Bush's claim was in existing case law, as well as reminding us that it's not clear why Bush had the standing to object to the injury he claimed to have suffered. Posner goes on to suggest even more sweepingly that "it was not only political harm to Bush that the stay averted, but harm to the nation, if we assume that the legitimacy of a President (which an unlawful recount would gratuitously have undermined) is a social good."[11]

Posner defines pragmatism as the willingness to weigh the practical consequences of a decision, but he gives no weight to arguments on the other side. Political legitimacy is often in the eye of the beholder, and my own view, for what it's worth, is that the Supreme Court cast a far darker pall over Bush's legitimacy than it would have done by refusing to intervene in the election. Bush was likely to become president by hook or crook because Republicans controlled the Florida legislature, the House of Representatives, and, most important, the Florida executive's office, whose determination about which slate was legitimate would have been binding on Congress in the event of a dispute between both houses. Although Congress might have named an electoral commission to resolve a disagreement between the House and Senate, in a reprise of 1876, we are less deferential to authority than our nineteenth-century predecessors were. And Sandra Day O'Connor would surely have been more vilified had she cast the tiebreaking vote on a Commission than on the Supreme Court. But if Bush had been handed the presidency by political actors, they could have been held politically accountable, and his own legitimacy would have been hard to dispute. (After all, someone had to break the tie.) By rushing unnecessarily to stop the recount, the Supreme Court created a far worse taste in the mouths of Gore supporters, who could

11. Ibid., pp. 164, 166.

suspect that the Court had prevented a fair recount from taking place, merely because the results of that recount can never be known. It's hard to think of an area where judges have less institutional competence than political punditry, and the sweeping and highly unconvincing display of Posner's own political predictions doesn't increase confidence that more ideological judges could do any better.

Clearly Congress is better equipped than the courts to make predictions about how best to choose a president who will be accepted by the public as politically legitimate, and whether or not efficiency, order, and political legitimacy are social goods that outweigh other social goods (such as the effort to discern the intent of voters.) As in the election of 1876, these are political questions masquerading as legal questions, not fit for the wrangling of lawyers. But Posner is unable to recognize this because of his undisguised contempt for Congress. The most jarring parts of his book are those in which he sneers openly that "Congress is not a competent forum for resolving such disputes" because "Title III is a statute, indeed a difficult and intricate one and . . . congressional resolution of a slate of electors would be a process of statutory (and constitutional) interpretation and application, the sort of thing that courts are equipped to do but Congress most emphatically is not."[12]

It is surprising to see Posner invoke a statute that assigns responsibility for resolving electoral disputes to Congress rather than the courts as a justification for entrusting the resolution of the same electoral disputes to the courts rather than to Congress. He has turned the statute on its head. But Posner goes further. "We learned recently that the elaborate constitutional provisions governing the impeachment and trial of a President—provisions that assign a judicial role to Congress—do not work very well because legislatures are not courts and legislators are not judges," he writes. "We should endeavor to keep Congress out of the picture, so far as that is possible to do. It is a

12. Ibid., p. 145.

large, unwieldy, undisciplined body (actually two bodies), unsuited in its structure, personnel, and procedures to legal dispute resolution."[13]

Posner's contempt for Congress has blinded him to the fact that it is better equipped than the Court to resolve disputes that involve a mix of political and constitutional questions. In fact, Congress—or at least the Senate—did relatively well in adjudicating the presidential impeachment, and in balancing the complicated mix of political and constitutional questions that are inevitably implicated by a decision about whether or not to remove the president. Certainly, the Senate did far better than the Supreme Court, whose overconfident and unfounded prediction that the *Jones* case "appears to us highly unlikely to occupy any substantial amount of petitioner's time" stands as a daunting reminder of the shortcomings of ivory tower judges who fancy themselves to be armchair empiricists.[14] The Senate was able to respond to the widespread popular distaste for what the House Republicans had done, and this political responsiveness was clearly reflected in the decision to acquit. An electoral dispute, like an impeachment, is a political rather than a constitutional crisis, despite Posner's claims to the contrary, and it requires a blend of legal and political judgments— certainly far more political than legal if one tries to disentangle the two. Precisely because the standards for a recount are so malleable, because the baselines so fluid, and the possibility of confidently preferring one legal framework to another is so remote, the question is political in both the conventional and jurisdictional senses. Why Posner trusts judges more than Congress is hard to fathom, given the fact that few judges have proved better than elected representatives at voting anything short of the party line.

The speculative and unconvincing nature of Posner's predictions about political chaos remind us with special force why pragmatic considerations should play little role in a judge's decision to intervene in

13. Ibid., pp. 145, 250.
14. *Clinton v. Jones*, 520 U.S. 681, 702 (1997).

cases that arguably raise political questions. As the Supreme Court's inability to keep up with fast-moving legal issues has demonstrated, judges have no more institutional competence than pundits to predict how a rapidly changing political event is likely to unfold or to balance the costs of political uncertainty against other political values. This was the core of the initial response by traditional legal scholars to Bickel: they argued that the decision about whether to reach the merits of a case ought to be made on the basis of principle rather than politics.[15]

Bush v. *Gore* also suggests that the political question doctrine should weigh heavily on judges at the remedial stage of a lawsuit. Bickel is ambiguous here: if the political question doctrine is understood as a counsel of pure pragmatism—cautioning judges not to order school desegregation if they fear white flight, for example—it invites bullying of judges. But if the political question doctrine is understood as a counsel of judicial humility and self-doubt, it points in a very different direction. Professor John Hart Ely has famously suggested that judges should intervene in politics to correct political process failures.[16] But a self-doubting judge should skeptically consider the effects of a judicially ordered remedy as well as a judicial decision to intervene in the first place. In *Bush* v. *Gore,* it wasn't clear whether the remedy ordered by the Florida court might have precipitated new political process failures in the course of trying to correct old ones. For this reason, I believe the Florida court was wrong to order the relief that it did: by changing the counting standards in midstream rather than deferring to the counting standards imposed by individual canvassing boards, it arguably corrected one equality violation at the cost of creating another. Whether or not you believe this violation rises to the level of a constitutional error—and I don't—it shows that judicially mandated

15. See, e.g., Wechsler, Principles, Politics and Fundamental Law 11–14 (1961).
16. See John Hart Ely, Democracy and Distrust: A Theory of Judicial Review (1980).

remedies for political process errors may have perverse effects because the underlying right that is being violated is so elusive and hard to define.

Nevertheless—and for the same reason—the Supreme Court was also wrong to correct the errors of the Florida court. As I argued in November, the proper body to correct the unjustified intervention of the Florida Court was Congress rather than the Supreme Court.[17] When it stopped the recount, the Supreme Court, like the Florida court, could not be confident that it was avoiding political process failures rather than precipitating them: the decision turned on highly contested questions about the nature of the right to vote that were political rather than legal in nature. And both the justices who voted to stop the recount and those who would continue it were unsuccessful in articulating a coherent principle of equality of representation to justify either course.

The same skepticism about the underlying principle that the court was vindicating informed Bickel's discussion of *Baker* v. *Carr.* "What is the dominant principle" that the Court was seeking to vindicate, he asked? Unlike *Brown,* where the anti-caste principle could be articulated with clarity, the Court never managed to identify precisely what equality required in the apportionment cases, which necessarily involved "a very high percentage of politics with a very small admixture of definable principle." But although the Court in *Baker* had trouble identifying a dominant principle, its intervention could be excused because of its restraint on the question of remedy: instead of ordering the Tennessee legislature to adopt a particular apportionment scheme, Bickel noted approvingly, the Supreme Court had "opened a colloquy, posing to the political institutions of Tennessee the question of apportionment, not answering it for them."[18] By inviting the legislature to

17. Jeffrey Rosen, "Florida's Justices Went Too Far," New York Times, November 23, 2000, at A43.
18. Bickel, The Last Dangerous Branch, pp. 196, 193.

pass a new apportionment statute, the Court left the ultimate political question—the question of drawing an electoral map that could be reconciled with the equal protection clause or the republican form of government clause—up to the legislature itself. All this suggests a new pillar of the political question doctrine: to the degree possible, remedies for political process failures should be designed by the political branches themselves. And in *Bush* v. *Gore,* the impossibility of asking the Florida legislature to devise uniform standards for a recount provided an additional reason that the Court should have refused to intervene in the first place, allowing the excesses of the Florida court to be corrected by Congress.

Posner, of course, concedes the weakness of the equal protection argument; but he argues that *Bush* v. *Gore* should have been decided on the very different grounds set out in the separate concurrence of Chief Justice Rehnquist, who was joined by Justices Scalia and Thomas. Article II of the Constitution, they said, forbids a state court to change the rules for choosing presidential electors established by the state legislature. There was no need to worry about whether the recount would be supervised by the court or the legislature; because the rules had been changed, the recount had to stop. I can imagine a situation where a state court so clearly and unequivocally changes the electoral rules laid down by the legislature that a higher court might have to intervene to restore the status quo. There would be no political question, for example, if a state court in a contest proceeding refused to count votes from African Americans, in clear violation of the equal protection provisions of the state and federal constitutions. (This, incidentally, exposes the weakness of Bush's suggestion earlier in the litigation that a state court in an electoral dispute may not rely on its own constitution without violating Article II.) But if the political question doctrine is understood as a doctrine of judicial humility rather than judicial heroics, it counsels judges to restrain themselves from concluding that a state court has acted unreasonably in cases where reasonable people can disagree about whether a particular interpretation is beyond the pale. I think the Florida court was wrong to change the counting standards, but the change was not so obvious a departure from a confusing statutory scheme to constitute an obvious or unequivocal violation of Article II. (After all, the Article II argument, like the equal protection argument, was essentially unprecedented: both were made up in the heat of litigation.) A justice with some sense of her own fallibility would have abstained from intervening in *Bush* v. *Gore* on the grounds that reasonable people could disagree about whether the Florida court's interpretation was lawless, and those who believed that it was lawless could take their case to the Florida legislature and ultimately to Congress: there was always a political remedy available for the political wrong.

The political question doctrine, in short, should be viewed as an argument for deference in the face of contestability. It embodies a presumption of abstention and strongly rejects the suggestion that a decision to abstain is just as political as a decision to intervene. From the perspective of judicial humility, abstention is the baseline, and any deviations from it bear a strong burden of justification.

In arguing for a resurrection of a political question doctrine that focuses on judicial self-doubt rather than on judicial heroics and is extended to remedies as well as rights, I see additional reasons to criticize the voting rights cases of the 1970s and 80s that culminated in the racial redistricting cases. Abandoning its dialogue with state legislatures, the Court soon got into the business of ordering particular apportionment schemes, not only striking down particular arrangements as a violation of the equal protection clause but inviting lower courts to impose specific alternatives that would then be submitted to the Supreme Court for its approval. Bickel, however, viewed this as the worst of all forms of entanglement in the political thicket. "In some future case," he wrote after *Baker*, "the Supreme Court may see as its function, not merely to let an apportionment be, but to legitimate it. This . . . would be grave error. If one may use proper nouns to name judicial errors, as is sometimes done with diseases, we should call this *Plessy* v. *Ferguson's* Error, after the case that legitimated segregation in 1896."[19]

When the Rehnquist court refused to treat political gerrymandering as a nonjusticiable political question, it committed the *Plessy* error that Bickel feared.[20] And this error was extended and compounded in the racial redistricting cases, where the Court presumed to evaluate each apportionment on its own terms, approving some, rejecting others, and inviting the lower courts, rather than the legislature, to draft acceptable alternatives.

Bush v. *Gore* gives us additional reasons to fear the *Plessy* error in cases involving voting rights. When judges take it upon themselves to legitimate a particular method of vote-counting or to impose an alternative method, their decisions are likely to be perceived through partisan lenses, because the underlying right is so elusive and abstract. But *Bush* v. *Gore* also reminds us that judges shouldn't abstain from deciding political questions out of a self-aggrandizing concern for the legitimacy of the Court or the fate of the country. These pragmatic considerations, as Posner's overconfidence inadvertently demonstrates, aren't ones that judges are institutionally equipped—let alone constitutionally authorized—to make. Instead, judges should abstain from deciding political questions for reasons of judicial humility. Self-doubting judges can't trust themselves to be guided primarily by law rather than politics in cases where the proportions of both are so dramatically unbalanced.

19. Ibid., p. 197.
20. See *Davis* v. *Bandemer,* 478 U.S. 109 (1986).

MARK TUSHNET **10**

The Conservatism in *Bush* v. *Gore*

Journalists find it easy to say that a Supreme Court decision is "conservative" or "liberal." When the Supreme Court divides narrowly over whether the Constitution allows Congress to make states pay damages to employees who were fired because they were thought to be too old for the job, people write of the Court's "conservative majority" and "liberal dissenters." These characterizations are not simply descriptions; they also attribute cause: the majority ruled as it did *because* its members are conservatives, and similarly for the dissenters.

Political scientists have developed a formal model for what they think happens on the Supreme Court. They call it the attitudinal model. Its basic idea is that justices have values and preferences *before* they consider any particular case, and they apply those values and preferences to the facts of the cases they decide.

Some legal academics, drawing on the thought of the American Legal Realists of the 1920s and 1930s and critical legal scholars of the 1980s, think Supreme Court decisions exemplify the proposition that "law is politics."

So why were some journalists, some political scientists, and many legal academics surprised to the point of outrage by *Bush* v. *Gore*? Five Republican justices awarded the presidency to the Republican candidate. Why should people who think that constitutional law is politics or who accept the attitudinal model be surprised?

On first glance, *Bush* v. *Gore* seems to be different from the run of cases because politics in a quite narrow sense—crude partisan preferences—are apparent on the decision's surface. Appearances may be deceiving. Perhaps the justices in the majority decided as they did not because their most immediate preference was that George W. Bush become president, but because they had an understanding of the law according to which George W. Bush was legally entitled to become president.

We must examine what can be said in favor of the Court's holding to address that possibility. The decision's defenders point out that two justices appointed by Republican presidents dissented from the Court's decision, and that actually seven justices agreed that the recount ordered by the Florida Supreme Court failed to satisfy the Constitution's requirements. Those points, while accurate, plainly fail to describe the decision's obvious political dimensions. They often seem to be made halfheartedly and with a certain amount of embarrassment. (Even more striking, I think, is the strong tendency among Bush's partisans to defend, not the decision *the Court* rendered, but the concurring opinion written by the chief justice.)

But, the opinion's defenders might say, the Court majority reached its conclusions not because the five justices were Republicans picking a Republican to be president, but because they were faithfully following what they believed the law to require. At the very least, they assert, the majority's holdings were within the range of reasonable interpretations of the law. Law—real law—rather than politics explains what the Court did.

Full consideration of that claim would require a quite detailed exposition of the legal arguments made by, or even available to, the majority. Short of that, I provide some summary comments, dealing with the decision to end the recount process and with the Court's equal protection holding.

I have not yet seen a decent legal defense of the majority's decision to preclude Florida authorities from conducting a recount that would be consistent with constitutional requirements. The majority said that the Florida legislature had set an absolute deadline of December 12 for completing a recount, and that a constitutionally adequate recount could not be completed before that deadline. But, as was widely observed in the immediate aftermath, the U.S. Supreme Court's interpretation of Florida law rested on statements made by the Florida Supreme Court in a legal context quite different from the one created by the U.S. Supreme Court's constitutional holding. The Florida Supreme Court said, at most, that the legislature set December 12 as an absolute deadline on the assumption that a constitutionally acceptable recount could be completed by that date.

Defenders of the holding that terminated the recount are few. We can find more defenders of the Court's equal protection holding. Some Republicans may do so strategically, hoping to provide some legal legitimacy to the presidency of George W. Bush. Some liberals may do so equally strategically, hoping to use *Bush* v. *Gore* in challenges to other aspects of our election system. But the equal protection holding is indeed defensible in principle.

An equal protection violation occurs when one person is unjustifiably treated differently from another. In *Bush* v. *Gore* the question was whether it was unjustifiable to count the votes of some qualified voters who cast "legal votes"—made marks on their ballots clearly indicating their preferences—without counting the votes of other qualified voters who did the same.

What is the problem with the recount ordered by the Florida Supreme Court? It is hard to say that anyone was "deprived" of a vote in the usual sense. The classic cases of vote deprivation fall into two groups. First, a statute or social practice denies an identified group— for example, African Americans, women, and so on—access to the ballot box. Members of the group simply cannot cast a vote. The harms caused by these practices are evident. Members of the group lack any opportunity to influence the election's outcome, and the practices themselves signal to the group's members that they are not full members of the political community.

A second form of vote deprivation occurs when ballot boxes are "lost" so that one candidate can win the election. Here people in the precincts with lost votes enter the voting booth, but their votes do not count. As some Republican partisans saw the case, *Bush* v. *Gore* exemplified this sort of vote deprivation. In their view, the Florida Supreme Court had gerrymandered the recount process so that the voters whose votes were added during the recount were predominantly Democrats and those whose votes were not added were probably predominantly Republicans.

Had the Court seen *Bush* v. *Gore* in those terms, the case would have been fairly easy. The Court has held that political gerrymanders violate the constitutional right to equal treatment. The Court's standard for determining when an unconstitutional political gerrymander has occurred are exceedingly stringent. If similar standards had been applied to the Florida Supreme Court's actions, it would have been impossible to conclude that that court engaged in the equivalent of partisan gerrymandering. But, in any event, nothing in the Court's equal protection analysis even hinted that the problem with which the Court was concerned was partisan gerrymandering of the recount process.

Gerrymandering in general raises a different sort of constitutional problem. Everyone can vote and every vote is counted, but the votes of the minority group—partisan or racial—in a gerrymandered district are wasted in the sense that voters in that group do not have an effective voice in government. The language courts have developed for this problem is that it involves vote *dilution* rather than vote deprivation.

Bush v. *Gore* was a case of vote dilution, but in a peculiar sense. In the usual gerrymandering case, we know whose votes are diluted: people who live in cities, Democrats in a district gerrymandered to favor Republicans, and the like. In *Bush* v. *Gore*, understood as the

Court understood it, identifying the group whose votes are diluted is tricky. *Bush* v. *Gore* does not suggest that Florida had to have *any* recount procedure at all. So, the problem cannot be that people who clearly intended to vote for Bush or Gore but mismarked their ballots are treated differently from people with the same intentions who marked their ballots correctly. Rather, the problem arises because of different treatment of people *within* a particular group. Simplifying a bit, the disadvantaged group consists of people who clearly intended to vote for one or another candidate but who marked their ballots in ways that the voting machines could not read. That group's influence on the election's outcome is reduced when the votes of only some group members are counted.

The question then becomes, Why does it violate the Constitution to dilute the votes of members of that group? Given the way the Court approached the problem, the answer cannot be that there is systematic bias in recounting some but not all ballots. The constitutional violation must be this: the Constitution requires that voters with identical intentions have the same amount of influence on election outcomes unless there are strong reasons for allowing differences, as there might be for a decision not to allow any recounts. Florida's process was designed in a way that made it possible to identify the clear intent of some voters—those who correctly marked their ballots and some of those who incorrectly marked them—but not the clear intent of all voters, and without any reasonably strong justification. That is clearly a defensible—indeed, an attractive—view of what equality demands in the voting process. It is a significant extension of prior holdings dealing with vote dilution, and it is quite far-reaching in its implications for the use of different types of voting machines, absentee voter rules, and the like.

That argument, the strongest one in favor of the Court's equal protection holding, actually undermines its decision to foreclose the completion of a recount that complied with the Constitution. Recall that the decision to stop the recount rested on the Court's conclusion that the Florida legislature had set December 12 as an absolute deadline for the completion of any recount. But a legislative decision to impose an absolute deadline under the circumstances presented by *Bush* v. *Gore* would violate the very constitutional right recognized in that case. Treating December 12 as an absolute deadline barred Florida authorities from discovering whether there were additional lawfully cast votes that could be added to the existing count.

The reason for setting such a deadline was to ensure, as far as the Florida legislature could, that the results reported to Congress would be protected from challenge. The applicable statutes certainly did not envision a case in which a state submitted a return only because the Supreme Court had intervened to stop the recount. On these facts, Congress was perfectly free to reject Florida's return on the ground that no final decision had been reached consistently with the Constitution. In other words, complying with the December 12 deadline did not enable Florida to guarantee that its electoral votes would be counted for a specific candidate. As a consequence, the reason for setting an absolute deadline does not seem terribly strong.

Unfortunately, we can have no confidence whatever that the justices in the *Bush* v. *Gore* majority actually accept *as a principle* the principle justifying the equal protection holding. To accept a legal proposition as a principle is to be committed to applying that proposition in similar cases when they arise. The Court's disclaimer that it was dealing only with the circumstances presented in *Bush* v. *Gore*—a statewide recount conducted under the supervision of a single judicial officer—does not alone show that the majority was not committed to the principle justifying the equal protection holding. The Court's defenders might suggest that the disclaimer may reflect only caution about pointing out a principle's implications for unforeseen cases.

Yet some of the cases were hardly unforeseen. The Court had before it arguments that applying equal protection principles to methods of counting votes once they were cast required the application of the same principles to the methods of casting the votes in the first place:

If divergent standards for counting ballots were constitutionally impermissible, why are not divergent methods for casting votes? The Court's effort to cabin its decision to the facts before it bespeaks, not caution, but unwillingness to treat the equal protection holding as a principle.

In addition, the principle that justifies the equal protection holding is innovative. Well-established, though rarely enforced, equal protection doctrine precludes states from arbitrarily depriving people of their rights. The Court said that it was concerned about arbitrary deprivations of the fundamental right to vote. But characterizing the adverse effect of the recount procedure on anyone's right to vote is a substantial extension of previous cases dealing with vote dilution. The five justices in the majority have been reluctant, to say the least, to develop innovative interpretations of the equal protection clause, or even to push existing interpretations slightly beyond the point at which equal protection doctrine rested a decade or two ago.

To summarize what is an already condensed version of a complex argument: it is quite hard to account for the result in *Bush* v. *Gore* in purely legal terms. Although there *are* legal principles that might justify the equal protection holding (but probably not the preclusion of a recount conducted according to constitutionally permissible standards), it is exceedingly difficult to conclude that the five justices in the majority were committed to legal principles that required the result they reached.

The journalists, political scientists, and legal academics mentioned earlier might say, "So what else is new? We've always said that legal principles don't account for outcomes; politics does. *Bush* v. *Gore* is just another example of the usual way of doing business."

Perhaps it is not. I consider two possibilities. The first explains why people who accept the strong view that crude partisan politics accounts for the outcome in *Bush* v. *Gore, and* who believe that law really is politics, might nonetheless be surprised by the case's outcome. The second suggests that something other than crude partisan politics, but something fairly described even so as politics, might account for the outcome.

That obvious partisan politics accounts for the Court's action might be surprising if the view that law is politics takes a sophisticated rather than a simpleminded form. The sophistication comes in two varieties. The first, taken primarily by political scientists, sees Supreme Court justices as political actors no different from senators or presidential candidates. The second, taken by some political scientists and legal academics, sees the Court as one of many political institutions whose task is to construct the ideological frame within which a wide range of more discrete political issues fit.

Consider first the view that justices are political actors. *Bush* v. *Gore* might be surprising to a person holding this view because the justices usually seem to be reasonably astute political actors, but *Bush* v. *Gore* seems politically inept. After all, justices differ from senators and presidential candidates in many ways, two of which are particularly relevant to this discussion: justices don't have to worry about reelection, and they must enact their policy preferences in ways that can fairly be described as law not politics—as society understands that vexed distinction.

The latter difference makes surprising the legal weakness in the Court's holdings in *Bush* v. *Gore*. The decision might be defensible in principle, although the opinion hardly does the necessary work, even taking into account the time pressures that the Court thought it faced. Legal weakness implies that the justices, though acting as politicians, were not acting as *good* politicians, that is, as people able to achieve the policy goals they desired within the institutional constraints they faced. It is as if a presidential candidate centered a campaign on a proposal that had no hope of surviving the legislative process.

The other difference between justices and other political actors, life tenure, means that justices can take a longer view of how best to enact what they want. The justices' political resources are rather limited, consisting primarily of public deference to judgments that the public has come to believe are fairly described as resting on law rather than politics. The more apparent it is that the line between law and politics is hard to discern, the fewer political resources the Court has and the less likely it is that the justices will be able to achieve their goals over the long period they ordinarily have in which to do so.

Bush v. Gore might be surprising to one who sees judges as political actors because it seems calculated to undermine rather than sustain the Court's political resources by making it apparent that law is politics in the crudest partisan sense. Of course, justices thinking about retiring within the short-term might have fewer reasons to sustain the Court's long-term political resources; they are in the position of someone who has one last chance to achieve an important policy goal and who is indifferent to what might happen later. And, in the specific context of *Bush v. Gore,* such justices might hope that their replacements, nominated by the person they were placing in the presidency, would agree with their general policy orientation. And yet even politically compatible replacements would find themselves limited in what they could accomplish if *Bush v. Gore* impairs the Court's political resources.

In this connection we can contrast *Bush v. Gore* with the Court's earlier, and unanimous, decision in *Bush v. Palm Beach County.* In context that decision had to be taken as a rebuke to the Florida Supreme Court, even though the Court did not accept Governor Bush's position that it should immediately call a halt to all disputes over the election. Yet the fact that every justice on the Court joined the opinion eliminated the possibility that it would be seen as a partisan decision. When the Court reached the dispositive question in *Bush v. Gore,* the justices divided along what everyone understood to be partisan lines, notwithstanding efforts by Republican partisans to emphasize that seven justices agreed that the procedures approved by the Florida Supreme Court violated the Constitution. The resource of respect for the Court as an institution above politics, carefully husbanded in *Bush v. Palm Beach County,* was dissipated in *Bush v. Gore.*

Surveys immediately after *Bush* v. *Gore* showed no net decrease in general public support for the Court. But political resources are needed for the long term, and what happens a day or a week after a political event may not be a good measure of the event's full political significance. The surveys did reveal one interesting fact that might have longer-term implications: the absence of a change in public support for the Court overall concealed political polarization over the Court as Republicans became more supportive and Democrats less so. If that polarization persists, we may see the public treating the Court roughly in the way it treats a Senate divided between Republicans and Democrats.

The political calculations associated with deciding *Bush* v. *Gore* are quite complex. In many ways, the Court's political standing will turn on whether the decision proves successful, that is, whether President George W. Bush has a successful presidency. Here, too, a person who regards the Court as a political actor might be surprised at seeing one political actor putting its fortunes in the hands of another.

Rendering the Court hostage to the Bush presidency might make sense if the stakes were high enough. The narrowness of the policy differences between the major presidential candidates makes it implausible to think that in 2000 the fate of the Republic turned on which candidate became president. But perhaps something else was at stake.

The second, more sophisticated, view of law as politics may produce useful insights here. According to that view, the Supreme Court develops ideological structures that underlie policy outcomes. So in saying that the present Court has a conservative majority, we might mean not that the justices seek to enact conservative policies directly into law but that they have a general perspective on law and lawmaking that reflects conservative values. Precisely how that conservative perspective will affect specific cases is often not obvious, particularly because conservatism comes in many varieties.

Bush v. *Gore* might seem surprising to someone who thinks the

Court was conservative in this sense. The Court's concern for equality seems hardly connected to the kinds of conservative policy outcomes typically associated with conservatism. Perhaps the conservative elements in *Bush* v. *Gore* lie beneath the surface.

Suppose *Bush* v. *Gore* cannot be defended as law. The political practice of breaking the bonds of legality in the service of compelling needs is common enough to have a name: *raison d'état*. The particular raison d'état available in *Bush* v. *Gore* was not the compelling need to make George W. Bush president. Rather, it was the compelling need to avoid chaos. Of course, nothing in the Court's opinion refers to that need, for to do so would be to force the extralegal concept of raison d'état into legal form. Commentators on the decision, particularly its defenders, do regularly refer to matters being out of control. Sometimes they say that the Florida Supreme Court was out of control; sometimes they suggest that the process of recounting ballots was out of control, with partisans shouting at the vote counters in an entirely disorderly proceeding.

What is striking about this concern is the apparent belief that the *Court* had to intervene to avert chaos and disorder. After all, there was a standard process for determining who won Florida's electoral votes. The Constitution and federal statutes set out a procedure under which the members of Congress would decide which votes to count for whom. That procedure had some intriguing gaps in the circumstances presented by *Bush* v. *Gore,* but there was little reason to think that the members of Congress could not handle the problems in an orderly fashion. The crisis that *Bush* v. *Gore* intended to avert, then, was not rioting in the streets—it was the crisis of democracy operating in its usual fashion, not with geometrically precise order but with real people talking with one another and then deciding what to do.

Understanding *Bush* v. *Gore* as arising from the Court's discomfort with the messiness of democracy allows us to place it among a number of cases in which the Court has expressed skepticism about the possibility that Congress could act in a constitutionally responsible manner. For example, in 1991 the Supreme Court rejected earlier decisions and held that the Constitution's protection of the free exercise of religion did not invalidate general laws that did not target religious practices. Congress responded with the Religious Freedom Restoration Act, which attempted to require courts to apply the approach the Court had rejected. The Supreme Court immediately invalidated the act, rejecting the proposition that Congress and the Court share responsibility for identifying precisely which rights the Constitution protects. The Court has required that, at least in some areas, Congress compile a substantial factual record as the basis for its enactments. But, for example, when Congress relied on an extensive investigation of discrimination in enacting the Americans with Disabilities Act, the Court nitpicked the factual record in holding the act unconstitutional in some of its applications.

The contemporary Court appears to see itself as the guardian against the disorders to which democracy is prone—at least, as the justices see democracy working as it necessarily does. The clearest expression of this distrust of democracy has come in a *liberal* decision: *Planned Parenthood* v. *Casey.* When the Court upheld what three justices called the "core holding" of *Roe* v. *Wade,* Justices O'Connor and Kennedy, who were pivotal in *Bush* v. *Gore,* joined Justice Souter in an opinion that "call[ed] the contending sides of a national controversy to end their national division by accepting a common mandate rooted in the Constitution"—where, of course, the Constitution's "mandate" was specified by the Court itself.

Concern for avoiding a different kind of disorder may also underlie *Bush* v. *Gore.* The three justices who joined a separate concurrence expressed some disdain for voters who were unable to follow directions. As they saw it, fairly interpreted, Florida law required that only those votes cast in ways that machines could read them should be counted. Here the justices may have been juxtaposing the order that results from the use of technology with the disorder associated with human action.

Historically, one facet of conservative thought has been a generalized suspicion of democracy. In this sense *Bush* v. *Gore* is an ordinary and unsurprising conservative decision. The role of technology in conservative thought is more ambiguous, but certainly one strand of conservatism has seen technological advance as an attractive and stabilizing feature of capitalist economic systems, which technology serves in part by increasing society's material well-being and thereby diminishing the risk of social disorder occasioned by competition for limited resources.

From this angle, the difficulty with *Bush* v. *Gore* is that legal conservatism has only been selectively suspicious of democracy and selectively committed to technology over human action. When it suits the cause, legal conservatives become populists, decrying the arrogance of a liberal elite in imposing its will on the more sensible public. Dissenting in *Casey*, Justice Scalia said, "The Court should return this matter to the people—where the Constitution, by its silence on the subject, left it." In a case involving gay rights, he wrote, "When the Court takes sides in the culture wars, it tends to be with the knights rather than the villains—and more specifically with the Templars, reflecting the view and values of the lawyer class from which the Court's Members are drawn."[1]

There is a suggestion here that legal conservatism reflects not a generalized suspicion of democracy but only a suspicion of democracy with respect to matters about which the Constitution speaks. But the Court's federalism decisions have been almost proud of the fact that the conservative majority is enforcing what the justices see as the unwritten postulates of the nation's federal system. In short, legal conservatives' suspicion of democracy seems not generalized but opportunistic.

A similar opportunism over technology appears in the Court's decision refusing to allow census figures to be adjusted statistically—that

---

1. *Romer* v. *Evans*, 517 U.S. 620, 652 (1996).

is, scientifically—from the count produced by mail-in responses and face-to-face surveys.[2] Notably, the Court divided in the census case exactly as it did in *Bush* v. *Gore*. As in *Bush* v. *Gore*, the division seems partisan in the narrowest sense, because it was generally believed, certainly by Republicans, that statistical adjustments would end up favoring Democrats. Although the five justices in the *Bush* v. *Gore* majority may have felt, at a level below conscious articulation, that technology and science are ways of controlling the messiness of human action, the same five justices in the census case appear to have felt, at the same level, that human actions are preferable to technology and science.

Political actors are always ideologically sincere *and* opportunistic, though sometimes opportunism evidently prevails over sincerity, as it perhaps did in the census case. *Bush* v. *Gore* may be more illuminating when understood as a case in which some dimensions of contemporary legal conservatism—its suspicion of democracy and its interest in technology—can be discerned than when understood as a case in which law was reduced to politics in the narrowest partisan sense.

The equal protection principle underlying the Court's decision is attractive enough, even if one harbors suspicions about the majority's commitment to it. *Bush* v. *Gore* gave us a president, but it may be more important for the light it sheds on the nature of contemporary conservatism. Excavating the opinion, we can find in it not only sheer partisan preference but also deeper concerns conservatives have about the messiness of democracy. In the longer run, it may be more important for true democrats to understand that today's conservatives, like those in the past, have misgivings about democracy than it is for members of the Democratic Party to decry the Court's imposition of George W. Bush on the American people.

2. *Department of Commerce* v. *House of Representatives*, 525 U.S. 316 (1999).

11

Does the Constitution Enact the Republican Party Platform? Beyond *Bush* v. *Gore*

The Current Situation

Bush v. *Gore* has already become a case for the history books. Of course the decision amounts to a black eye for an extraordinary institution. The essentially lawless character of the Court's decision ought not to be forgotten.[1] At the same time, there is a looming risk. The risk is that some independents and Democrats, in the academy and elsewhere, will be too focused on the Court's decision—that they will seem, and be, sore losers, defining too much of their agenda in reaction to Election 2000 and assessing political life in large part by reference to the Court's decision in *Bush* v. *Gore*. It is not hard to detect the smell of sour grapes.

I believe that much of the importance of *Bush* v. *Gore* lies not so much in what it did as in what it reveals about the nature of the federal judiciary in the current period. Because of *Bush* v. *Gore*, it should finally be possible for the American public to disregard the ludicrous Republican rhetoric about "liberal judicial activism"—something that has not been an active presence in American life for well over a

---

1. For my own views, see Cass R. Sunstein, "Order without Law," in The Vote (Cass R. Sunstein and Richard A. Epstein, eds. 2001).

decade. We are now in the midst of an extraordinary period of right-wing judicial activism, in which federal judges, far too sure that they are right, feel too free to reject the judgments of other branches of government.

For the future, the task is to restore the courts to a more humble and legitimate place in American government—a place in which judges accord more respect to democratically elected branches, proceed incrementally and cautiously, and attempt to protect rather than to displace democratic processes. *Bush* v. *Gore* fits all too well with a large number of other cases in which the Supreme Court has essentially played politics by other means, rejecting reasonable judgments by other branches by reference to its own, often parochial, conception of the law. An especially unfortunate aspect of the situation is that the Court seems oblivious to the extent to which its own political preferences are playing a role in the relevant decisions. In too many places—and this is one of my principal themes here—the Constitution, as interpreted by federal judges, is looking uncomfortably close to the Republican Party platform.

To improve the situation, it is necessary to rethink the issue of judicial appointments, and in particular to rethink the Senate's role. And to do this, it is necessary to go well beyond *Bush* v. *Gore.* I certainly do not believe that fair-minded independents, Democrats, and Republicans should impose an embargo on nominations by President Bush or that they should take *Bush* v. *Gore* as a reason to reject any and all choices emanating from the White House. Such a course would seem, to too many, to be the path of sore losers. But I do believe that it is appropriate for the Senate to impose a high burden of proof on presidential nominees, so as to ensure that the current tendency toward judicial hubris is dampened rather than extended. No one has a right to a federal judicial appointment.

The bottom line: in the near future, the Senate should refuse to confirm any Supreme Court nominee who is unable to demonstrate basic respect for democratic prerogatives, of the sort that the current

Court has been unwilling to show. The Senate should take the same approach to lower court nominees. Even more, the Senate should insist, under current conditions, on its right to provide "advice" to President Bush so as to become an active participant in creating the overall character of the federal judiciary rather than being a passive observer. More particularly, the Senate should use its advisory function, not to veto most of President Bush's choices, but to ensure the federal judiciary has an appropriate mix of views. It should attempt, in short, to sustain intellectual diversity on federal courts.

A Remarkable Historical Shift

There is an important tale in the background here, one that has yet to be told in any detail. The tale involves the self-conscious, highly successful transformation of the federal judiciary, brought about by high-level Republican officials. To a degree that has been insufficiently appreciated and is in some ways barely believable, the contemporary federal courts are fundamentally different from the federal courts of just two decades ago. I offer some brief notations here.

During the past two decades, a significant difference between Republicans and Democrats has been that high-level Republican officials, unlike their Democratic counterparts, have been obsessed with the composition of the federal judiciary. For President Ronald Reagan's White House, remaking the federal judiciary was a top priority. Presidents Reagan and George Bush had a distinct agenda for the nation's courts: to reduce the powers of the federal government; scale back the rights of those accused of crime; strike down affirmative action programs; and diminish privacy rights, including the right to abortion. They sought judges who would interpret the Constitution, and other federal statutes, in a way that would promote this agenda (parts of which, incidentally, seem attractive to me as a political matter).

I will say more below about the vexed terms "judicial activism" and "judicial restraint." For present purposes, the key point is that

Republican presidents have wanted federal judges whose views of the law, and the Constitution, would stay relatively close to the terms of the Republican Party platform. President Reagan in particular attempted to stock the federal bench with young conservatives, many of them having some enthusiasm for the social movements associated with Reaganism. Of course Justice Scalia is the principal symbol of this effort by the Reagan White House. But consider as well Judges Richard Posner and Frank Easterbrook, two of the best and most heavily cited judges on the lower courts. Neither is a doctrinaire conservative, and both have independent streaks. But both judges must be counted, in general, as having done essentially what the Reagan White House hoped they would do. (It counts as a special bonus that Judge Posner, with the prestige of a judicial appointment, has written one book defending the outcome in *Bush* v. *Gore* and another book amounting, in large part, to a defense of the impeachment era attack on President Clinton.)

But the effort to reshape the federal judiciary has not been limited to Republican presidents. Under President Bill Clinton, Republican senators were equally singleminded. Showing extraordinarily little respect for presidential prerogatives, they did a great deal to block Mr. Clinton's judicial nominees. Sometimes Republican senators justified their actions by labeling Clinton nominees (whatever the facts) as "liberal activists." Sometimes they offered no reasons at all and simply refused to schedule confirmation hearings. Senator Orrin Hatch was especially firm, showing a general, across-the-board opposition to "liberals." (According to one report, Senator Hatch told prominent Democratic senators: "No liberals."[2]) One result was that many moderate Clinton nominees received no serious consideration from the Hatch-led Senate Judiciary Committee.

By pointing to these efforts, I do not mean to suggest that Democrats have not been concerned with the composition of the federal judiciary.

2. Personal communication from a Democratic senator.

Of course many Democratic voters have been attentive to that issue, especially during election years. The nature of the federal judiciary and in particular the future of *Roe* v. *Wade* have been central campaign issues for Democratic candidates. But in contrast with their Republican counterparts, Democratic officials have been remarkably passive, reluctant to attempt any transformation of the federal judiciary or to insist on continuity with the Warren Court. As an exhibit-in-chief, consider the fact that President Clinton chose two centrist justices, Ruth Bader Ginsburg and Stephen Breyer—two people whose views are very far from those of, say, William Brennan and Thurgood Marshall. Ginsburg and Breyer are extremely distinguished choices, and in my view they have the right view of the role of the Supreme Court in the constitutional order.[3] But they cannot be counted as "liberals," or as the Democratic counterpart to Justices Scalia and Thomas. With respect to the lower federal courts, President Clinton followed the same basic pattern. I have not done a systematic study, but it is hard to think of a single Clinton appointment of a "liberal" judge, corresponding to the conservative Posner or Easterbrook. I speculate that President Clinton actually wanted centrist judges, not liberal judges. And it is not speculative to say that the Republican Senate would not have easily stood for liberal equivalents to Posner or Easterbook—say, Laurence Tribe, Bruce Ackerman, or Jack Balkin. As I will suggest, it would be best if the Court had at least one such liberal equivalent—not (in my view) because those views are right (I believe that they are wrong) but because they are likely to add something valuable to the Court's deliberations. Of course President Clinton should not be faulted for failing to attempt to reshape the judiciary under circumstances in which Republican Senators simply would not have permitted the reshaping to occur.

For their part, Democratic senators, largely unwilling to base rejection of nominees on political disagreements, have usually deferred to Republican presidents. They have rarely made an issue of right-wing

3. See Cass R. Sunstein, One Case at a Time (1999).

nominees, especially but not only on the lower courts. To be sure, there have been prominent exceptions, the most visible of which was the sustained effort by the Democrats to defeat President Reagan's nomination of Robert Bork to the Supreme Court. But the success came at a high price. Partly because Judge Bork was treated so unfairly by liberal interest groups, the process infuriated and energized Republicans. The process also chastened the Democrats, who feared seeming obstructionist and who generally became more passive in its aftermath. The intense political effort to prevent the confirmation of Justice Clarence Thomas is a prominent counterexample. But in general, the Democrats have been willing to acquiesce in the choices of Republican presidents, whereas Republicans have taken an exceedingly aggressive stand.

The result of all this? We are now in the midst of a remarkable period of right-wing judicial activism. The Supreme Court has moderates but no liberals—no one who stands as a jurisprudential successor to Justices William Brennan and Thurgood Marshall. The so-called liberal wing actually consists of two moderate Republicans (John Paul Stevens and David Souter) and two moderate Democrats who represent centrist thinking (Ruth Bader Ginsburg and Stephen Breyer). *In fact the Rehnquist Court has struck down more federal laws per year than any Supreme Court in the last half century.* Consider a few brief illustrations:

- The Rehnquist Court has reinvigorated the commerce clause as a serious limitation on congressional power, for the first time since the New Deal itself. As a result, a number of existing federal statutes have been thrown into constitutional doubt.
- The Rehnquist Court has sharply limited congressional authority under Section 5 of the Fourteenth Amendment, in the process striking down key provisions of the Americans With Disabilities Act, the Religious Freedom Restoration Act, and the Violence Against Women Act, all of which received bipartisan support.

- The Rehnquist Court has imposed serious barriers to campaign finance legislation—with Justices Scalia and Thomas suggesting that they would be prepared to strike down almost all legislation limiting campaign contributions and expenditures.
- The Rehnquist Court has thrown affirmative action programs into extremely serious question, raising the possibility that public employers and schools will not be able to operate such programs.
- In many cases, the Rehnquist Court has interpreted regulatory statutes extremely narrowly, choosing the interpretation that gives as little as possible to victims of discrimination, pollution, and other misconduct.

Republican politicians have been equally interested in the lower courts because the vast majority of rulings never make it to the Supreme Court. Conservative judges in these lower courts, many appointed by President Reagan, are now determining the current direction of the judiciary, and here the Republican Party platform, in any of the past years, gives a clue to that direction.

A Jurisprudential Notation, or Were the Framers Reaganites? The close resemblance between the positions of conservative federal judges and the Republican Party platform raises many questions, and I will not attempt to answer those questions here. A crude version of the view that "Law is politics," enjoying an academic rebirth in the aftermath of *Bush* v. *Gore,* would ask: So what else is new? On one view, any position on the meaning of the Constitution is inescapably "political." But many contemporary conservatives, including some of the current justices, would undoubtedly respond that they are speaking for the Constitution as it was originally understood, and not for any party position in the least. They would urge that they are "originalists," or "textualists," speaking for the document and for history.

This response has some validity. It would be ludicrous to contend that Justices Scalia and Thomas are simply voting their political convictions and that their pretense to legality is a mere fraud. But there are several puzzles here. The adoption of any particular approach to constitutional interpretation, including "originalism" or "textualism," has to be justified and not merely asserted. Any effort to justify an approach would have to speak at least partly in terms of the consequences; it must be contended that the system would, in one sense or another, be better if that approach were adopted. To the extent that Justices Scalia and Thomas prefer textualism and originalism, it must be, in part at least, because those approaches make the world better from their own point of view. On what other ground could an approach to interpretation be defended?

But there are other problems. It is extremely difficult to justify the equal protection holding in *Bush* v. *Gore* on originalist grounds; the votes of Justices Scalia and Thomas, without even a brief nod to history, stand as a large embarrassment to their purported jurisprudential commitments. Nor is the case isolated on this count. Justices Scalia and Thomas have made plain their constitutional opposition to affirmative action programs. But they have yet to explain, in even a brief paragraph, how "originalism" justifies that opposition. Both justices are also opposed to campaign finance regulation, but they have not explained how the First Amendment, interpreted in originalist fashion, justifies their views or their votes. Both justices have suggested that the Constitution forbids Congress from granting citizens a right to sue, but they have not investigated the relevant history, even though they have voted to strike down democratically enacted legislation, and even though the history seems to argue against their positions.

In these circumstances, the general resemblance between the Republican Party platform and the view of conservative federal judges stands unexplained on traditional legal grounds. I do not believe that law is, in any sense, "just politics," but it seems clear that right-wing political commitments have been playing a significant role on the Supreme Court—not just in *Bush* v. *Gore*, but far more generally.

What Should Be Done

If President Bush follows the path set by his predecessors, and if Democrats remain passive, the federal judiciary will lurch ever more rightward. What might the future look like? We could easily imagine a situation in which federal judges

- Strike down affirmative action programs, perhaps eliminating such programs entirely
- Strike down campaign finance reform
- Invalidate portions of the Endangered Species Act and the Clean Water Act
- Reinvigorate a controversial understanding of the Second Amendment, so as to prevent Congress and the states from enacting certain gun control legislation
- Elevate commercial advertising to the same basic status as political speech, thus preventing controls on advertisements by tobacco companies (among others)
- Further reduce congressional power under the commerce clause
- Generally limit democratic efforts to protect disabled people, women, and the elderly from various forms of discrimination
- Significantly extend the reach of the "takings" clause, thus limiting environmental and other regulatory legislation
- Ban Congress from allowing citizens to sue to ensure enforcement of the law
- And much more

Should anything be done about such prospects? In an ideal world, neither Democrats nor Republicans would have to think, most of the time, about the political convictions of judicial nominees. In such a world, both Republicans and Democrats would insist on high-quality judges who would decide cases based on legal grounds that could be accepted by people with diverse views. In my view, rule by left-wing judges is no better than rule by right-wing judges. In the 1970s, I believe, Republicans were right to attack undemocratic, overly ambitious rulings of the Warren Court. Yet by focusing so carefully on judicial appointments, Republicans have also produced an undemocratic judiciary, one with far too little respect for the prerogatives of the elected branches.

If President Bush seeks judges with political missions, there is only one remedy. As a minimal step, the Senate should be prepared to block any effort by Mr. Bush to fill the courts with people of a particular ideological stripe. Of course the Senate has the power to refuse to consent to a presidential appointment, and the Senate should deny its consent to nominees who cannot demonstrate that they have a healthy respect for democratic prerogatives and will refuse to participate in the general effort to engraft new constitutional limitations on congressional power. Justices Scalia and Thomas have been distinguished members of the Court, and their voices deserve to be heard. But a Court that marched to their tune would make unacceptable inroads on democratic self-government. The Senate should not permit this to happen.

The Senate also has power to provide "advice" to the president. Indeed, the Constitution's framers intended the Senate's "advice and consent" role to provide security against what they greatly feared: an overreaching president willing to dominate the judiciary.[4] In fact, the framers were strongly opposed to an exclusive presidential role in the selection of federal judges, and they gave the appointment power to the president with considerable reluctance, and only with the understanding that the Senate would be playing a significant role as well. During important periods in the past, the Senate has in fact asserted a strong role as adviser.[5] In 1932, for example, Herbert Hoover's choice

4. See David A. Strauss and Cass R. Sunstein, The Senate, the Constitution, and the Confirmation Process, 101 Yale L. J. 1491 (1992).
5. See Laurence H. Tribe, God Save This Honorable Court (1989).

of Benjamin Cardozo was greatly influenced by senators who insisted on a liberal justice to replace Oliver Wendell Holmes.

The Senate should reclaim its advisory role, collaborating to ensure the creation of a modest, and properly balanced, federal judiciary. There was real ugliness in Senator Hatch's occasional refusal to hold hearings for Clinton nominees. If Democratic senators replicated Senator Hatch's aggressive approach, there would be far less ugliness in it, if only because the replication could be justified not as retaliation but as an effort to produce more in the way of balance within the federal judiciary. It is ironic but true that Senator Hatch's repeated and quite ludicrous complaints about "judicial activism" make far more sense as an attack on Justices Scalia and Thomas than on Justices Ginsburg and Breyer. The Senate would be well within its rights to complain about conservative judicial activism and to insist on a role in "advising" the president about the appropriate mix of federal judges, on the lower courts as well as the Supreme Court.

What does this mean in particular? It suggests, above all, that the Senate should attempt to ensure a sensible mix of views, and to promote intellectual diversity within the federal courts. This does not mean that the Senate should attempt to block all or most nominees whose views seem unacceptable. The president is due a measure of deference. Nor does it mean that the Senate should insist on "liberals" of any kind. But it does mean that the Senate should ensure that the Supreme Court, and the courts of appeals, will show a high degree of intellectual diversity, so that particular courts are not "stacked" with judges of a certain stripe. Thus, for example, an appointment of a conservative and a moderate, to any particular court of appeals, should be regarded relatively sympathetically, whereas an appointment of two extreme conservatives should be regarded skeptically, especially if the relevant court is already stacked with conservatives. An appropriate balance is especially desirable because like-minded people, not forced to confront opposing positions, tend to move in quite extreme directions.[6] Intellectual diversity is necessary both to avoid extremism and to ensure that issues are adequately ventilated in the process of judicial deliberation.

Of course, the ideas of "appropriate balance" and "sensible mix" are not self-defining. People with different views on what is correct will also have different views about what is an appropriate balance. I mean to suggest, by such ideas, that the federal judiciary should not be entirely out of line with the pattern of responsible opinion within the legal culture—and that it should include a spread of views corresponding, at least roughly, to the existing spread within that culture. A Supreme Court that moved in the directions outlined above, or indeed that continued the most disturbing current trends toward right-wing judicial activism, would represent a large-scale departure from the pattern of responsible opinion.

A clarification: in making these points, I do not mean to offer any general, context-independent points about the appropriate relation between the Senate and the president. Much depends on what kind of federal judiciary, and Supreme Court, we now have. If the Court were properly balanced, and if it were not so willing to intrude into democratic processes, it would be entirely appropriate for the Senate to confirm President Bush's choices. If the Court lacked anyone with Justice Scalia's views, and if it was tilted to the left, it would be appropriate to confirm someone like Justice Scalia, and perhaps even appropriate to insist on someone like Justice Scalia. In some circumstances, the president should care a great deal about "ideology" and seek justices who would move the Court in a certain direction. I believe that it would have been fully appropriate for President Clinton to choose at least one such justice, though of course this was not feasible as a political matter. My plea for an aggressive senatorial role, designed to ensure against right-wing hubris, is a particular reaction to the recent highly successful effort, by Republican politicians, to recast the fed-

6. See Cass R. Sunstein, Designing Democracy ch. 1 (2001).

eral judiciary in a certain mold. A successful effort by Democrats, to create a left-wing judiciary with similar hubris, would properly meet with an aggressive Republican response.

Two Brief Definitional Notes

I have used several terms that deserve some definitional attention. The idea of "judicial activism" is an unusually vexed one, above all because any claim that judges are "activist" seems to depend on accepting a certain theory of legitimate interpretation. If originalism is the right approach to constitutional law, then Justice Scalia is no activist. If democracy reinforcement is the right approach to interpretation, then Earl Warren was hardly an activist. Here is the problem: if we need to agree on a theory of interpretation in order to know whether judges are activist, discussion of the topic of "activism" will become extremely difficult and in a way pointless. A disagreement about whether judges are activist will really be a disagreement about how judges should be approaching the Constitution; the notions of activism and restraint will have added nothing.

To avoid the problem, I am using a neutral definition here. A court is activist when and to the extent that it is willing to strike down legislation or other acts and decisions by other branches of government. On this view, to call a court "activist" is not necessarily to condemn it. It is on this view that the Rehnquist Court counts as the most activist in the nation's history, simply because and to the extent that it has struck down more federal laws, on an annual basis, than any of its predecessor courts. To be sure, this statistic does not tell us everything we need to know. But it is highly suggestive about current tendencies and trends.

I have also said that the current Court has moderates but no liberals. Of course terms of this sort are extremely crude and can be quite confusing. If we are to use such terms, as a kind of helpful shorthand, there is a further problem, for we seem to lack a neutral way of defining them. In this chapter I have used the terms to refer to the range of reasonable professional opinion. Along that range, William Brennan and Thurgood Marshall count as liberals; such academics as Bruce Ackerman, Jack Balkin, Derrick Bell, and Frank Michelman are in the same basic category; Ruth Bader Ginsburg, Sandra Day O'Connor, David Souter, and Stephen Breyer are in the center; Antonin Scalia, Clarence Thomas, and Stephen Williams are genuine conservatives. The Court has no liberals in the sense that none of its members would follow in the path set by Brennan and Marshall. I have lamented this situation, not because I believe that this is the correct path but because a Court that lacks anyone committed to it is missing something important—just as a Court lacking the views of Scalia and Thomas would be missing something important. By these measures, a significant problem with the current Court is that despite its unusually high level of intellectual distinction, it has a heavy right wing, a heavy center, but no left at all.

I am not suggesting that the Senate should insist this problem be corrected. Under the constitutional plan, the president is entitled to a certain measure of respect, and President Bush is simply not going to choose a liberal Supreme Court justice. The Senate should not require that vacancies be filled by those on the left but should instead see to it that any nominees have a proper respect for democratic prerogatives and that the judiciary as a whole will not continue to trend toward right-wing judicial activism.

The (Ir)Relevance of *Bush* v. *Gore*

In defending an aggressive role for the Senate, I have said little about *Bush* v. *Gore*. In fact I believe *that the argument for this aggressive role would be exactly the same if Bush had won Florida decisively, and if* Bush v. Gore *had never been decided.* The basic problem is the nature of the federal judiciary, not the risk that the current Court will have "picked its successors." I do not entirely lack sympathy for the provocative suggestion, pressed most prominently by Bruce Ackerman, that the Senate should declare a kind of moratorium on the confirmation of new Supreme Court justices. But on reflection, this proposal seems to me to appear, and to be, unduly rigid and obstructionist. The Court functions best if it has nine members, and so long as the Senate is allowed to act as a partner in choosing the Court's membership, constructive engagement is the far better path.

I add one qualification to my general plea for the irrelevance of *Bush v. Gore.* The decision stands as the most prominent illustration of the most disturbing current tendency within the federal courts—a tendency to play politics by other means and, without the slightest hesitation, to second-guess the judgments of other officials. There is an eerie resemblance between large-scale current trends within the federal judiciary and the Republican Party platform since the days of Ronald Reagan. This tendency can be seen in multiple arenas, within the lower federal courts as well as the Supreme Court. It is placing a cloud over democratic judgments of many kinds, involving campaign finance, federalism, affirmative action, environmental protection, and much more.

For those troubled by *Bush v. Gore,* the real task is to look forward, not backward. It is past time to get over *Bush v. Gore* as such. It is time to think instead about the Supreme Court's alarming and increasingly immodest conception of its role in the constitutional system—and of how to use the various branches of government to restore the federal judiciary to its appropriate place.

Off Balance

We are in the fourth phase of the Republican Revolution. The first began with Newt Gingrich's victory of 1994. The Contract with America expressed the ambition, shared by every generation in our history, to rewrite the terms of the social contract between the People and their Government. Gingrich's government shutdown provided a wonderful way of dramatizing the aspirations of the rising movement: let's go cold turkey on the nanny state inherited from FDR and LBJ, and the American people will hardly notice; or if they do, they will jubilate in their new-found market freedom.

The moment bore comparison with Martin Luther King's March on Washington or Franklin Roosevelt's presidential victory in 1932. The only difference was that Gingrich lost the battle for public opinion. Such failed constitutional moments have occurred quite often in American history, with the losing side reluctantly retreating to the standard deal-making of normal politics.

But this time the Republicans refused to admit defeat. A small sign was a remarkable decision handed down by the Supreme Court in the immediate afterglow of Gingrich's rise to power. In *Lopez* v. *United States,* a sharply divided Court struck down an act of Congress as beyond the powers of the national government. This was the first time since the New Deal that the Court asserted such an authority.

The majority was composed of the same five judges who would later decide *Bush* v. *Gore*. But at this point they were far more cautious. They targeted a minor statute—the Gun Free Schools Act—which did not have powerful political defenders who would launch an immediate counterattack on the Court's effort to limit the power of Congress to solve national problems. But the decision did put the legal mandarins on notice of the Court's revolutionary intentions. Its open-ended opinion potentially undermined the powerful national government that Americans had built over the course of the twentieth century.

When *Lopez* came down in 1995, nobody could tell whether it was the opening shot in a great battle or a strategic feint soon to be forgotten—least of all the five justices who signed the opinion. This would depend on the subsequent course of constitutional politics in general, and the fate of judicial nominations in particular. To sustain a serious assault on the twentieth-century state, it would not be enough for Gingrich to make revolutionary gestures from his perch in the House of Representatives. He—or somebody like him—would have to win the presidency and convince the Senate to replace the aging justices from the Ford-Reagan era with a new generation bent on pressing forward with the assault against the twentieth century.

Immediate prospects were dim. Reeling from the popular repudiation of the government shutdown, the Republicans' ardor was fading on Capitol Hill. To symbolize a retreat to normal politics, the party chose Robert Dole as its presidential nominee—that most unrevolutionary of pols.

But paradoxically, Clinton's reelection served to provoke a recrudescence of mobilized Republican commitment. As in the case of the government shutdown, the constitutional separation of powers set the stage for some grand political theater. Once again the House leadership drew deep from its armory of constitutional weapons of last resort—but this time, its weapon of choice was the power of impeachment, and the aim was not to turn the tide against the welfare state but to signal a definitive return to an older morality of truth-telling and sexual probity.

Future generations of legal scholars will be scratching their heads in disbelief at the suggestion that the Lewinsky episode amounted to a "high crime or misdemeanor." But the public's reaction was much more important than any scholarly opinion. As the proceeding marched on to its tragicomic conclusion, ordinary Americans made it emphatically clear that the Republicans were overreaching. Whatever one may think of the president's effort to cover up his sexual transgressions, it was not just cause for ejecting him from the White House.

There are few iron laws of American politics, but here is one of them: the off-year elections inevitably show a victory for the party that does not control the White House. During the twentieth century, there was only one exception to this rule—1934, when a Democratic landslide confirmed the signal given by Roosevelt's victory two years before. And 1998 proved another exception: in response to the Republicans' impeachment plans, the voters handed the party a significant defeat.

But the revolutionaries in the House refused to listen. They went right on to impeach the president in a lame duck session. The fact that they were going to lose votes in the new Congress only made them more eager to rush while they could still ram the bill of impeachment through the House.

This second phase of the Republican Revolution was no more successful than the first. But it was far more disturbing from the vantage of democratic principle. The Republicans did win big in the 1994 elections, and if Speaker Gingrich wished to claim a mandate for revolutionary change, he was doing no more than other popular leaders had done before him. Most of these leaders have been presidents, but if we go back to the nineteenth century, we can find a fascinating precedent for Gingrich's effort to lead a revolution from the House of Representatives. This was precisely the institutional dynamic after the Civil War, when Thaddeus Stevens led the Republican majority in the House to launch a successful campaign for the Fourteenth Amendment. Gingrich was acting well within the precedents when he made a similar effort on the basis of the sweeping Republican victory in 1994.

But Henry Hyde and Ken Starr pushed on without any such popular mandate, asserting the right to disrupt the normal course of presidential government. Their willingness to take extraordinary constitutional actions in the teeth of public opinion is very disturbing. But their efforts failed, and for that, I suppose, we should be grateful.

Until we turn to *Bush* v. *Gore,* which marks the third stage in the Republican Revolution. Like the House's decision in *Ken Starr v. Bill Clinton,* the Court's decision in *Bush* v. *Gore* represented a shocking revision of prevailing constitutional understandings surrounding presidential succession—except that, as a matter of law, the decision was much worse.

In moving forward with the impeachment, the House managers did advance coherent legal arguments to justify their precedent-shattering step. The question—not a small one—was whether these arguments were outweighed by the legal arguments on the other side. Whatever one's view, at least the managers could put coherent sentences and paragraphs together as they explained why Clinton's coverup was the legal equivalent of "Treason, Bribery, or other High Crimes and Misdemeanors."

This is not true in *Bush* v. *Gore.* I do not suggest that the majority's equal protection rationale is silly. It isn't. The Constitution obviously applies to vote-counting, and the Court has an obligation to intervene if a recount is systematically skewed in favor of one side. The majority's application of this basic principle was controversial, but this is often true. And if the Court had simply ordered the Florida recount to proceed under its newly minted standards, I would not be protesting in the name of the rule of law.

Bush v. *Gore* does not veer off the tracks until the next stage: where the Supreme Court refuses to allow Florida to continue its recount under the new standards required by equal protection. *To demand equal protection but to prevent Florida from satisfying this demand*—this is not bad legal judgment; this is sheer willfulness.

The Court's defense—that no time remained for Florida to meet the state's own December 12 deadline—is simply preposterous. Florida law contains no such "deadline." Every lawyer knows that the Supreme Court should have sent the case back to the Florida courts to determine the next step after weighing all the relevant legal factors—including the 1960 precedent established by Congress when it allowed Hawaii to change its electoral vote on the basis of a recount as late as December 28. By plucking a deadline out of thin air, the Court was willfully preempting not only Florida but also Congress—to which both the constitutional and statutory text has, as Steven Calabresi emphasizes, confided ultimate decision-making authority.

And the Court gave *no* legally valid reason for this act of usurpation.

Not even the House managers proceeded in such an arbitrary fashion in *Starr* v. *Clinton*. And if they had, they could have pointed to the precedent of President Andrew Johnson's impeachment, when the principal House manager told the Senate: "You are bound by no law, either statutory or common, which may limit your constitutional prerogative. . . . *salus populi suprema est lex.*"[1]

But the Supreme Court is a court. It has never asserted the sovereign prerogative to transcend the rule of law for "the good of the country." And this was a particularly bad time to indulge such pretensions. After all, the Democrats had already seen their last president destroyed by an impeachment that struck many as grossly disproportionate to the offense. Was this really the right time for the Court to hurl a second thunderbolt at Democratic pretensions to the White House?

Whatever difficulties Congress may have had in resolving the electoral college crisis in January—and these are easily exaggerated[2]—the Court was risking something far more precious: the losers' confidence in the integrity of the system. *Starr* v. *Clinton* was bad enough

1. I discuss this episode in We the People: Transformations 227–30 (1998).
2. I discuss this matter further in Anatomy of a Constitutional Coup, London Review of Books, pp. 4–8 (February 8, 2001), reprinted in Arthur J. Jacobson and Michel Rosenfeld, The Longest Night: Polemics and Perspectives on Election 2000 (2001).

without the knockout punch of *Bush* v. *Gore*. Better for the Court to leave the rule of law intact, and let the chips fall where they may, rather than raise awkward questions: With Bill Clinton *and* Al Gore destroyed by extraordinary constitutional actions, will the next Democratic president be allowed to govern with the deference regularly accorded Republican presidents? Or will Democratic presidents regularly find themselves exposed to extraordinary constitutional assault by the other branches?

The Court's offense against the rule of law cannot be excused, then, by a hand-waving appeal to the "national interest" in rapid resolution of the presidential contest. Of course, it was nice to resolve the matter on December 12 rather than sometime in January. But not at the cost of creating a pattern of extraordinary interventions that systematically disparage one side in the ongoing contest for the presidency. This point would be irrelevant if the Court's decision to call it quits on December 12 was plausibly grounded in legal reasoning.

But it wasn't.

It is a mistake, then, to liken *Bush* v. *Gore* to other great cases—*Dred Scott* or *Lochner* or *Brown* or *Roe*—where the Court handed down a decision of ramifying political consequence. In the other cases, the justices made great efforts to enunciate enduring principles rooted in the nation's historic constitutional commitments. Such efforts are inevitably controversial, both in the short and long run, but these controversies are an intrinsic part of the practice of judicial review. In contrast, the scandal surrounding *Bush* v. *Gore* involves not the Court's principles but the refusal by the five-judge majority to give Florida a chance to live up to them.

Bush v. *Gore* is different in a second way. When the justices handed down other major decisions, their initial pronouncements never operated as the final word. They served to precipitate a great democratic debate that ultimately determined the fate of the judicial initiative. If the justices failed to persuade a broad majority of the rightness of their reading of our enduring principles, their judgments have not survived—and a good thing, too.

Bush v. *Gore* disrupts this ongoing process of political contestation. In our democracy, there is one basic check on a runaway Court: presidential elections. As the wheel of mortality turns, presidents can reshape the constitutional agenda by nominating new justices who are critics of the reigning jurisprudence. If the president can convince the Senate to send them to the high court, he can successfully realign the Court's jurisprudence and lead the Court to abandon great cases that have failed to command sustained support in democratic politics.

Bush v. *Gore* liberates the Court from this ultimate check on its authority. It is one thing for unelected judges to exercise the sovereign power of judicial review; quite another for them to select the president who selects their successors. By taking this extraordinary action, the reigning judicial majority has insulated its constitutional doctrine from the fundamental democratic check on the abuse of its authority.

And at an especially sensitive moment. As we have seen, the Court joined the first phase of the Republican Revolution with a 5–4 decision that, for the first time since the New Deal, struck down a federal statute as beyond the powers of Congress. Since 1995, it has followed up with a series of decisions chipping away at the constitutional foundations of national government. The reigning majority has chosen its targets carefully—it has not yet invalidated a major statute in a way that would catalyze a massive political reaction. Even its recent decision striking down the Violence Against Women Act involved a relatively minor remedial provision. But taken together, these opinions are adding up to an intoxicating jurisprudential brew. While the general public may suppose that only *Roe* v. *Wade* is in jeopardy, the Court is laying the groundwork for a wide-ranging assault on a host of statutes protecting the environment, guaranteeing equality, and furthering social welfare.

More precisely, *five members of the Court* have committed themselves to this remarkable project—the very same "Five" making up the majority in *Bush* v. *Gore*. Though their revolutionary opinions run roughshod over the eloquent protests of the dissenting four, the dominating Five are perfectly aware of the risks they are running. The Five's actions speak louder than their words: their refusal to strike down any major statutes shows they are well aware that the time is not yet ripe for an all-out effort to repeal the constitutional law of the twentieth century.

To take an example almost at random, the Endangered Species Act seems endangered by the Five's emerging doctrines: Does Congress's power over interstate commerce embrace such noncommercial regulations as a ban on taking animals? How can this act to *preserve* Nature from commercial exploitation be reconciled with the Five's narrow reading of the "commerce" clause?

Don't expect the Five to answer anytime soon. Before the Court strikes down pivotal statutes like the Endangered Species Act, the Five will need reinforcement from a new generation of vigorous conservative jurists, eager to carry the recent pathbreaking jurisprudence to its "logical" conclusion. Only after the Five are refreshed with some young blood will the Court have the intellectual energy, and the lengthy period of control, required to take the conservative struggle against the twentieth century to a new stage.

Here is where the Five's decision in *Bush* v. *Gore* enters. By intervening in the presidential contest, the Five have dramatically changed the future prospects of their revolutionary jurisprudence. To put the point operationally, suppose that Al Gore had made it into the White House, and was faced with the task of filling a vacancy opened by the resignation of Chief Justice Rehnquist or Justice O'Connor. Does anybody suppose that any of his nominees would seriously contemplate joining an opinion striking down the Endangered Species Act?

A Gore presidency would have done more than stop the Five's revolutionary jurisprudence in its tracks. It would have forced their enterprise into reverse gear. Justices Breyer and Ginsburg are mainstream moderates, not aggressive liberals, when measured against the likes of Justices Brennan and Marshall. But it doesn't take a liberal to dissent from the Five's revolutionary doctrines—as the steady stream of vigorous opinions by Breyer, Ginsburg, Souter, and Stevens demonstrates. One more judicial appointment cut from Clintonian cloth would have sufficed to tip the balance of judicial power—generating a series of 5–4 decisions overruling the recent 5–4 cases marking the Five's premature push for a decisive turn in the path of the law. A Gore presidency, in short, would have dashed the deepest hopes of the present majority on the Supreme Court.

The crucial question is the constitutional status of this thought-experiment. One thing is clear: we will never know who would be president today if the Supreme Court had allowed the Florida vote count to proceed—perhaps Bush, perhaps Gore. It was the Supreme Court Five, *and nobody else,* who resolved this uncertainty and made my Gore scenario only a thought-experiment. By taking this action, the Court has revolutionized its relationship to the rest of the government as well as the voters. As every schoolchild knows, the voters elect the president and the Senate, who then select the justices. But when the justices intervene to determine the presidency, they have shattered these well-established lines of constitutional authority and have left the Senate as *the* institution with a normal relationship to the voters.

This simple point provides the way out of our unprecedented situation. In exercising its constitutional authority to "advise and consent," the Senate should not conduct business as usual when confronting presidential nominations to the high court. Because the Court has destroyed the normal constitutional equilibrium, it has placed the Senate in an extraordinary position. *As the only institution with an undisturbed relationship to the electorate, the Senate has a special obligation to protect the People from a runaway Court.*

There are different ways to discharge this special responsibility—if you are persuaded that it exists. Before moving to these (important) questions of strategy, a careful scrutiny of basic premises is in order. First off, the Senate's special constitutional responsibilities do not depend on speculative accounts of the Five's motives in deciding *Bush v. Gore*. Even if they were as pure as the driven snow, noble motives cannot change hard facts: judicial intervention has disrupted the constitutional equilibrium, leaving the Senate as the only institution in a normal relationship to the electoral process.

Nor does the Senate's special responsibility depend on my previous claim that the Five's abrupt termination of the recount was without *any* basis in law—though surely this doesn't help matters! To establish the existence of constitutional disequilibrium, it is more than enough to say that the Court's intervention was open to profound legal question—the chapters in this book surely establish this much. After all, nominations normally come from presidents whose claim to office is *completely* independent of the will of the reigning Supreme Court majority. It is this condition of complete independence that makes his power over nominations such a basic tool in the ongoing effort to keep the Court under democratic control. But this normal situation does not exist today, and it will not recur until the next president is selected on election day of 2004.

By the same token, the Senate's special responsibility does not require anybody to challenge President Bush's constitutional authority to hold office. The Supreme Court's decision in *Bush v. Gore* was accepted by Al Gore and Congress when the time came to count the electoral votes. The underlying difference in Florida was vanishingly small, and the right thing to do is to grin and bear it. Although one would hope for cautious moderation from George Bush, he is the only president we have, and he is entitled to exercise his legal powers to the full.

But the Constitution gives Bush the power only to make judicial nominations. It is entirely up to the Senate to reject any or all of them. And in making its confirmation decisions, it is perfectly appropriate—nay imperative—for the Senate to confront the fact that *Bush v. Gore* has thrown the appointments process into constitutional disequilibrium. The point is a structural one—instead of two independent checks on the Court, there is now only one. With the president's relationship to the citizenry mediated by the Court, only the Senate retains a normal connection to the electorate, and this requires it to accept an extraordinarily heavy burden of leadership on judicial appointments until normal conditions are reestablished. Q.E.D.

Now is the time to take the next step: How should the Senate discharge its special responsibilities during constitutional disequilibrium?

There are two options. The first, which I favor, is that Senators should wait for the system to regain equilibrium on its own before confirming any new justices to the Court. Before President Bush can expect to place any of his nominees on the Court, he should be required to win the 2004 election fair and square, without the Court's help. Alternatively, the Senate might consider first-term nominations on the merits, but without any of the deference accorded ordinary presidents. The burden should be on each nominee to establish that he or she will serve with the judicious moderation of David Souter rather than the revolutionary zeal of Clarence Thomas.

I reach the first approach by eliminating the second. After all, the confirmation hearings before the Senate Judiciary Committee were never designed to function as the *principal* check on a runaway Court. To the contrary, and for good reason, the Senate normally understands itself as a backstop to the president and designs its hearings with this function in mind.

After all, the president ran in all fifty states and won a mandate from the People to govern. An important part of governing is to consider how well the Court is doing and to use judicial nominations to keep the Court in line with prevailing public opinion. When the president exercises this prerogative, the Senate has in fact given his choice a lot of deference. At best, the hearings before the Senate judiciary committee serve as a secondary check, and it is a fair question whether they accomplish even this much.

Take the two nominations of the elder Bush: David Souter and Clarence Thomas. Put yourself in the position of a thoughtful senator peering through the smoke and mirrors of media hype surrounding the confirmation hearings. Could you confidently predict that it was going to be Thomas, and not Souter, who would become a right-wing extremist?

I'm not so sure. One could plausibly believe that Souter was a right-wing "stealth candidate," whom Bush nominated to exploit senatorial deference in the absence of seriously damaging evidence. One could also think that Thomas's experience as an African American would temper his conservative leanings once he had liberated himself from his presidential handlers. Although the present level of strategic obfuscation is much too high, perhaps it is barely tolerable under normal conditions—when the president *properly* takes the leading role in the appointments process. As the president and his headhunters narrow the list of nominees down to a single name, they are privy to all sorts of confidential information (including private interviews with the candidate). This provides them with much better information than is available to the Senate later on. Because it is normally up to the president to take the leading role in deciding whether the Court's makeup requires substantial readjustment, one can only be happy that he has better information than does the Senate.

This is definitely not the case during our present period of disequilibrium. If the Senate has a special responsibility to take the leadership role until the next presidential election, it simply lacks the tools to make case-by-case assessments in a thoughtful manner. This might not be so serious if the younger Bush showed serious signs of recognizing the unprecedented situation the Supreme Court has placed him in. But, to put it mildly, this seems to be the last thing he has in mind.

Given the remarkable events surrounding his ascent to the presidency, the path of constitutional statesmanship for George W. Bush was clear. Govern from the center with moderation. Propose a sensible reform of the electoral college, and campaign for its enactment by Congress and the states. Make it a first priority of your administration to guarantee the American People that the election of 2004 will not involve a replay of the fiasco of 2000.

This has not happened. The present administration is pretending that George W. Bush has a broad popular mandate to continue the Republican Revolution. It is as if the American People had elected Newt Gingrich by a landslide and Republicans in the House and Senate had won big majorities in the 2000 elections. During its first months in office, the Administration showed no interest in changing the law to guarantee that the presidential election of 2004 will not generate another crisis in the electoral college. Instead, it has focused its energies on rushing a tax cut of Reaganesque proportion through the Congress.

The president's initial moves on judicial appointments were no less troubling. As one of his first acts, he peremptorily dismissed the American Bar Association from its traditional role in vetting candidates for judicial nomination—a position the ABA has been accorded by every president since Eisenhower. The new administration cited the ABA's role in the Bork nomination as its principal reason for eliminating this check on presidential authority. Not that the ABA was a lion in the Bork affair—a majority of its committee found the nominee qualified to serve. But its endorsement was lukewarm, and this was enough: better to take the heat early for breaking with tradition than run the risk of ABA resistance to some future Bork-like nomination. No administration with moderate ambitions for the Supreme Court would have the foresight, or the determination, to make such a costly decision so early in its tenure—when so many more immediate matters were pressing for attention.

The constitutional response to this display of Gingrichian pretension does credit to the system of checks and balances. If President Bush had taken the path of constitutional statesmanship, Senator Jeffords would never have abandoned the Republican Party, handing the Democrats control of the Senate. But by pretending to a mandate that he did not receive, he pushed Jeffords to take action that began to repair the constitutional disequilibrium left in the wake of *Bush* v. *Gore*. The question is whether the Senate will continue to take the necessary steps to stabilize the system when Supreme Court vacancies arise.

The Republicans' loss of the Senate makes it even more likely that the president will not nominate somebody like Robert Bork—whose voluminous writings made plain his intention to lead the Court's revolutionary assault on the constitutional law of the late twentieth century. Instead, he will follow in his father's footsteps and try to deflect public attention from his nominee's substantive constitutional commitments. Just as his father put Clarence Thomas on the bench, the son will be tempted to nominate a right-wing Latino—diverting public attention from the nominee's right-wing creed to whether the Democrats dare to reject the first Hispanic nominee to the Supreme Court. And if the Democrats say no, the president can always nominate a "stealth candidate"—making sure this time that his cipher is more like Anthony Kennedy than David Souter. Or he may nominate a right-wing senator and invite the Senate to ignore mere matters of ideology and allow a fellow member of the "greatest club on earth" to ascend to the marble palace. This strategy worked for the president when he nominated John Ashcroft as attorney general, and—who knows?—it may work again.

But it shouldn't. The Senate should not defer to President Bush to the same degree it deferred to his father's nominations of Clarence Thomas and David Souter—for the simple reason that the father won the 1988 election without the assistance of the Supreme Court, while the son did not. Given this fact, the Senate must operate as the principal check on a runaway Court until the next presidential election can rectify the existing disequilibrium. Because there is abundant reason to doubt that the Senate will be able to discharge this high responsibility through case-by-case determinations, it should follow the old Hippocratic maxim: *do no harm.*

It should simply refuse to hold any confirmation hearings until nature take its course and the present constitutional disequilibrium resolves itself with the presidential election of 2004.

There is no compelling need to fill vacancies before 2004. The Supreme Court has often functioned perfectly well without its full complement. During the 1990s, the justices have cut their work load dramatically and now deliver only eighty opinions of the Court each year. They can easily maintain this pace even if two or three vacancies open up. There will be time enough for President Bush to fill these positions if he wins the 2004 election without the Court's assistance.

The remedy I propose is unprecedented, but so is our situation. There is, however, a historical episode that comes close enough to shed some light. When President Lincoln was assassinated, he was replaced by Andrew Johnson, who threatened to nominate justices who would consolidate the conservative wing of the Court. The Reconstruction Congress responded with a statute providing that retiring justices could not be replaced. By the time Johnson left the White House in 1868, the Court was reduced to seven members. After the election, Congress returned the Court's size to nine, giving Ulysses S. Grant the power to fill the vacancies that it had denied his predecessor.[3]

The Reconstruction Congress explained that it was John Wilkes Booth, not the American People, who had transformed Andrew Johnson into the president. They would not have deprived Abraham Lincoln of the power to make appointments. A similar logic applies today. The five-judge majority that presently dominates the Court should not be permitted to extend its control for a decade or more simply because it has put George W. Bush into the White House.

Given the temporary character of the present disequilibrium, there is no need for Congress to pass a new statute to make this point. It is enough for the Senate Judiciary Committee to announce that the confirmation hearings it conducts are simply inadequate to discharge the high responsibilities thrust upon it by the present constitutional

3. See my We the People: Transformations 239 (1998).

disequilibrium and that it will simply wait until this condition is cured by the routine operation of the electoral calendar.

But suppose the committee decides to move ahead? Then this decision should be understood as tentative. If the hearings generate a media circus, deflecting the debate onto irrelevant matters, it would be perfectly appropriate for the committee to refuse to forward the nomination to the floor. Without a compelling informational basis for the nomination, the committee will simply be failing to respond to the high responsibilities cast upon it by *Bush* v. *Gore*.

Even if the committee does send a nomination forward, Senate rules give forty-one members the power to block consideration on the floor—and normal notions of deference to presidential prerogatives should not deter senators from using this power to force a delay until the next election.

And if none of these checks on precipitous action prove efficacious, individual senators should be encouraged to reflect on the existing disequilibrium and invoke it as the basis for a consistent "No" vote on all Supreme Court nominations proffered during President Bush's current term in office.

There is an even better way out. All nine justices should simply remain on the bench until the next election. Death waits for no man, but—mortality aside—this is no time for a justice casually to precipitate a constitutional disequilibrium. All of them managed to remain in office for the last six years of Clinton's administration. They can do the same for four more years. Judicial restraint doesn't often require judges to hang on to power for as long as they can.

But life can be surprising.

Suppose, however, that the justices decline my invitation and choose to realize my worst fears. Rather than holding on for dear life, three incumbents—Chief Justice Rehnquist and Justices O'Connor and Stevens—call it quits. The Senate, in turn, ignores my plea and allows President Bush to smuggle three hard-right replacements onto the Court through an artful mixture of stealth candidacies, ethnic politics, and senatorial courtesy. The three new appointees join the Scalia-Thomas faction, and as the 2004 election draws near, Justice Scalia has become the chief—if not in name, then in reality.

Secure in their control of the Court for the next decade, the Scalia Five no longer have to bother with Justice Kennedy's anxious dilly-dallying. They proceed boldly to transform provocative dicta in recent cases into slashing attacks on the law of the late twentieth century.

The Republican Revolution moves into its final phase. With much talk of judicial restraint, *Roe* v. *Wade* is consigned to the dustbin of history. With much talk of the original intention of the founders, the Court tightens the constitutional straitjacket on the powers of the national government to pursue social and economic equality. As environmental protection is cut down to size to make room for the rights of private property, the power of the government is enhanced when it comes to the prosecution of Christian morality in the schoolrooms and bedrooms of the nation.

And then something funny happens: come 2004 or 2008, the Democrats sweep to power in the presidency and the Congress.

Perhaps the Democratic ascendancy will lead the Five to moderate a bit, but perhaps not.

The old-timers among them will recall the bad old 1990s when they outlasted President Clinton until he was discredited. Maybe this will happen again?

The rush of new case law has a dynamic of its own. By now the Five have written so many opinions establishing the "plain meaning" of the constitutional text that they will have forgotten how contestable their interpretations really are. It may seem to them like treason to abandon the "intention of the framers" merely because Americans of the twenty-first century insist on enhanced environmental protection, increased social equality, and greater powers for the national welfare state. Better to stay the course and uphold their version of the rule of law.

As six justices come together to strike down new statutory initiatives of the Democratic majority, the president calls upon Congress and the nation to consider how they have reached this impasse: "My fellow Americans, it would be one thing if the present Court had been selected in a fair and democratic fashion. But this is not the case. The president who created the present majority did not owe his office to the People. He owed it to the Supreme Court, which then allowed him to name its successors by resigning during his first term. When President Bush named these men and women to the high bench, they hardly gave an inkling of their intentions to make war on modern government. Yet this is what they have been doing."

What happens next?

Nothing good—that's for sure.

How likely is this scenario?

Your guess is as good as mine. But if you think the chances are significant, a temporary Senate moratorium on Supreme Court appointments begins to seem like a modest proposal at preemptive damage control.

Constitutional disequilibria have a nasty habit of spinning out of control.

JACK M. BALKIN **13**

Legitimacy and the 2000 Election

On December 12, 2000, the Supreme Court of the United States illegally stopped the presidential election and handed the presidency to George W. Bush.[1] Much of the anger about the 2000 election has been directed at the five conservatives on the Supreme Court. But it is important to remember that the Supreme Court would not have had the opportunity to intervene if there had not already been an equally serious problem of legitimacy on election day—massive black disenfranchisement in the crucial state of Florida. There is already enough evidence to suggest that Florida state officials violated the Federal Voting Rights Act and, in the process, denied Al Gore the presidency.[2]

Together, the combination of black disenfranchisement in Florida and the Supreme Court's decision in *Bush v. Gore* seriously undermines the legitimacy of the 2000 election. Nevertheless, on January 20, 2001, George W. Bush was sworn into office as the forty-third president of the United States by Chief Justice William Rehnquist—

My thanks to Bruce Ackerman, Sandy Levinson, and Reva Siegel for their comments on previous drafts of this chapter.

1. This claim is defended in Jack M. Balkin, Bush v. Gore and the Boundary Between Law and Politics, 110 Yale L. J. 1407 (2001).

2. See the report of the United States Civil Rights Commission, http://www .usccr.gov/vote2000/stdraft1/main.htm (last visited on July 24, 2001).

who, not coincidentally, helped deliver the presidency to Bush—and Bush began to govern as the nation's president for a full four-year term.

Then, only eight months into the new administration, on September 11, 2001, the United States was attacked. Terrorists bombed the Pentagon in Washington and destroyed the World Trade Center in New York. Thousands of people were killed. The country quickly rallied around its new president, who promised to bring those responsible to justice and to wage unremitting war against international terrorism. The crisis brought on by the events of September 11, and the need for national unity at this bleak hour, might seem to settle the question of the election's legitimacy once and for all. The nation must look to its president to lead it through the difficult times that lie ahead. Whether or not his ascension to power was entirely aboveboard, George W. Bush is, quite literally, the only president we have.

But events are far more complicated. Whether people like it or not, the politics of the next four years—and perhaps for years to come—will be shaped in subtle ways by doubts about the legitimacy of the 2000 election. There has been, and will continue to be, an ongoing dispute over the meaning of these events and the legitimacy of the Bush presidency. That dispute, in turn, will be shaped by how well the political parties handle the crises, difficulties, and opportunities of the next several years. By themselves the terrorist attacks do not decide the eventual verdict—they merely help define the terrain in which the dispute over legitimacy will be played out. The election of 2000 is over. But the struggle over its meaning will continue for a long time to come.

Presidents and Parliaments

The American Constitution deals with claims of illegitimacy differently from many other democratic systems. If the 2000 election had occurred in a parliamentary democracy, a prime minister who had been elected with razor thin margins under a cloud of suspicion would face an endless series of votes of no confidence, until new elections were called. Those elections would settle the question of legitimacy. But the U.S. Constitution has no provision for dissolving the government and holding new elections to determine who has the right to rule. It has a fixed constitutional calendar. Presidents are elected once every four years. And the Clinton impeachment has demonstrated, if any demonstration were necessary, that a sitting president is almost impossible to remove. Impeachment and removal simply does not play the same role in our system as a vote of no confidence. Once an American president is installed in the Oval Office, even under questionable circumstances, he or she will control the levers of executive power for four years, absent death or disability.

As a result, the debate over the meaning and the legitimacy of the election of 2000 will be played out through the only devices available in the American constitutional system—the separation of legislative and executive power and the fixed constitutional calendar, which provides for elections in 2002 and 2004. In a parliamentary system, the prime minister is thrown out of power along with his party. But in the American system of separated powers, divided government—a president of one party and a Congress controlled by another—is not only possible but commonplace. Through varying the president's support in Congress, We the People can send signals of relative confidence or lack of confidence in the president and his party. For example, in 1994 Americans expressed lack of confidence in Clinton's presidency, throwing both houses of Congress to the Republicans for the first time in fifty years. In 1998, at the height of the Lewinsky scandal, the American people expressed confidence in Clinton by awarding the Democrats five seats in an off-year election in which the Republicans would normally have been expected to win twenty or more. And, of course, the greatest demonstration of confidence that We the People can offer a president is reelection to a second term.

To be sure, the meaning of these elections is constructed; their significance is generally appraised after the fact. It may not correlate with any particular voter's actual intentions or reasons for voting. All politics, it is often said, is local. But the construction of these meanings is an important part of the way a democratic system works, both for outside observers and for the participants themselves. Ascribing a meaning to an election is how politicians understand their mandate, and, to a large extent, it is how members of the public understand what they have done collectively.

The meaning of the 2000 election—and hence the legitimacy of the Bush presidency—has yet to be determined. If the Democrats win both houses of Congress in 2002 and then regain the presidency in 2004, they will have delivered as solid a rebuff to Bush's legitimacy as is possible in the American system of government. We the People will have rejected the Supreme Court's imperious decision to hand Bush the White House. In hindsight, the election of 2000 will have been judged a mistake, and—for reasons that I will explain shortly—the more mistaken it seems, the more it will throw into doubt the legitimacy of how Bush obtained power in the first place. On the other hand, if George W. Bush wins a second term in office by a decisive margin, this will bestow legitimacy on his first term retrospectively, and will tend to confirm the wisdom of the Supreme Court's intervention, if not the precise reasoning of *Bush v. Gore*. The election of 2000 will be considered at most a tie, which gave Bush the opportunity to establish that he truly did represent the will of the People. Because there was no constitutional harm, there was no constitutional foul.

With the ashes of the World Trade Center still smoldering as I write these words, the country is likely to give George W. Bush every opportunity to demonstrate his qualities of leadership. If he makes the most of that opportunity, he will be rewarded with reelection and the mantle of legitimacy. But as every politician understands, a great deal can happen in four years. No one knows how long the current crisis will last, how well the new president will lead, or whether economic and domestic problems will eventually overtake concerns of foreign policy. Make no mistake: the meaning of the 2000 election—and the legitimacy of the Bush presidency—is still very much up for grabs.

Unplanned and unexpected events will test the mettle of both parties and shape the meaning of the Bush presidency. If the Democrats play their cards right, and the Republicans are foolish, the Republican Party will be punished for overreaching and the verdict of history will be that the election was illegitimate or at least dubious. *Bush* v. *Gore* and black disenfranchisement will be viewed as blemishes on the American system of justice that were corrected by a wise citizenry. On the other hand, if the Republicans rise to the occasion and the Democrats misplay their hand, George W. Bush will win the White House in 2004 and establish his legitimacy. *Bush v. Gore* will be seen as badly written but irrelevant, and black disenfranchisement in Florida will be excused or conveniently forgotten.

Because the American constitutional system is not a parliamentary system—because it has fixed election cycles and no explicit or practical method of removing an illegitimate president, all political events for the next several years will carry a dual meaning. They are both part of ordinary politics and part of the continuing struggle over the legitimacy of the 2000 election. If one thinks that black disenfranchisement was a scandal and that *Bush v. Gore* was a travesty, the last thing one should do is concede this struggle without a fight. The 2000 election is long since over. But both sides can still win the contest over its meaning.

Procedural and Political Legitimacy

How will this struggle be played out in the next few years? To answer this question we need to take a brief detour into the mechanisms of legitimacy. Legitimacy is a complicated concept with many different elements. Lawyers are mostly concerned with procedural legitimacy—whether the rules were properly adhered to. That is one reason why so many lawyers and law professors are disturbed by *Bush* v. *Gore*. They feel—and I think, quite rightly—that rule of law values were clumsily discarded to achieve a particular result. The Supreme Court's decision in *Bush v. Gore* looked like a judicial opinion, but it was so shoddy and so badly reasoned that it seemed lawless. Equally important, the disenfranchisement of tens of thousands of black voters in Florida in apparent violation of the Voting Rights Act casts serious doubt on the procedural legitimacy of the result. If *Bush v. Gore* violated canons of juristic practice to decide who would gain power, black disenfranchisement violated precious individual liberties to the same end.

But in a democracy, political legitimacy involves far more than adherence to procedural niceties. In very large part, it is a function of the trust and confidence that people have in their elected representatives. That trust and confidence, in turn, depends on many factors—including whether the official seems genuinely concerned about the interests of the country rather than the official's personal or political interests, and whether the official seems competent and able to handle the challenges of the job.

Procedural legitimacy—with its focus on fair procedures—and political legitimacy—with its focus on trust and confidence—are analytically distinct in theory but related in practice. Obviously, if politicians seize power by unlawful means, people may distrust them. But the converse is also true: the more trust and confidence the public has in its elected officials, the less it will be interested in worrying about their misconduct or the corners they cut to gain power. In addition, the less trust and confidence people have in their elected officials, they more they are likely to credit conspiracy theories and allegations of misbehavior, and the more they will worry about a politician's right to wield power.

The psychological connection between popular confidence and procedural legitimacy is quite important. It is very difficult for people living in a proud and long-standing democracy like the United States to accept that they are ruled by persons who have no right to their office. The tendency to reduce cognitive dissonance is very strong: it is less disturbing to believe that people who control the government are lawfully in place. This fact explains much of the quiescence that followed December 2000: Given that Bush was going to sit in the Oval Office anyway, most Americans simply didn't want to think about whether he had been lawfully elected.

For this reason, claims of procedural illegitimacy may well be most plausible after people have lost trust and confidence in their elected officials. That is why Richard Nixon's downfall came not when everything was going swimmingly in 1972, but when the economy had turned sour in 1974. It was easier to believe that Nixon was a crook when people had lost confidence in his ability to govern. To be sure, he had lost the ability to govern in large part because his administration was consumed by scandals. But if the economy had been humming along—as it was during Bill Clinton's presidency—the distractions might not have mattered as much.

Indeed, Clinton provides the best recent example of the complicated interaction of procedural and political legitimacy. Throughout much of his tenure in office he received very high marks from the American public even though his administration was repeatedly charged with improprieties. Large numbers of Americans liked him, believed that he cared about them and their lives, and had confidence in his ability to govern the country. His private life was a mess, his campaign fundraising practices were suspicious and at best skirted the edges of the law, and his actions during the Lewinsky flap were simply scandalous. Yet his approval ratings remained high throughout his second term, zooming to stratospheric heights as he was impeached by his political enemies. (And, in contrast to Nixon, he was helped immensely by a booming economy.)

People who had confidence in Clinton as a public servant were willing to give him the benefit of the doubt when it came to allegations of illegal conduct. They either didn't believe or didn't care that he broke the law, partly because they had confidence in his abilities as president and partly because they regarded his political enemies— who repeatedly raised charges of illegality—as worse than he was.

On the other hand, almost from the beginning of Clinton's tenure as president many Republican stalwarts felt that he did not deserve his office. In their eyes his election in 1992 was a fluke caused in part by the erratic antics of Ross Perot, and his reelection in 1996 was the direct result of his reckless flouting of the campaign finance laws. For these Americans, Clinton was a liar and a crook. They had no confidence in him from the word go. This lack of confidence led people to credit any number of conspiracy theories about the man. They believed that there was no one he would not lie to, and no law that he would not break. Even before conservatives accused him of perjury and obstruction of justice, they whispered rumors among themselves about rape and murder. For these Americans, Clinton's character simply undermined his right to rule. It is admittedly difficult for many liberals to understand the horror that many conservatives felt toward Clinton as a man they believed had no respect for the rule of law. It is perhaps equally difficult for many conservatives to understand why most Americans did not wish to throw the rascal out of office.

If procedural and political legitimacy are connected in the way I have described, we can better understand the problems now facing the Democrats and the Republicans. It makes little sense for professional politicians of either party to place the procedural legitimacy of the 2000 election at the center of public debate. The Republicans do not want to call attention to the question, which they regard as settled. The Democrats face the problems of cognitive dissonance and the facts on the ground: they cannot remove Bush, and they must not appear obstructionist, especially following the terrorist assaults on the World Trade Center and the Pentagon. Although many in their base may doubt Bush's legitimacy, they will not get many other people to agree that Bush lacks the right to rule until people have lost confidence in Bush as president. As a result, the political battles of the next four years may not focus overtly on who really won the election. Instead, the two parties will try to gain the greater trust and confidence of the

American people. For this reason much of the next four years will resemble ordinary politics. The one exception is judicial nominations, which I will discuss in more detail later on.

The events of September 11 greatly raise the stakes for both political parties and may ultimately define how Bush's presidency will be understood. A national emergency can establish a leader's legitimacy because in moments of crisis and difficulty the public wants and needs to rally around its leaders. If Bush shepherds the nation successfully through the present turmoil, he will gain immeasurable stature, and his political legitimacy will be greatly enhanced. That will significantly increase his chances of reelection, although it will not guarantee it. After all, his father, George H. W. Bush, led the country to victory in the Persian Gulf War and was nevertheless rejected by the voters only a year and a half later because of a weakened economy. If George W. Bush is unable to rise to the occasion or if his leadership proves unpopular, as Lyndon Johnson's did during the Vietnam War, he may actually lose legitimacy and be punished politically for his failures. Nevertheless, even a protracted struggle against terrorism need not doom his chances for reelection: if a war drags on, the voters may be unwilling to change horses in midstream. The Democrats are in a symmetrical position. They must be patriotic and support the president in times of national crisis. Yet this does not necessarily prevent them from winning the elections of 2002 and 2004, even if the struggle against terrorism continues for many years. After all, the Republicans displaced the incumbent party in the White House in 1968 during the middle of the Vietnam War.

From the Constitutional Trifecta to the War Against Terrorism

George W. Bush entered office with a cloud on his title of president. Even absent that cloud, he entered the Oval Office having lost the popular vote. As his administration began in January 2001, Bush had two basic choices. The first strategy was conciliation and the forma-

tion of a government of national unity. Bush could openly acknowledge the controversy surrounding the election, govern from the center, and devote his first term to rectifying the country's inadequate
voting system, perhaps even working for constitutional reform of the
electoral college. The second strategy, which Bush actually adopted,
was steadfast promotion of the Republican agenda. Bush made no
excuses or concessions about the outcome of the election. He expressed no doubts about his authority to rule. He simply claimed that
he had a mandate and dared the Democrats to prove otherwise. Although Bush promised to change the tone of politics in Washington
and spoke in friendly terms to his opponents, he showed no interest
in compromising his basic policies. His basic strategy was to speak in
the language of conciliation but to deal in the language of power.

Why did Bush adopt the second strategy rather than the first? One
reason is that he is simply a much more ideologically conservative
politician than he appeared to be in the election. Second, he and his
advisors probably assumed that drawing attention to the controversial
nature of his accession to power would not enhance his legitimacy,
but would detract from it. The more he admitted that his right to hold
office rested on shaky grounds, the more the Democrats would demand concessions. And the more concessions he offered, the more he
would anger the base of strongly conservative Republicans who were
his most steadfast supporters. Because he entered office with a minority coalition of popular support, Bush and his advisors may have
judged it prudent not to risk fracturing that coalition.

A third reason why Bush did not consider governing from the
center concerns the separation of powers. After the Supreme Court
installed Bush in office, the Republicans had won what I call the
"constitutional trifecta": they now controlled all three branches of
government. This has not happened frequently in American constitutional history after the Era of Good Feelings ended in the 1820's, and it
has been particularly rare in the last half century or so. Winning the
constitutional trifecta allows one party to push its agenda relatively

unimpeded, because the president, Congress, and the Supreme Court are all working in roughly the same direction ideologically. Normally a party wins the trifecta only during moments of widespread popular support and widespread popular mobilization. The last time was from 1960 to 1968, when liberal ideals dominated American politics. Even winning both the presidency and both houses of Congress (a sort of mini-trifecta) is relatively infrequent in modern times—and if it is not accompanied by widespread popular support, the party out of power soon takes control of the presidency or one branch of Congress.

Moreover, because of the peculiarities surrounding the 2000 election, the Republicans not only won the constitutional trifecta, but the president, the congressional leadership, and a majority of the Supreme Court were much more ideologically conservative than most Americans. Yet there was no consensus or mobilization for the hard right wing of the Republican Party, and no way of mistaking the results as a clear electoral mandate for its undiluted conservatism. Indeed more people voted for Al Gore or Ralph Nader than for George W. Bush or Patrick Buchanan. Given the tenuous connection between rulers and ruled, Bush decided to push a conservative agenda quickly during the limited window of one-party rule, a window that closed when Senator Jim Jeffords of Vermont defected and became an independent. Jeffords's defection effectively ended the constitutional trifecta.

There are two ways to interpret Bush's early strategy. One is that it was an act of desperation—knowing that the American people were not behind them, the Republicans tried to get as much done as they could in the limited time available to them. That included slashing taxes in order to forestall and cripple future federal spending initiatives, beginning an expensive missile shield program that would be difficult to walk away from, adopting a national energy policy that favored the interests of oil companies and large business organizations, and stocking the federal judiciary with ideological conservatives who would enjoy life tenure and fundamentally reshape American constitutional law. But a more charitable reading is that the Republicans tried to lead in the hopes that most Americans would follow. They chose a strongly conservative path in order to win the approval of the American people by demonstrating that they could get things done and move the country in a direction that most Americans would eventually support. In other words, they were attempting to establish the grounds of their legitimacy for the next decade.

By the beginning of September 2001, however, the results of this strategy were decidedly mixed. The Jeffords defection and the loss of the constitutional trifecta simply confirmed what one would have expected. In a politically divided country, a president without a genuine electoral mandate—indeed, one who was actually rejected by the majority of the voters—will find it difficult to push a program very far out of the mainstream. The bitterness of the 2000 election, and the suspicion among many Democrats that the election was effectively stolen, remained buried beneath the surface of everyday politics. Bush was unable to generate approval ratings much larger than the percentage of people who supported him in the election. The administration's clumsy handling of foreign relations raised doubts about the president's leadership. The sinking economy undermined confidence in his domestic policies. Barely eight months into his new administration, much of his agenda was sidetracked, and the remainder appeared stalled.

Then came September 11. The terrorist attacks gave George W. Bush a chance to detach his presidency from the controversial 2000 election and to demonstrate the quality of his leadership. Ironically, although the attacks made much of the Bush domestic agenda irrelevant, in the process they diverted politics, at least in the short run, to questions of national security, in which presidential and executive prerogatives tend to dominate. George W. Bush and his party have been given a golden opportunity to win the trust and confidence of the American people. Nevertheless, this opportunity also creates enormous risks both for himself and for the country. A self-declared war on terrorism has no simple ending point or exit strategy. The public may eventually bristle at a policy of domestic security that is too heavy-handed. If George W. Bush and his party can show strong, effective leadership, they will be rewarded generously at the polls. His ascension to power will be legitimated, and his right to rule will be successfully detached from the election of 2000. But if he overreaches in the domestic arena, if his leadership proves inept and his military adventures ineffectual, the public will not be forgiving. The basic weaknesses of his political position will reassert themselves, greatly amplified by his subsequent failures, and questions about the legitimacy of the 2000 election will reemerge in the public consciousness like Poe's telltale heart.

The Task Ahead: The Case of Judicial Appointments

Suppose, then, that one believes, as I do, that the election of 2000 was effectively stolen through the disenfranchisement of African Americans and the hubris of five conservative Supreme Court justices. Suppose one believes that although Bush cannot be removed and, indeed, that the nation must rally behind him in the wake of the terrorist attacks, he did not legitimately win the 2000 election and that five members of the Court have betrayed their oaths of office. What is the proper political response for the opposition party to take under our constitutional system?

Let me break this question down into two parts. The first is whether the opposition should adopt a strategy of intransigence or propose a positive agenda. The second is what to do about judicial appointments.

The structure of the American Constitution provides the answer to the first question. The Democrats cannot bring the government down as they might in a parliamentary system. They face a fixed constitutional calendar. The remedy that the Constitution offers for an illegitimate presidency is forward looking—a new election at a fixed time, and not backward looking—the removal of a president. Therefore the opposition party's strategy must be much the same strategy as in any other moment in politics—to win the next election and the election after that. The American people are forward looking as well. Despite any qualms about the 2000 election, they will return George W. Bush to office in 2004 if they feel he has done a good job. And they will punish obstructionism by the Democrats as surely as they punished the Gingrich-led Republicans in 1996 and 1998.

Thus, the Democrats must pursue the methods of ordinary politics. In foreign affairs, they must work hand in hand with the president and support American troops in the war against terrorism. In domestic affairs, they must offer their own positive agenda and attempt to force the president to compromise. They must demonstrate that their values are more in tune with the majority of the American public and therefore that they are the appropriate party to lead the nation. They must prove to the American public that the wrong party has gained control of the White House and is pushing the wrong agenda, and that although there is nothing that can be done about the past, there is much that can be done about the future.

None of this means that the Democrats must accept the election of 2000 as fully legitimate. It means only that they must wisely utilize the limited remedy that the Constitution provides. Their position is symmetrical to that of the Republicans—who can establish the procedural legitimacy of the 2000 presidential contest by winning reelection in 2004. If Democrats win the battle of political legitimacy—if they can convince the American people that Bush is a failed president whose leadership was deficient and whose agenda was out of touch with the mainstream—the question of *procedural* legitimacy will take care of itself. They will win the verdict of historical judgment. No one, least of all the Republicans, should confuse this with "getting over" the 2000 election.

The case of judicial appointments is special. Here the Democrats have not only the right but the duty to obstruct the president's conservative agenda. That is so regardless of their support of his efforts in the world of foreign affairs. If their objections are principled and reasonable, they will suffer no punishment from the American people for derailing extremist judicial appointments, especially appointments to the Supreme Court. And fighting over judicial nominations—particularly to the Supreme Court—offers them the most appropriate platform on which to discuss *Bush* v. *Gore* and the procedural legitimacy of the 2000 election. First, the question of procedural legitimacy can be raised more forthrightly in the case of judicial nominations when the president was installed by judicial fiat. Second, the public is likely to view opposition to the president on judicial appointments quite differently from opposition on questions of war and foreign policy.

In a thoughtful chapter for this book, Cass Sunstein has argued that Bush should not be allowed to appoint judges who are out of the mainstream because he will throw the federal judiciary and the United States Supreme Court out of balance. The danger, Sunstein argues, is that Bush will appoint judges and justices who will remake the Constitution to reflect the Republican Party platform. In Sunstein's view this is wrong because the Court should always have an appropriate balance of conservatives, moderates, and liberals. It is the duty of the elected branches not to stray too far from that balance. The need for maintaining that balance, Sunstein suggests, would apply whether Bush's legitimacy was doubtful or clear, and whether or not the Supreme Court had decided *Bush* v. *Gore.*

I agree with Sunstein that the current Supreme Court majority has been altogether too disrespectful of democratic processes, that their political values are badly skewed, and that their invocations of text and original intention are opportunistic, ideologically biased, and self-serving. I also agree with much of his general indictment of their decisions. But I do think that *Bush* v. *Gore* makes a considerable difference here. I think that the question of legitimacy is crucial in explaining why the Democrats can and should fight over judicial appointments with energy and vigor.

Unlike Sunstein, I don't think that the issue is preserving a natural balance on the Court. Indeed, I don't think that there *is* a natural ideological balance to the Court that must be preserved over the generations. I see no reason, for example, why Lyndon Johnson should have appointed a conservative segregationist to replace Justice Tom Clark in 1967 rather than a liberal egalitarian like Justice Thurgood Marshall. It is true that the Warren Court was getting rather liberal by 1967, and adding Thurgood Marshall would push it even further to the left, particularly on issues of race. But I don't see this as particularly troubling. In my view, Johnson's 1964 landslide victory gave him the political authority to appoint Thurgood Marshall.

The problem today is not that the current Court is unbalanced—it surely is. The problem is that George W. Bush lacks the political authority to appoint members of the federal judiciary to unbalance it further. That is why *Bush* v. *Gore* matters. George W. Bush is asserting a legitimate power to reshape the Constitution through judicial appointments that he simply does not possess. It is the obligation of the Democratic opposition in the Senate to resist his attempts.

The Constitution evolves and grows with the times. Alterations in constitutional meaning sometimes come from amendments, but in large part they come from changes in judicial interpretation. And those changes, in turn, come from changes in the personnel of the federal judiciary. In the American system of government, the appointments process is the great engine of constitutional transformation. There is nothing particularly illegitimate about this. The appointment of judges by politicians is the mechanism through which changing social and political mores and the demands of social movements eventually get reflected in constitutional interpretation. Presidents, who are elected by the nation as a whole, tend to appoint judges who reflect their political principles and constitutional values. The Senate plays an important role in moderating and shaping the president's choices, especially when it is controlled by the opposite party. The checks and balances provided by the Senate's advice and consent keep the judi-

ciary more representative of the country as a whole. Nevertheless, if
one party keeps being returned to the White House, over time its
appointments will inevitably shape constitutional interpretation. For
example, if the people keep supporting politicians with conservative
values, we really should not be shocked if conservative values begin to
surface in judicial interpretations. As I like to tell my students, if you
don't like what the Rehnquist Court has been doing for the past decade, you (or your parents) shouldn't have voted for Richard Nixon,
Ronald Reagan and the first George Bush. Perhaps the most important reason why the Constitution has started to look like the Republican Party platform is that the Republicans dominated presidential
politics between 1968 and 1992. The Democrats did not get a single
Supreme Court appointment between 1967 and 1994.

The president's authority to stock the federal courts with his ideological allies stems from his victory at the polls. The problem with
judicial appointments by the present administration is that George W.
Bush lacks just this sort of legitimacy. He may occupy the White
House by the grace of his brother the governor of Florida and five
justices of the Supreme Court. But he shouldn't have the right to
appoint life tenured judges who are out of the mainstream unless he
won a mandate from We the People. He won no such mandate. Indeed, more people opposed his candidacy than favored it.

Thus, judicial appointments are the central area in which *Bush* v.
Gore and the question of Bush's legitimacy will be directly raised and
should be directly raised in the next four years. It seems altogether fair
for the Democrats to remind the public that the Supreme Court put
Bush in office, and essentially picked the man who would select its
successors and colleagues. Not only will he replace Supreme Court
justices, he will select the lower federal court judges who are charged
with implementing the Supreme Court's decisions in the vast majority of cases.

The composition of the Supreme Court is especially crucial because America is in the midst of a constitutional revolution. In 1991,

George W. Bush's father appointed Clarence Thomas to the Supreme Court to replace Thurgood Marshall. Since 1991, the same five conservatives have been rewriting the law of federal–state relations, limiting federal regulatory power, protecting commercial speech, resisting campaign finance reform, eviscerating the great writ of habeas corpus, narrowing civil rights remedies for women and minorities, expanding them for white males, and making it increasingly difficult for citizens to sue states for violations of their civil rights. As a result, we live in the midst of a constitutional transformation that, if carried to its logical conclusion, could prove as profound as the rights revolution of the 1960s. Yet most, if not all, of these decisions were decided by a bare 5–4 majority in bitterly contested opinions—not coincidentally the same 5–4 majority that decided *Bush* v. *Gore*. The fate of this conservative constitutional revolution rests with the appointment of the next several justices of the Supreme Court. If Al Gore had won, the revolution would have been stopped dead in its tracks. Democratic appointments to the Supreme Court and the federal judiciary would have cut back on some of these doctrinal innovations and overruled others.

By handing Bush the presidency however, the five conservatives did their best to keep their revolution going. By stopping the recounts in Florida, they gave themselves the chance to add a sixth vote and move constitutional doctrines even further to the right. As I have noted, constitutional revolutions are usually backed by electoral majorities who repeatedly return a political party to power. If George W. Bush had received an electoral mandate, he would be in a position little different from that of his father. He could have appointed a Thomaslike conservative and dared the Senate to refuse to confirm him or her, resting on the authority of the Republicans' electoral mandate. George W. may well try the same thing anyway, appointing a conservative Hispanic rather than an African American. But there is a crucial difference between 1991 and 2001. His father clearly won the election. George W. did not.

Even if George W. Bush had won a clear electoral majority, he would still face the problem of lacking a mandate for his judicial politics because he lost the popular vote. After all, there is little evidence that a majority of the American public supported the far right wing agenda of either the five conservatives or the Republican Party. But *Bush* v. *Gore* exacerbates the problem of legitimacy. By delivering the presidency to George W. Bush, the Five Conservatives entangled his fate with theirs. He should not be permitted to reshape the Constitution without a legitimate mandate from the People. They should not be permitted to profit from their own wrong.

Contributors

BRUCE ACKERMAN is Sterling Professor of Law and Political Science at Yale University. He is a member of the American Law Institute and the American Academy of Arts and Sciences.

JACK M. BALKIN is Knight Professor of Constitutional Law and the First Amendment at Yale Law School, and the founder of Yale's Information Society Project. His books include *Processes of Constitutional Decisionmaking* and *Cultural Software: A Theory of Ideology*.

GUIDO CALABRESI is a judge of the United States Court of Appeals for the Second Circuit. Before joining the court, he was dean of Yale Law School, where he continues to teach as Sterling Professor of Law Emeritus.

STEVEN G. CALABRESI is the George C. Dix Professor of Constitutional Law at Northwestern University. He was a co-founder of the Federalist Society and served in the Justice Department and White House during the Reagan and Bush administrations. He has published widely in leading law reviews.

OWEN FISS is Sterling Professor of Law at Yale University.

CHARLES FRIED has taught at Harvard Law School since 1961. He served as solicitor general of the United States in the second Reagan administration, and from 1995–1999 was an associate justice of the Supreme Judicial Court of Massachusetts. His books include *Order and Law: Arguing the Reagan Revolution* and *Contract as Promise: A Theory of Contractual Obligation*.

ROBERT POST is the Alexander F. and May T. Morrison Professor of Law at the School of Law of the University of California at Berkeley (Boalt Hall). He is the author of *Constitutional Domains: Democracy, Community, Management* and *Prejudicial Appearances: The Logic of American Antidiscrimination Law.*

MARGARET JANE RADIN is William Benjamin and Luna M. Scott Professor of Law, Stanford Law School, and director of Stanford's Program in Law, Science and Technology. She is the author of *Contested Commodities* and *Reinterpreting Property.* As one of the organizers of Law Professors for the Rule of Law, Professor Radin coordinated the publication of the law professors' protest against the decision in *Bush v. Gore.*

JEFFREY ROSEN is associate professor at George Washington University Law School, legal affairs editor of *The New Republic,* and author of *The Unwanted Gaze: The Destruction of Privacy in America.*

JED RUBENFELD is Robert Slaughter Professor of Law at Yale University and a United States representative to the Council of Europe. He is the author of *Freedom and Time* and many leading articles on constitutional law.

CASS R. SUNSTEIN is the Karl N. Llewellyn Distinguished Service Professor at University of Chicago Law School. He is the author of many books, including *Designing Democracy: What Constitutions Do, Republic.com,* and *Risk and Reason: Safety, Law, and the Environment.*

LAURENCE H. TRIBE is the Ralph S. Tyler, Jr., Professor of Constitutional Law at Harvard Law School. He is the author of *American Constitutional Law,* the most cited law book over the past half-century, and other influential works. Professor Tribe has also served as lead counsel in many important Supreme Court cases over the past two decades.

MARK TUSHNET is Carmack Waterhouse Professor of Constitutional Law at Georgetown University Law Center. He has published widely in constitutional law and legal history.

Index

deadline for completion of recount, 34–37, 96, 98, 116–18, 144, 195–96; decision choices, 7–8, 20–21, 34–38, 59–66, 94–95, 198, 227; decision criticisms, 72–75, 81, 85, 88–89, 92, 99, 108–9; embarrassment, 114, 184; equal protection decision, 12–14, 51–53, 56–57, 165–69, 176; Florida legislature, 65; Florida Supreme Court, 7–18, 23–26, 81–82, 104, 114–15, 137, 165, 171; ideological construct, 170, 172; judicial activism, 189; judicial judgment, 146–48; liberalism, 174, 189–90; motivation, 6, 28, 81, 94, 201; nominations, 101, 143, 171, 178–79, 180–81, 224; partisanship, xi, 113, 120, 122, 145, 164, 171; polarization, 172; political question doctrine, 147; politicization, 143–44, 145–46, 155, 224, 227; presidential selection, 96, 99, 102; reasoning, 6, 8, 28–29, 72, 88, 213; recount standard, 45, 51–53, 86–88; remand order, 11, 65, 90–92, 116; reversal of stay decision, 86; right-wing view, 184; role, 57–58, 68, 93, 142–44, 170–71, 191; state law interpretation, 10, 18–19, 22, 48–49, 54–56; television's role, 42, 65; termination decision, 21, 53, 165, 167–68, 201; unsought responsibility, 57–58. See also Bush v. Gore; judicial intervention; majority opinions; stay of recount proceedings

technology, xii, 57, 174–76
television, ix, 41–44, 56–57, 132. See also mass media
termination decision. See stay of recount proceedings
terrorist attacks, xiii, 211, 217–18, 221–22
textualism, 183–84

Thomas, Clarence, 80, 122, 205; appointment of, 227; concurring opinion, 54, 63, 137, 160; confirmation hearings, 182; political view, 183–84, 190, 202–3
tiebreakers, xi, 129–35; Congress, 134–35, 140; congressional partisanship, 135; county canvassing boards, 132–33, 140; electoral college, 130; Florida legislature, 133–34, 140; Katherine Harris, 131–33, 140; political question doctrine, 60; Roberts Rules of Order, 130
time constraints, 55–57, 96
Timmons v. Twin Cities Area New Party, 39–40, 61, 106
Trademark Remedy Clarification Act, 62
Tribe, Laurence, 5, 181
trifecta, constitutional, 219–20

United States v. Morrison, 18
United States v. Nixon, 87
United States v. Virginia et al., 8
unprincipled decision making, ix–x, 11, 27, 72–83, 87–89, 92–93, 99, 117
USA Today, 86
U.S. Code: dispute resolution, 93, 138–40, 156; Title 3, 9, 16–17, 24, 52–55, 134. See also safe harbor provision

Violence Against Women Act, 85, 92, 119, 182, 198
Virginia Military Institute (VMI) case. See United States v. Virginia et al.
vote deprivation, 165–66
vote dilution, 166–67, 169
voter intent, 55, 167; ballot design, 46, 48, 50; manual recount, 42–44, 88, 118; standards, 13–14, 52–53
vote tabulation, 9–11, 14–15, 21; accuracy, 44–47, 70, 90; ballot

One in Christ's love!
Ruth C. Stapleton